By J. R. Hawthorn and C. Macdonald

ROMAN POLITICS, 80–44 B.C.
A Selection of Latin Passages with
Historical Commentary and Notes

THE REPUBLICAN EMPIRE

BY

J. R. HAWTHORN, M.A.

SENIOR CLASSICAL MASTER AT BRADFIELD COLLEGE

LONDON

MACMILLAN & CO LTD

NEW YORK · ST MARTIN'S PRESS

1963

MACMILLAN AND COMPANY LIMITED
St Martin's Street London WC 2
also Bombay Calcutta Madras Melbourne

THE MACMILLAN COMPANY OF CANADA LIMITED
Toronto

ST MARTIN'S PRESS INC
New York

PRINTED IN GREAT BRITAIN

PREFACE

'THE Roman Empire' is a highly ambiguous phrase. Sometimes it means the government of Rome by Augustus and his successors, the men we usually call emperors, sometimes it is the government by Rome of non-Roman provinces. It is easy to be led by this ambiguity into assuming that the foreign empire was the work of the emperors, or at least that what was done before them was only a tentative beginning, ill-thought-out and ill-administered: there must be something contradictory and unsatisfactory about a Republican empire.

The study of politics at Rome in the last century of the Republic does not always do much to remove this feeling. Men sometimes went to the provinces reluctantly, with one eye on a speedy return, and it so happened that one of the most reluctant was also the most vocal; we readily assume that while there they must have done their work badly. Men sometimes became richer by governing provinces; we believe that governors spent the greater part of their energies extorting money from their luckless subjects — the phrase 'gold-rush' has been used. Much of our information comes from the proceedings of the extortion court, the object of which was to detect and punish peculation; it is easy to think that these cases were typical.

Yet the histories of the western world are full of the blessings of Roman rule and the spread of Graeco-

Roman civilisation which it made possible; the photographs of aqueducts and amphitheatres with which they are embellished draw our attention to the period of impressive imperial architecture, and the maps give prominence to the frontiers of Trajan. The result is a contrast between the beneficence of the emperors' Rome and the rapacity of Republican Romans which needs to be examined. We are asked to assume a sudden change of heart, and to attribute to the emperors, collectively, remarkable gifts of wisdom and virtue. It is time we made a more serious attempt to find out whether this is true. It is possible, of course, that morality did come in with Augustus, that Horace was right in saying of the new age

neglecta redire virtus

audet.

But it is also possible that virtue had been less neglected than he would have us believe.

This book is an attempt to assess the nature of the Republican empire. For that it is not enough to study the laws and regulations, to set out what a governor or tax collector could legally do and what were the processes for preventing or punishing illegality. These things can be found in the compressed pages which the history books devote to the subject, but important though they are they do not answer our question. We have to try to find out not only what *could* be done but what usually *was* done, not only whether bad (or good) things happened, but how bad (or good) they were. And when we come to judge, as we must, we should also give some thought to the standard by which we judge. Should it be that of the British foreign service of the twentieth century? Or of the eighteenth? Or of other peoples of the ancient Mediterranean world? We must also be asking what the provincials thought about the empire. They have left little record of this themselves, apart from the readiness with which they accepted it or the violence with which they fought against it; though in passing we may notice that revolts did not cease with the accession of Augustus. An effort of the imagination is required.

We are more likely to arrive at a reasonable judgement if we read the ancient literature at some length; not in isolated sentences, selected to prove a particular point, but in extracts long enough for us to feel the strength of the ideas which lie behind. We can then see the deeds against the background of contemporary thought, with a much fuller understanding than we could otherwise have. At the same time our appreciation of the literature will be the better if we see it as the expression of Roman thought; if we realise that the grace of a letter or the periods of a speech were, to their author, means of persuading friend or audience, and that the persuasiveness of the language is related to the justice of the case. Both our reading of the ancient authors and our study of history will gain if they are closely related.

In this book I have made as fair a selection as I can of the ancient evidence, remembering that normal practice and attitudes of mind are more important for the purpose than detailed points of law or occasional eccentricities. It is true that any selection may have the effect of distorting; I can only say that I have tried to play fair, and that although considerations of space have compelled me to omit many interesting passages, I have not omitted them because I disagree with them. Where our only sources of information are seriously biased, I have tried to suggest what allowances should be made. We are fortunate in their literary quality, since the great bulk comes from Cicero himself; fortunate too that we can learn from him both about Verres in Sicily and his own tour of duty in Cilicia, so that the same witness is testifying on both sides of the case. But the more ably a case is presented, the more carefully we must read.

In the notes on the texts I have neglected points of grammar and concentrated on matters of historical interest. On points of detail the evidence is often inconclusive, and to understand the general picture we have to ask the difficult questions: How good? How much? How often? Where possible I have preferred to state my opinion of what the answer should be, rather than be for ever taking refuge in a scholarly vacuum. There is the less danger in this since the texts which are the foundations of our knowledge are here printed at some length, and themselves provide the means of judging the views I have expressed. To assist the translator, I have in places given an indication of what the difficult sentence is about, but I have avoided providing the ready-made idiomatic translation which is so often accepted without further thought. For the Greek passages in Chapter VI, I have provided a full translation.

To Mr F. A. Lepper, of Corpus Christi College, Oxford, I owe a debt of gratitude which I am glad to acknowledge. He has read the historical introductions in manuscript, and made many helpful and important suggestions. Mr. E. Badian, of Durham University, has read the book in proof with a vigilant eye, and with great patience and generosity assisted me to remedy many of its defects.   In thanking them for their help I must point out that of course they bear no responsibility for the heresies and perversities which remain.

CONTENTS

LIST OF MAPS

PART ONE
THE REPUBLICAN EMPIRE

I

THE GROWTH OF THE EMPIRE

FROM the maps on pp. 289–291 it is possible to follow in outline the growth of the Roman empire, and to see when the decisive steps were taken; to visualise the extent of the empire in the time of the Scipios, of Sulla, of Pompey, and the boundaries planned by Augustus. And although a political and military account of the expansion is no part of the scheme of this book, since the way in which an empire is acquired is likely to affect the spirit in which it is administered, some remarks on imperial policy may assist our understanding.

First in the long list of provinces was Sicily, and the motive for the annexation is clear; at the cost of much blood and treasure the Carthaginians had at last been driven from the island, and it was necessary to make absolutely certain that they did not gain a foothold there again. It was felt that alliances were not enough; some form of permanent control was essential, and the presence of Roman troops. We have little detailed information about the early years, but from 227 onwards a praetor, colleague of the praetors at Rome, was in charge, and in the second Punic war his province was enlarged by the inclusion of the kingdom of Hiero. The island was used by Scipio as a concentration area for the invasion of Africa. But though the province was acquired for military purposes, some civilian administration, in particular the collection of taxes, could not be avoided. It was fortunate for the empire-to-be that so early in their expansion the Romans stepped into the shoes of Hiero. It is probable that nowhere in the Mediterranean world were higher standards of accuracy and integrity to be found in the public service; for their first education in empire the Romans had a good model.

In Spain, the motive for annexation was the same, to deny the peninsula to the Carthaginians. It had been there that the Barca family had revived the Punic fortunes, and from there that Hannibal and Hasdrubal had marched into Italy. But with this the similarity ended. Beyond the civilised cities of east and south the Romans had to deal with a congeries of warlike hill tribes, and a large mountainous country where a pursuing army might find itself in mortal danger. The framework for settled peaceful administration did not exist. Their experiences in Spain, while draining their military manpower, did not whet their appetite for empire. Fifty years later, it was with reluctance, and only after other methods had been tried, that they made the province of Macedonia; the final conquest of Carthage was long bitterly advocated and obstinately opposed at Rome.

So far, decisions on imperial matters had been made by the senate, and it is reasonable to conclude that this was not only the normal but also the right practice for the Roman state; Polybius understood. But the annexation of Asia was different. While the senate was hesitating about accepting such a surprising legacy, and prudently counting the cost of a distant province, the people acted. The senate's authority was challenged, and challenged successfully, just where it had always been strongest, and the Roman empire entered the continent of Asia.

The Gracchi were murdered, the senate regained control, and the dangers of a people's empire were averted. The next provinces, Narbonese Gaul and Cilicia, were soberly planned for military and naval purposes. But with the appointment of Pompey the position changed again, and with it the map of the world. His commission was to defeat Mithridates, and it would naturally be assumed that he would organise, advised by the usual commission of ten senators, the new province of Bithynia on which the senate had already decided. It would not be surprising, too, if the senate considered the possibility of annexing the kingdom of Mithridates, as having been the cause of two wars; if they decided to do this, Pompey would be instructed to put the plan into effect. What happened was not that at all. Pompey did not owe his command to the senate, who had in fact bitterly opposed it, and did not consider it necessary to wait for instructions from them. Instead, the Roman proconsul made his own plans, organising the affairs of Asia to his own liking. Not only a greatly enlarged Cilicia and the provincialisation of Bithynia and Pontus, but campaigns into the heart of the Caucasus, alliances which almost amounted to domination beyond the Euphrates, and the new province of Syria, including Judaea. A new scale of empire has been created. The Romans, who had once hesitated to occupy Macedonia, must now march their troops through it and beyond, across the whole length of Asia Minor. And this growth of power was matched by a growth of wealth. The Romans now discovered on a grand scale that empire could be a profitable business. There could be no return to the timidity of the second century. When Pompey came back from the east, he expected the senate to ratify his whole system by one comprehensive vote; to take it as read. We are tempted to think of this as a reasonable request; but the senators saw themselves losing control of foreign policy, and did not see why a general appointed in a fit of enthusiasm by the urban assembly to defeat Mithridates should presume to redraw the map of Asia. They insisted on a detailed point-by-point examination of his arrangements, and in the end there was no examination at all.

Pompey soon found an imitator, and Rome gained an addition of territory in the west to match the new conquests in the east. Again the proconsul was the people's appointment, again the major decisions were made by him. By the time the question of ratification arose, the opinion of the senate was no longer important. The place of cautious corporate reluctance has been taken by the opportunist ambitions of the great commanders, until the power of Augustus at last decided this conflict which had developed between the government and the individuals, and incorporated the grand but sporadic advances in a coherent, viable empire.

This book is concerned with administration, not conquest, so that it will naturally deal more with the normal senatorial machinery than the spectacular advances of the Gallic and Mithridatic wars. We shall, however, expect to find that the names of Caesar and Pompey frequently occur. For Roman generals were not just soldiers; they were the same men who were senators and consuls, and for the greater part of their lives they were civilians. Rule by these men is not rule by the army; they also had their contribution to make to the processes of government; the *lex Julia de rebus repetundis* was one of the most important laws on the subject, while it is not unreasonable to believe that the legislation of 67 had Pompey's blessing. In the different methods of government established in Bithynia and Gallia Comata we see the minds of Rome's greatest generals at work on problems of civilian administration.

To return to the early days, when Rome had provinces rather than an empire, and before they had any idea of the size and permanence of the building whose foundations they were in fact laying. We must banish from our minds the notion of the inevitable growth of the empire,[1] and view the occupation of each province, as they did, as a new and dangerous undertaking, bringing probably more trouble than profit. We shall then be in a position to sympathise with their reluctance, and to understand why there were times when they were able to annex a new province and chose not to do so; a choice which some will call civilised and restrained, others cowardly and unenterprising.

In 196, when Flamininus made his famous proclamation at the Isthmian games, Greece had come into their hands as the spoils of war, and if the Romans had wanted to make it a province there was no power that could have prevented them. The Greeks had evidently feared that Roman troops would remain in their country, but in fact the Romans decided otherwise. They were busy organising two new provinces in Spain, which they dared not abandon to the Carthaginians, and had only entered on the Macedonian war reluctantly. They were, however, determined to keep the king of Macedon out of Greece, and their declaration served notice that he would invade it at his peril. They found, too, that having undertaken to protect the Greeks against foreigners they could not avoid the task of protecting them against each other; the Greeks, on their side, found that they could be free from everyone except the people who had made them free.

When the Romans did make a new province, this was usually the result of a period of war or diplomacy which left its legacy of obligations, friendships and animosities. Very often the area which was to constitute the province was not already organised as a political unity, but contained a number of communities which had independent and often conflicting backgrounds, and stood in different relations to the new overlords. The Aedui and the Veneti were incorporated in the same province, but that did not obliterate their different histories. Even when, in 133, Attalus bequeathed the united kingdom of Pergamum to the Romans, they inherited also his various relations with the Greek cities of the coast and the tribes of central Asia Minor.

Besides this, the communities which they were going to incorporate in a new province might be organised cities on the Graeco-Roman model, or tribes with little cohesion or political system. Had the Romans been theorists they might have attempted to settle all alike in some grand general plan for the empire. Being, above all, practical men, they faced each particular problem as it arose, and sent out to each province a commission of senators, usually ten in number, who were to examine each local difficulty on the spot and make recommendations on the basis of which the charter for the province was drawn up in Rome.[2] This charter, though it was confirmed by a resolution of the senate and not by a law of the people, was known as the *lex provinciae*, and it regulated, in great detail, the administration of the province.

When, within the area which was being provincialised, there were communities with which Rome already had a treaty, this treaty was respected. The terms of these treaties naturally varied; some were treaties between nominal equals, in which the obligations undertaken were strictly mutual, others openly admitted the preponderance of Rome, and bound the other contracting party to further the interests of the Roman people;[3] all seem to have included the provision of military assistance — though for Messana in Sicily it was limited to the furnishing of one ship. When there were other communities which had aided Rome in the preceding struggle, or whose status was for some other reason peculiar, the senate sometimes left them outside the normal provincial administration of the province by declaring them free states. When the kingdom of Attalus was taken over, Greek states in Asia Minor which had not been included in his kingdom were allowed to retain their freedom, except for some which had opposed the interests of Rome. In Sicily there were five free cities, some because they had given assistance to Rome in the first Punic war, others for reasons which we do not know; one of them, Segesta, was proud of claiming that it had been founded by Aeneas. The people of Termessus in Pamphylia distinguished themselves in resisting Mithridates, and we have the text of the law by which special clearly defined privileges were given them as a reward. Mitylene obtained its freedom from Pompey, on his way back from the east, because it was the birthplace of his new friend Theophanes.[4]

These states, whether *foederatae* or *liberae*, retained their status. It would not be true, however, to say that they were not affected when a Roman province was organised around them. On the one hand there was a gain in security both from foreign enemies and from local brigandage. The Roman governor had troops at his command which though not adequate for all emergencies were more powerful than the *civitas* itself could maintain, and in the event of a major invasion, assistance from Rome was more certain.[5] There was a gain in prestige also, since status is always measured by comparison with the neighbours, and citizens of these states could consider themselves superior to the ordinary provincials around them. More important, they were probably exempt from the normal provincial taxation. They might not be financially quite free; it was not impossible for a *foedus* to stipulate the payment of some form of tribute, and the phrase *libera et immunis* implies that a state could be *libera* without being *immunis*;[6] financial burdens were certainly imposed on some of them: we know that in Sicily they were liable to provide the *frumentum emptum*,[7] but at least they were exempt from the tithe.

But there was also a loss. Previously these states had dealt directly with the distant senate and magistrates of Rome, occasionally with a commander-in-chief in the field. Communications were slow, interference sporadic and confined to the barest essentials. Now there was a Roman proconsul permanently stationed near at hand, controlling the affairs of their neighbours; it was inevitable that their dealings with Rome should be through him; interference could be frequent and detailed. True, they had their special status, and could protect themselves from him, as Cicero says, *praesidio foederis*,[8] but that they needed this protection was a new thing. The scrupulous governor, of course, respected their rights, but against the unscrupulous, who was not deterred by the terms of their treaty, they could only appeal to Rome and in the meantime do what they were told.

The truth is that, in this context, both *libertas* and *foedus* had by the time of Cicero become something of a sham. During the conquest of Italy these relationships represented diplomatic realities, and when the Romans first crossed the Adriatic or the Pyrenees they were still valid. But as the empire grew, in these agreements all the power was on one side, and, whatever the juridical terms might be, an equal relationship was impossible.[9] The Romans came to prefer the declaration of *libertas* to the making of a *foedus*, since, though they were in honour bound to defend the *liberi* against attack from without, they were not specifically and irrevocably committed to anything, whereas a *foedus* might impose obligations which they could not evade; however it was clear that the *foederati* were equally indebted to the magnanimity of the imperial power. Their true station was one which was familiar to Roman society, that of the client. The Roman noble was accustomed to the role of patron, conferring benefits of his own free will and expecting services in return,[10] and it was natural for the senate to carry this way of thinking into foreign policy. By this, the patron power, like the individual *patronus*, was bound in general to protect and assist, but free to determine for himself the nature of the protection and the assistance. The special status of these *civitates* conferred distinction, which was valued, and some material advantages, but with the formation of the provinces it no longer corresponded to the facts of the time. The free states are a survival of the Greek city-state into an age in which the city-state is no longer powerful enough to play an independent part in world affairs.

The *lex provinciae* did not confine itself to defining the limits of the province. Apart from the recognition of states with special status — if there were to be any — it laid down detailed regulations for the administration of the rest of the province. And here we come to the most characteristic thing about Roman rule. The Republic had nothing in the least resembling a colonial civil service, and never thought of creating one. For that matter their home civil service was rudimentary in the extreme by our standards. To govern a province they sent out one governor with *imperium,* one quaestor to keep the accounts, up to three legati to act as the governor's deputies and a small number of semi-official *comites*. All of these, quaestor, legati, comites, arrived with the new governor and left with him — if they did not leave before him; and his normal term of office was two years. Clearly, the great bulk of the administrative work must still be done by the provincials. The governor dealt directly with the governments of the separate *civitates* which made up the province — for the province as a whole had no central organisation until the Roman emperors laboriously set about making one.

The composition of the local governments was therefore of great interest to the Romans, and careful provision was made in the charter for this. They were always happiest when dealing with cities like their own, and in some parts of the empire they founded cities, or declared that stretches of the countryside were to be the territory of a neighbouring city,[11] but where, as in Gallia Comata, they had to deal with non-urban tribes, they adapted themselves to this, and did not impose a foreign system.[12] In the towns they concentrated on the local senate, and made, or confirmed, the regulations for membership. Since they intended not to interfere in local politics, but to work through the established government, their regulations inevitably favoured the classes already in possession of power, and it suited the Roman senate that the governments should be in the hands of the well-to-do. The empire is therefore open to the charge that it retarded social and political progress in the provinces, though from the best of motives. There are times when non-interference is itself a kind of interference.[13] In tribes, the important person is usually the chief; hence the names of Dumnorix, Diviciacus, Indutiomarus colour the pages of the *de bello Gallico*. A single chief might be less stable than a body of aldermen, but chief it had to be, and it was vital to Caesar that he should be favourable to Rome.

Having made — or confirmed — regulations for the personnel of the government, the Romans gave them as much freedom as possible in administration, the governor only interfering for certain specified purposes or when things were going wrong. His special spheres of activity will be the subjects of the following chapters; defence, the administration of justice, and taxation. In the first of these, the system had to be flexible, but the principles were well known; for the other two, detailed provision was made in the charter, with careful regard to the local conditions and local practices. Nevertheless, however careful the framers of the charter might be, a great deal depended on the interpretation of the man on the spot. The Roman system of the *imperium*, concentrating as it did all executive authority in the hands of its holder, put great temptation in his way. For the magistrate at Rome there were restraints — colleagues, tribunes, public opinion; for the governor in the province only the distant possibility of a trial before a court far removed from the scene of his misdeeds. Our evidence shows us the conduct of two governors, one careful and conscientious, the other selfish and rapacious. We shall do well to remember that neither Cicero nor Verres was a typical Roman.

II

DEFENCE

It used to be said that there were three things which subject peoples required of an imperial power: peace, justice and low taxation. This is a practical man's definition. Others would say that the goodwill which inspires loyalty is the essential thing; or a creative urge to mould and educate. But perhaps the practical man has the better of the argument; at least it brings the target within reach, and if an imperial power can achieve these things it will be in a better position to receive the loyalty of its subjects than if it is continually worrying about what they are thinking. And the deliberate teaching of backward peoples can hardly begin until the elementary conditions of settled living have been created; once they are created, there is much to be said — within the Mediterranean world — for leaving them to do the rest for themselves. We will therefore postpone to our last chapter the consideration of the 'imponderables', of loyalty, affection and enthusiasm, and return now to the three practical requirements of peace, justice and low taxation. In this and the following chapters we will deal with them separately, in that order. And we shall be starting at the right place, because on the first depends the possibility of achieving the other two. What we are studying now are the policies which enabled the Mediterranean world to enjoy the *pax Romana*.

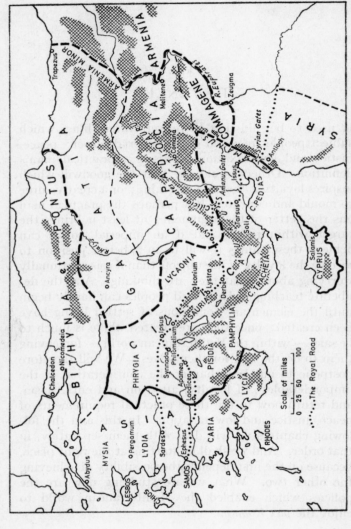

Map 1. ASIA MINOR 51 B.C.

Not least among the benefits of Roman rule was that the various peoples within a province were not allowed to make war upon one another.[1] We know enough of the turbulent history of Gaul before the Roman conquest to realise that civilised living was always in danger. It was only when the Transalpine province was created that the people of Marseilles could breathe freely, and only permanent occupation by Rome restrained the exhausting struggle for supremacy between the Aedui and the Sequani. The subsequent growth of the prosperity of Gaul was tremendous, and, outside Provence at least, the chief Roman contribution was the maintenance of peace.[2] Life in free Spain was probably even more insecure, if we judge by the difficulty the Romans had in finding an organised government with whom they could treat, and there is perhaps no greater transformation in the empire than that which happened in Spain between the lifetimes of Viriathus and Trajan.

Once a province was formed, keeping the peace in it was a responsibility of the governor. For this he might have troops from Italy, and certainly had the right to demand them from the provincial communities themselves. The supplying of troops at need was a condition of any alliance with Rome. But in most provinces he would seldom need troops for this. The knowledge that he was a magistrate of the Roman people, the memory of the wars by which they had been conquered, the certainty of punishment if they were disloyal, these things were normally sufficient.[3] The Spanish provinces were for long exceptions to this, but in most provinces of the Republic internal security did not depend on the sight of Roman troops. The states themselves were not disarmed; such a thing was not practicable before the days of efficient civilian police forces. Nor would it always be wise, since it would increase the immediate responsibility of the governor for the suppression of brigandage or minor riots, and the Romans had no wish to undertake the burden of such elementary police work.[4] When Mithridates invaded Asia in 88, the Roman armies were already defeated, but the cities were not altogether without the means of fighting — though it is noticeable that the stoutest resistance came from outside the Roman province: Termessus in Pamphylia and Rhodes were the heroes of that dark hour; the cities of the province, especially in Lydia and Mysia, had not unnaturally come to rely on the Romans.

Internal security, then, was not normally a pressing problem. External security was another matter altogether. Its gravity varied of course very greatly from one province to another, and nothing short of a complete account of the foreign policy of the Republic would adequately describe it. Here we must be content with understanding its main principles. The province had three lines of defence: alliance with the peoples beyond the frontier; the army stationed in the province; the forces which Rome could, if necessary, send out to deal with an emergency. If the first of these was successful, it was likely that war would never come to the province at all, and it might therefore be the least costly as well as the least unpleasant method of defence. An alliance with Micipsa might be the best defence of the province of Africa; what is more, if war did come, the troops of the king would be a welcome addition to the Roman army — especially his cavalry.[5]

Since, on most frontiers, the neighbouring tribes were

governed by kings or chiefs, and since their alliances with Rome were of necessity one-sided, we commonly talk of the Client Kings; especially when the occupant of the throne owed his position to the gift of the Roman people. Deiotarus was a *socius et amicus* of the Roman people; Ariovistus was — remarkably — *rex et amicus*. But where there was no such personal ruler the Romans were quite willing to declare that the Aedui were collectively their *socii et amici*.[6]

Alliances with these client peoples might prevent the province from becoming a battlefield, but it did not therefore prevent the battle. The client might be attacked from the other side, and then the patron had both an interest and an obligation to protect him. The Aedui were the defence of the Transalpina, the defence of the Aedui involved the Romans in the Gallic war. And if the Romans found that they were compelled to keep troops in the client territory or to control it closely, they might in the end decide that it was simpler for the client to become a province.[7] In fact, all the client states mentioned in this book had become provinces by the time of the emperor Claudius.[8]

Behind the frontier were the troops of the province itself. About them our information is not as full as we could wish. Besides local levies, whose services he was entitled to demand, the governor might have under his command a Roman army, consisting of one or more legions of Roman citizens and a number of cohorts of the allies of Rome.[9] But the Roman Republic did not station an army in a province unless there was work for it to do there, and therefore never built the great permanent depots such as those whose remains bear witness today to the standing armies of the empire. When

B

a province was being established, and for as long as continuous fighting was needed to hold its frontier, the governor was given forces adequate, but not more than adequate, to the tasks expected. If no military action was likely, there would be no Roman army. Nevertheless we must not underestimate the size and permanence of the armies defending the frontiers, and must beware of assuming that the helplessness of Asia was typical.[10] It is certain, for instance, that the Spanish provinces were never in the time of the Republic without Roman troops, and probable that there were seldom less than two legions in each; Macedon, with its long exposed northern frontier, was known for the number of triumphs earned by its governors;[11] in Cilicia, as we shall see, Cicero took over an army in being. Inevitably, therefore, Rome developed what was in practice a standing army, and, as conditions were not continually altering, legions were in fact stationed for long periods in their provinces.[12] In 60, Transalpine Gaul, exposed in situation but with no immediately dangerous enemy (as far as men could then see), had one legion; Syria, the eastern bastion of the empire, had two. That the status of the governor depended normally on the size of the army he was to command shows how important in Roman eyes was the military aspect of the empire.[13]

Normal pacification and defence, then, were achieved by the troops at the disposal of the governor, and for the usual border warfare they had to be enough. But when a major war had to be fought, and the provincial army was inadequate, the Republic had no strategic reserve permanently mobilised under arms. They had in Italy a large reserve of trained manpower, including

many ex-servicemen, who could be immediately enrolled, mustered into legions, and sent to the threatened
spot. This took a little time, of course, and has given
rise to the legend that the Republican empire had no
defence policy.[14] But it is surely not unlike what we do
today. It is an exorbitant form of insurance to maintain permanently under arms in peacetime an army
large enough to fight a major war. Before Marius the
Romans could not possibly have done so even if they
had wanted to, and for some time afterwards their
practice was still governed by the civilised, though
perhaps naïve, assumption that peace was the normal
state. The first Roman to assume that there would
always be a major war was the builder of the *ara pacis*.

If the emergency was not a very serious one, so that
a small additional force would be enough, and provided
that no ambitious noble was looking for a field in which
to display his talents, the governor might be authorised
to enrol further cohorts himself, perhaps an extra
legion.[15] But in a real crisis it became the practice to
send out a new governor, who levied new legions which
he took with him, and if the war transcended the bounds
of one province he was naturally given wider powers.
It was when this commander returned to Rome vic-
torious, with an army to demobilise, that the civilian
government was in danger.[16] Naturally these armies
have overshadowed in our sources the less spectacular
work of the normal provincial armies.

In one respect Roman security measures were for a
long time woefully inadequate. They were by nature
landsmen and soldiers, and though merchandise
travelled in ships, troops marched. They were therefore slow to recognise that they were in fact building

an empire whose centre and artery was the sea. Their armies went to Cadiz via the Riviera, to Thessalonica via Apollonia, and the governors of Narbonensis and Macedonia had as an important part of their duties the protection of the *via Domitia* and the *via Egnatia*. Cicero's Cilicia, as we shall see, controlled the land route to Syria. Consequently they were less interested in safe passage by sea, either in the upkeep of harbours or the suppression of pirates.

The Carthaginians had kept the western Mediterranean safe for their traders, and the fleets of Rhodes and Egypt had been fairly successful in the east. The Romans destroyed Carthage, allowed the power of Rhodes and Egypt to decline, and disbanded their own fleet.[17] They had always regarded it as ancillary to their land forces, and after the organisation of southern Illyricum in 167 their military communications by sea were reduced to a minimum.[18] The interest of the government in protecting traders was only spasmodically aroused by particular events, such as the massacre of Italians at Cirta in 112. It is not surprising that the century which followed the impoverishment of Rhodes was the heyday of ancient piracy. The Balearic Islands in the west, Crete and the Levant in the east were their haunts. Since seaborne trade in the east was much the richer, the pirates were correspondingly more prosperous, and their favourite bases were along the southern coastline of Asia Minor. Here they were protected from the landward side, which meant that they were protected from a Roman army, by the long mountain range behind them, and all the trade of the west with Phoenicia and Egypt was at their mercy. The district was known to the Romans as Cilicia, so that the name Cilician was often used as a general term for a pirate.

It was Roman indifference which allowed the menace to grow; most of the carrying trade was not in the hands of Roman citizens, the senators were not interested. They were in fact debarred by law from owning merchant ships themselves. Most of the Italici who are recorded in the inscriptions of Delos before 88 were natives of southern Italy, not of Rome.[19] After 122 the equestrian *societates* acquired a general interest in the prosperity of the eastern Mediterranean; even so, it was some time before the Roman state took any action, the equestrians having as a rule little direct influence on government policy. But behind Roman inactivity we may also see a more positive motive. Besides plundering the cargoes of ships, the pirates carried on another lucrative business, the kidnapping of natives of the coastal areas whom they sold as slaves. Many of these slaves found their way to Rome, where they provided, between the periodic gluts caused by the great wars, a steady supply of labour which made life pleasant for the rich men of Rome. The suppression of piracy would cut off this supply at the source.

Owing to this combination of indifference and self-interest, little action was taken against the pirates until eventually they went too far. Instead of confining their depredations to private traders, they allied themselves with the military enemies of the state. At the same time, by their attack on the slave port of Delos in 88 they did much to destroy their own usefulness to the Roman nobility. They were no longer a private nuisance which the Romans could overlook, but a direct challenge to the imperial power. Their success as pirates had incensed the equestrians, but it was their transformation into organised enemies which stirred the senate to action. Hence the command of Antonius in 74, the Romans waging war against their three enemies, Mithridates, Sertorius and the pirates.[20] Since there were few resources available for such a campaign, Antonius was not a success, and it was left to the energy of Pompey to clear the seas. Even so, he left no permanent organisation; except in wartime, the Roman system did not easily provide for commands which could not be exercised by the governor of a particular province. Though the civil wars did in fact call very large fleets into being, it was not until the time of Augustus that the seas were effectively policed in peacetime.

All the methods of empire defence can be seen at work in Asia Minor: the refusal to annexe any territory after Magnesia in 188; the greatest of the client kings, the kings of Pergamum, and later of Galatia and Cappadocia, and one of the most important of the free states, Rhodes; the peaceful province of Asia, which seems to have been left without a legion; intermittent and not very successful war on the pirates of Cilicia; emergencies — Mithridates and the pirates — which the local forces were quite unable to cope with; the special commands of Lucullus and Pompey, and the subsequent demobilisation problem; the army of Cilicia under strength in 51 and dependent for reinforcements on Deiotarus and Ariobarzanes; rumours of a Parthian invasion and the realities of the hill tribes; triumphs granted and refused; the unhappy involvement of the provinces in the civil war, and the impoverishment of

Asia in the cause of Roman nobles; fulfilment by the early emperors of a design implicit in the expansion of the Republic.

Since our illustrations of Roman defence policies are taken from the province of Cilicia, this is a good moment to take a closer look at the map of Asia Minor. It consists of a central plateau, difficult to cross and of no great wealth, the centre of the old Hittite empire. To the west it slopes down to the fertile valleys of Ionia, to the north and south it is separated from the sea by long mountain ranges, which in some places reach down to the sea, in others are separated from it by a narrow fertile strip; due east, mountains and then the unattractive uplands of Armenia; south-east, beyond two passes, wealthy Syria and the route to the east. It was by this last way that eastern armies must come,[21] crossing the Amanus by the Syrian Gates, and Taurus by the Cilician Gates, and continuing along the old Persian Royal Road.[22] The plain of Tarsus saw Xenophon and Alexander marching east, the armies of Orodes marching west. But though armies marched the whole breadth of the sub-continent, traders went by sea to Syria, putting in only at the hospitable coasts of Pamphylia and Tarsus. Greek influence had scarcely penetrated into the interior, which remained for long too backward in civilisation to be assimilated or coveted by the Romans.[23]

Cilicia properly so called is the strip of land between the Taurus range and the sea, extending from Syria to Pamphylia. The western end is rugged and inhospitable, appropriately named Cilicia Tracheia, the eastern end, Cilicia Pedias, is open and fertile, centred on the city of Tarsus. As a province it had a curious history. The name Cilicia was used as the title of Antonius' command

against the pirates in 102, and again by Sulla in
92; they had no territory to administer. In his re-
organisation of Asia in 84 Sulla made a territorial province of Cilicia, but it included no part of Cilicia proper;
it consisted of Pamphylia and Pisidia, the Hellenised
coastland where St Paul landed, an interval of civilisa-
between the ruggedness of Lycia and Cilicia Tracheia.
Its function was the defence of Asia from the south-
east, and to act as a base for naval action. Ancient
warships did not easily remain at sea for long periods
without landing, and Sulla had had personal experience
of the difficulties of a naval commander who has no
organised shore base. Here in 80 came Dolabella, with
Verres in his train; next, in 78, Servilius Vatia, to undo
the harm done by Dolabella and to triumph over the
Isaurians who lived inland of the Taurus range.[24]

Pompey transformed the map of Asia Minor. To
begin with, after his suppression of the pirates and
before he took over the Mithridatic war, he provincialised Cilicia Pedias, organising it as a group of city
states, some of which he increased in size by settling in
them the more pacific of the captured pirates. The
province now contained the two fertile enclaves of
the coast, Pamphylia-Pisidia and the Pedias. Of the
Tracheia nothing is known, but even within the bounds
of the Pedias there was the small client kingdom of
Tarcondimotus, and it may well be that the Tracheia
was governed — in so far as it was governed — in the
same way. So far, no radical change, except that the
defence can now be organised at the attacker's bottle-
neck. After defeating Mithridates, Pompey created
along the Black Sea coast the new province of Bithynia
and Pontus, including the wealthiest parts of the Pontic

empire; city-states again, where possible.[25] The coast-line of Asia Minor was now in the Roman empire, the uninviting interior he handed over to the kings Deiotarus and Ariobarzanes, who ruled Galatia and Cappadocia respectively. This is a typically Roman arrangement, by which the kings, in return for the honour and glory, look after parts of the empire where direct Roman control would be arduous and unpopular.

But it was the annexation of Syria which changed the function of Cilicia. Syria now became the first line of defence against the far east, and fighting must be expected on this new frontier. For the movement of troops the Romans required secure land communications, and this meant the road from Asia to the Syrian Gates. The boundaries of Cilicia were extended, to give the governor control of what was now one of Rome's major military routes. For this purpose the province must include Phrygia, stretching far to the north, since troops might be coming from Abydos; Lycaonia and Isauria, to guard the central stretch; then Cilicia Pedias. By the time he is at Laodicea, Cicero is already in his province, and the headings of his letters take us along Xenophon's route.[26] Only the Pamphylians are far from this road, and in one year at least they never saw their governor; for their assizes they had to travel to Laodicea. The result was the curiously shaped province shown in the map on page 16. A difficult province to administer, seeing that the Pedias was cut off from the rest of it in winter by the Taurus mountains; for six months of Cicero's year, not even a letter from the governor reached the cities of Phrygia.

The security of this long and difficult province

B2

involved also the kingdoms of Galatia and Cappadocia. It was part of the duties of the governor of Cilicia to act towards them as the representative of Rome, to support, if need be, their authority, and to make them contribute to the defence of Asia Minor. We should include their kingdoms in the area for whose security he was responsible. Small wonder that we find consular governors.[27]

By Pompey's conquests, the Republic had arrived at what Augustus later decided was the correct frontier for the empire in the east. Though the shapes of the provinces subsequently change, the frontier remains the same. The Pedias was transferred to Syria, a convenient arrangement for administration, and the chief responsibility for central Asia Minor was given back by Antony to the kings. On the death of Amyntas in 25 B.C. Augustus made the large province of Galatia shown in the map on page 291,[28] and it was left to Tiberius, in A.D. 17, to complete the pattern by the annexation of Cappadocia.

III
ADMINISTRATION OF JUSTICE

Once the military security and pacification of his province was assured, the most important task remaining
to the governor was the administration of justice.
Caesar fought the Gallic war in summer, and crossed the
Alps for the winter to hold his assizes in Illyricum and
Cisalpine Gaul; Cicero enters his province at the western
end in July, while his predecessor is still holding an
assize at Tarsus, and immediately starts hearing cases
as he moves eastwards; in the next February he is back
at Laodicea for a long session. The subject is inevitably
a complicated one, and much of our information comes
from chance references, not always unbiased, to particular cases. But the main principles emerge fairly
clearly.

First we must place respect for local customs. The
laws of a country are a reflection of its past history, of
the character of the people and of their economic
interests. On some of the most important matters
Syrians are likely to think very differently from Spaniards, and a law of commercial contracts, for instance,
which would work well in Antioch would be unlikely to
be understood in the highlands of Lusitania.[1] The im-
portation of Roman laws of inheritance would in many
places have been felt as an alien tyranny.[2] And not
only were there differences between provinces; there
were also differences within the province itself, since

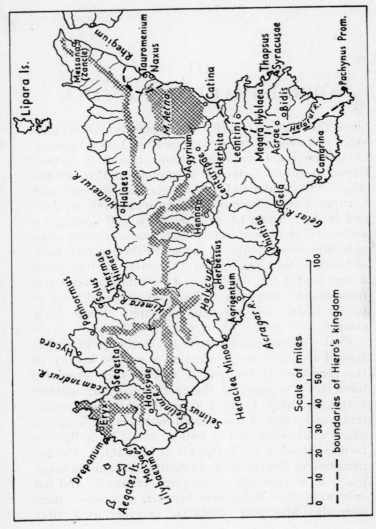

Map 2. SICILY

the province was essentially a group of *civitates*, independent of one another. There might well be differences in the law of property between Lilybaeum in western Sicily and the Hellenised agricultural communities of the eastern end of the island. What was required was a system stable enough to give the consistency essential to civilised communities and yet adaptable to the great variety of societies contained within the bounds of the empire.

It happened that the Romans had developed, very early in their history, a legal system which embodied to a remarkable degree these two requisites, stability and adaptability. In the edictal law of the praetors of Rome was found the basis of a system which combined Roman administration and Roman ideas of fair dealing with the local customs and rules of the provincial communities. Our extracts will show Cicero and Verres administering this law, and some knowledge of the working of the edict is necessary for their understanding.

At Rome elementary human rights were mostly secured by statute, notably by the Twelve Tables, and when it was claimed that one of these had been violated restitution could be obtained by a civil action based on the law, a *legis actio*. But as the condition of life became more complex, and a more sophisticated set of rules was required, it was felt that the passing of new laws would be a clumsy and inefficient way of providing them — as indeed it was, given the nature of the Roman assemblies. Instead, therefore, of evoking new legislation, the magistrates in charge of the courts, principally the praetors, issued their own interpretations of existing statutes, and announced how they would act in cases not covered by statute at all. They were enabled to do this because they were invested with the *imperium*, which gave its holders the power to issue orders to Roman citizens and to compel obedience. It came about therefore that the great majority of civil law cases were heard in courts which depended for their validity on the imperium of the praetor, not on statutes, and the way was open for a much more sensitive and practical development than could have been achieved by a succession of *leges rogatae*. There was, however, a danger in giving such discretionary powers to a magistrate, the danger that he might make up the rules as he went along, and that the people would not know what to expect. It became the practice therefore for the praetor to issue, when he entered office, a statement, in great detail, of the sort of conditions under which he would constitute a trial and the instructions which he would give to the court. He was expected, and after the year 67 he was compelled, to adhere to this edict.[3] There might also have been another danger; since the praetorship was an annual office, and no magistrate could bind his successor, every January might see a new set of rules; a contract, valid when it was made, might no longer be enforceable after a change of praetors. To meet this danger, it was the custom for a praetor to repeat in the main his predecessor's edict, making alterations only if experience was showing that present legal practice could be improved; and for these alterations, if not a lawyer himself, he would have no difficulty in securing expert advice. The edict became, therefore, just the combination of conservatism and innovation which was required.[4]

At Rome, if a citizen thought he had been wronged

by another citizen, he could go to the *praetor urbanus* and claim redress, either in accordance with a *lex*, or, much more frequently, under the terms of the edict. The praetor then summoned both parties, questioned them on the exact nature of the dispute, and decided which section of law or edict applied. If he decided that the case should proceed, he appointed a single *iudex* (or, in some cases, a board of three *recuperatores*[5]) to hear it. He gave to the *iudex* a written formula, exactly applicable to the parties to the dispute, which stated the questions the *iudex* had to answer, the grounds on which he should find guilty or not guilty, and the amount of restitution he should order:

> Let Lucius Octavius be the judge: if it appears that the estate in question is the property of Publius Servilius, then, if it is not restored to him, condemn Catulus to pay to Servilius the value of the estate; if it does not appear so, acquit him.[6]

The case is then heard by the *iudex*, without the further interference of the praetor.

The hearing may be a complicated matter, calling for legal knowledge and acuteness of mind. The *iudex*, who should be acceptable to both sides, is likely to be a lawyer; he has little in common with our jury of ordinary citizens, for which all that is required is 'good men and true'; it is judgement by the expert, not by the average man. The *iudex* will almost certainly sit with a *consilium* of expert advisers, whom he himself chooses, though he does not have to take their advice. But however skilled the *iudex* or his advisers may be, the authority of his judgement depends for its validity on the *imperium* of the praetor.

At Rome the most important edict was that of the *praetor urbanus*, who administered the law between one citizen and another. But with the expansion of Roman interests it was found necessary, in 242, to appoint a *praetor peregrinus*, who should take charge of cases between Romans and foreigners. Here no statute law existed, since foreigners could not be bound by the laws of Rome, so that the only authority was the *imperium* of the praetor. He of course issued his own edict, and for his inspiration he had to consider not what was legal at Rome, but what was right between two civilised human beings who might live normally under different codes. This notion, that there were things which were generally right independently of laws, was the notion of the *ius gentium*, and being the basis of peregrine law tended also to influence the edicts of the urban praetors Roman lawyers were never likely to be carried away by vague ideas, but the notion of the *ius gentium* acted, especially in the most formative period of Roman law, the generation before Cicero, as a humanising force, which made it easier for Roman ideas to be accepted all over the civilised world.

The first appointment of a *praetor urbanus* was traditionally dated to 366, that of a *praetor peregrinus* to 242. In 241 the Romans acquired their first province. It was military reasons which in the first place compelled them to send to the province a man with *imperium*, since it gave him the right to command armies, and the early governors were in fact praetors. It was natural that the praetor in the province, when he had to administer justice, should adopt the methods of the praetors at Rome. The Romans, as we have seen, did not apply their own statute law in the provinces; there is no *legis actio* there. All depends on the *imperium*, and the incoming governor, like the newly elected praetor, issued his edict. There was no systematic attempt to make the edicts in the different provinces resemble one another (the Republic always preferred the danger of chaos to the danger of regimentation), but common sense usually prevailed, and erratic changes were avoided. Cicero took expert advice at Rome (there was time between appointment and departure), modelled his edict on the famous Asiatic edict of Scaevola, and was prepared to make a modification when he reached his province, examined his predecessor's edict and listened to the men on the spot.

It must have been a difficult document to compose; it had to conform to the charter of the province — which the governor-designate could find out about — and take account of the different customs and laws of the *civitates* within the province. It must not be so detailed as to be always in conflict with the local laws, nor so general as to be devoid of meaning.[7] Small wonder that Cicero left an important part of his edict unwritten, announcing that he would be guided in general by the practice of the urban praetor. The edict of Cicero is the only one of which we have much information, yet even on this our knowledge is tantalisingly vague. Of all of his year's jurisdiction, of which he was so proud, there is only one case which he thinks Atticus will be interested to hear about, and that because it affects his friend Brutus. And when we are told about Verres' appointment of *iudex* or *recuperatores*, the presentation is so manifestly hostile that we have to be on our guard.

If the governor's *imperium* was the source of civil

law in the province, when one individual claimed restitution from another, even more did the criminal law depend upon it, when the state inflicted punishment on an individual. The Roman procedure with which we are most familiar, the *quaestiones perpetuae* and the *iudicia populi*, did not apply there, except when a very important case might have to be sent to Rome, when the governor must obviously make his decision on the basis of what the Roman court is likely to do. The practice seems to have been for minor cases to be settled by the *civitas* unaided, and this may have been laid down in the provincial charter, and for the governor himself, sitting with a *consilium* of his own choosing, to hear the rest.[8] Whereas in civil law cases the governor framed the *formula* and appointed the *iudex*, whose decision was then binding, in criminal cases he was himself both judge and jury. Again, if the matter was one covered by his edict, he was expected to observe it, but there was no way of compelling him to do so. Nor was there any appeal. A provincial who had powerful friends at Rome might try to bring pressure to bear on the governor before the trial, but once sentence had been pronounced there was nothing he could do, except submit and hope for revenge when the governor returned to Rome. Roman citizens were better off; if their status, their persons or a large sum of money was involved, they could appeal to the *populus Romanus*, so that the governor was likely to treat them more tenderly; but this appeal involved a journey to Rome, and a hearing before a not very satisfactory tribunal; and even they were in small matters at the mercy of the governor. Moreover, Gavius found that even the magic name of *civis Romanus* was not a certain guarantee.[9]

There remains a class of cases which are neither purely criminal nor purely civil; when the state itself is involved, but there is no question of the individual's having committed a crime; what is sometimes called administrative law. It arises when a citizen or subject is not, in his opinion at any rate, disobeying a legitimate order but contesting its legitimacy. If the magistrate has no doubts, he will normally decide the matter himself, and if he decides against the individual he will use his power of *coercitio* to compel obedience. We are then in the realm of criminal law, compulsion by the state, with punishments for disobedience. At Rome, the citizen had his right of appeal to the people, and a *iudicium populi* might result. The provincial had no such rights, and there the matter rested.

A more difficult problem is presented by agents of government other than the magistrate himself, notably by the *publicani* in the provinces where the taxes were farmed. In a general sense they were of course agents of the government, in that they collected its taxes. But since in fact they had already agreed what they should pay to the treasury, and what they were actually collecting went into their own pockets, not to the exchequer, they could also be regarded as private financiers; in the results of their negotiations with the taxpayers the state had no immediate stake one way or the other. Obviously it was in their interests that the governor should regard them as the agents of the state, and enforce their demands as if they were his own; to apply, if need be, the process of criminal law. The taxpayers, on the other hand, wanted him to treat the *publicani* as private financiers with no superior rights. The best guarantee of this impartiality would be the settling of tax disputes by the ordinary methods of civil law, and this was the correct procedure. In the Sicilian edict of Verres, and doubtless in other provincial edicts as well, was the promise to send such cases to a board of *recuperatores*. In the tax-farming provinces this was the most crucial of the governor's decisions. Best of all, for the *publicani*, was the one who exempted them altogether from the civil law, and himself helped to enforce their contracts; second best, was the one who in framing his *formulae* and selecting *recuperatores* favoured their interests. If he thought it his duty to protect his subjects, the equestrian class never forgave him.

A further extension of this problem is raised by the curious case of the Salaminians. Brutus, or a company in which he was interested, had lent money to the *civitas* of Cypriot Salamis, or rather to its representatives at Rome, at 48 per cent interest, although the normal rate on such loans was 12 per cent. Now Gabinius, in his tribunate, had not only made it illegal to lend money to provincials at Rome, but also made such a contract unenforceable at law, so that repayment could never be demanded in the civil courts. By the influence of Brutus, who was a *patronus* of the island, this contract was specifically exempted from both these disabilities.

Not surprisingly, the Salaminians were unable, or said they were unable, to pay up, and Brutus sent his agent Scaptius to endeavour to collect the money. Now there comes to light one of the more scandalous facts about Roman administration — the readiness of the nobles to use the machinery of government for their own personal ends. Brutus prevailed on Appius Claudius, governor of the province of Cilicia (in which Cyprus was incorporated) from 53 to 51, to treat Brutus' agent as if he was an agent of the state, and actually to give him troops to help him collect the money. The Salaminians suffered, but did not, or could not, pay up. In the summer of 51 there arrived a new governor, in whose edict was the clause that he would not recognise interest rates of more than 12 per cent. The Salaminians sat up and took notice; if they could pay the debt during Cicero's term of office the sum payable would be considerably reduced, and they would be saved from the worst consequences of their imprudent borrowing. Not only that; Cicero raised their hopes at once by recalling Scaptius' troops, thus serving notice that Scaptius was no longer to be regarded as an agent of the government; it was now a private suit between the two parties. When he reached Tarsus, there were the Salaminians, and Scaptius with them. Cicero began to hear the case, and after some argument they were prepared to pay up on the basis of 12 per cent, while Scaptius demanded 48. There is no suggestion in Cicero's narrative that he might have sent the case to *recuperatores*, and indeed there would have been no point; the facts were not in dispute; the only disputed point was the rate of interest to be allowed, and that would have been stated in the *formula*, and therefore fixed in advance by the governor anyway.[10] The decision had to be Cicero's and he should be given the credit for ruling that with the figure of 12 per cent in his edict he could not compel debtors to pay 48, even to oblige his friend Brutus; less credit, though, for undoing the fruits of his courage by putting off the whole transaction, knowing that it was probable that his successor would allow Brutus' claim in full. Of course the Salaminians had contracted originally to pay the high rate of interest, and may well have known all about Gabinius' legislation and hoped that thanks to it they might avoid payment altogether; and as soon as they saw a chance of getting out of part of it they produced a hundred and six talents with suspicious speed. We need not waste too much sympathy on them. But the whole affair shows both the influence which a Roman noble could hope to exert, and the chaotic effect which frequent changes of governor could have on the lives of the provincials.[11]

The system of provincial jurisdiction was not faultless. Too much depended on the governor, on his conscience, his ability and his strength of character. Expert legal advisers may not have been as easy to find in the provinces as at Rome. More central control of the edicts was probably desirable. On the other hand, too many fixed rules would have been an obstacle in a subject of such variety and complexity, and we must remember that our sources present to us almost exclusively the mistakes and the injustices. Of the thousands of cases successfully settled, and the continuous operation of the local courts, we hear almost nothing.

IV

TAXATION AND FINANCE

In the previous chapters we have seen how the Romans
endeavoured to ensure for their provinces the blessings
of peace and justice. We have now to consider how
these things were paid for. By now it should be clear
that we are unlikely to discover a uniform system — or
even perhaps a uniform principle — applied throughout
the Republican empire. What we may well expect to
find is, at the heart of the matter, an essentially Roman
idea, which may be adapted, expanded, modified, and
perhaps eventually submerged as a result of practical
contact with the different peoples of the Mediterranean
world.

The central idea can be simply stated. To the
Romans, military security was always a primary consideration, and in their alliances they made provision
for sharing the burden of future fighting. Their allies
had to provide troops, and it was natural that if the
fighting was far from Rome they should assist in one
way or another in the maintenance of Roman forces.[1]
From this it would not have been a long step to the
idea that a province should contribute a sum of money
to pay for its own defence. In this case, the amount to
be paid would have to be calculated on the basis of
future military requirements. In fact, however, when
the Romans first made provinces, in Sicily and Spain,
they inherited systems of taxation, and, as it was their

habit to use the instruments ready to hand rather than invent new ones, they simply diverted to themselves what the people were already in the habit of paying to someone else. This had great advantages; it did not appear tyrannical, and it saved them from having to experiment with new systems which might fail. True, it did not relate the size of the contribution to the likely cost of defending that particular province, but the Romans were seldom dogmatic in defence of a theory. They were presented with things which worked, and they worked them. And if they had stopped to consider it as a matter of justice, there were two sides to that question too. In any case, taking the empire as a whole, at least until the annexation of Asia, and perhaps until the eastern conquests of Pompey, the Romans took little more in taxation than the empire cost them.

Sicily must have yielded a surplus from an early date;[2] Sardinia too, perhaps, but a small one. But it must have been many a long year before the Spanish provinces ceased to be a burden, and it is doubtful whether Macedonia ever did. The corn of Sicily made possible the rapid growth of the city of Rome, but apart from that the Roman exchequer in the second century had small financial reward from the empire. War booty there was in plenty, but that is another matter; the second century wars were so profitable that direct taxation was abolished in Italy in 167.[3] But the treasury was not getting rich; much of the public expenditure at Rome during the next thirty years was done by the *triumphators* of Pydna and Corinth,[4] and it is clear that in 133 there was no great surplus. Individuals made money too, but the state took little interest in that.

The bequest of Attalus was different; Tiberius Gracchus, in the throes of an expensive agrarian programme, saw in it a financial windfall. Steeped as he was in the ideas of Pericles, he thought it perfectly natural to use the tribute of the allies to augment the domestic revenues of the imperial power. The gift was accepted; the money, after some vicissitudes, began to flow, and a new situation was created. In 66, when the Mithridatic war seems about to start all over again, Cicero can claim that the revenues of Asia are vital to the economy of Rome.[5] But this has still to be balanced against the unremunerative provinces, and, though it was small consolation to the *Asiani*, if we reckon only the sums which found their way into the treasury, the provinces as a whole cannot be said to have been overtaxed. Gaius Gracchus never proposed to *give* corn away in Rome; that was reserved for Clodius, after Pompey's annexations in the east had transformed the financial situation.[6]

But there is more to taxation than fixing the total amount to be paid. The way in which the burden is distributed and the way in which it is collected may be almost as important. But when we attempt to find out what was going on in the Republican provinces, we find that our information is disappointingly meagre. Historians in Republican Rome were nearly always senators[7] — on the principle that only when you had made history were you entitled to write about it — and senators were not normally interested either in financial details or in the feelings of the provincials. When Cicero governed a province for a year he wrote nearly sixty letters home, mostly on matters of public interest; yet there is so little on this subject that we still do not know the basis on which the taxation was assessed. Only when a senator was prosecuted for maladministration did it become necessary for these things to be talked about.

Because Cicero went to exceptional lengths to marshal the case against Verres, and because he published these speeches entirely, the taxation system of Sicily is fairly well known to us; because he did not publish the speech which he reluctantly delivered for Gabinius, that of Syria is not. In reading the Verrines, as of course we must, we have to bear in mind that this was the system in force in one financially important province. We shall learn that detailed regulations had been made in the beginning by the Roman government, that the spirit in which they were administered depended very largely on the governor of the moment, and that the whole matter was of the greatest importance to the provincials. It is likely that these things, at least, were true throughout the empire.

In most provinces Rome inherited a system of taxation, and found it expedient to make few changes. The eastern end of Sicily, the old kingdom of Hiero, was mainly agricultural, and the wealth from which the taxes had to be paid varied with the quality of the harvests. Hiero's taxation was therefore based on the harvest, the farmer being compelled to pay a tenth of his produce to the state. This worked satisfactorily; a farmer's acreage is easily known, the yield, whether in corn or cattle, can be estimated; no great evasion is possible. The Romans took over Hiero's system and applied it to agricultural land throughout their province. The Syracusan farmer need hardly know that the Romans have arrived. The Spanish provinces, which Rome inherited from Carthage, had been paying a fixed tribute, the same sum each year. They too continued as before. Macedonian tribute was based on the previous royal taxation, but here Rome took only half of what they had previously been paying to the king.

The Roman government was not rapacious. The provincials found themselves paying not more, and in some cases less, than before. But of course there is a difference between paying taxes to your own government, when the money is spent in the country, and sending it abroad. And though there might no longer be the expenses of a royal court, the provincial troops and local officials still had to be paid, and public buildings maintained. Tribute to Rome is not the only item in the provincial budget. To strike a financial balance for the allies, we shall have to take account of this, and include the customs dues, besides the other burdens of which we shall speak later.

We now come to the element of the taxation systems which caused most of the trouble — the methods of collection. We must first repeat that the Roman provinces had no central native governments. Even when they inherit a kingdom, which already has one, the Romans dissolve it; they themselves took the place of Hiero, Attalus, Nicomedes;[8] the princes, chamberlains, viziers, are sent packing. Even the extensive royal domains of Bithynia are no longer to be administered from the capital. But though the Romans took the place of the previous government, they had not the means themselves of carrying out the detailed administration which had to be done, nothing comparable to the great Hellenistic bureaucracies. The next chapter will make this clear. The governor had no Department of

Inland Revenue. For the collection of taxes one of two methods was used: either the individual *civitas* — city, prince or tribal chief — was responsible for collecting its own taxes and for paying them to the Roman governor, or the Romans employed a private firm to do the task for them. The first was probably the method employed in the Spanish provinces, and in Caesar's Gallic conquests. It put the burden and the expenses of collection on to the communities themselves, with the added risk that the load would not be fairly distributed among individuals, and that, from sheer inefficiency, the money would not arrive on time, since the *civitates* themselves were not likely to have the necessary trained staffs. In fact, when local taxes had to be collected, it was a common practice for the cities of the Greek east to employ private firms themselves, and Cicero points out that once, when a large lump sum was demanded of them, they had been unable to collect it by any other means.[9]

The second method was that which the Romans inherited in Hiero's kingdom. There the taxes of each city-state were collected by a private firm, but the firm was chosen by Hiero and worked under his instructions; it dealt directly with the individual farmers, and the city government had no part in the matter; if there was a dispute, the parties to it were the *decumanus* and the *arator*. The selection of the private firm was done by the normal method for a public contract, competitive tender. In fact an auction was held, at Syracuse, for the taxes of each state separately, but instead of saying how little they would charge for collection (which would compel the government to find out independently what the year's taxes would amount to), they had to say how much they were prepared to pay, as a lump sum, to the treasury.[10] The auction was held in early summer, when the prospects for the harvest could be assessed, and the contractors had to estimate the probable yield of the tax (because they could only demand from a farmer one tenth of his crop), and subtract their expenses and profits. They are in the position of fixing their own profits, but so does any firm which tenders for a contract, and if the auction is truly competitive they cannot fix them too high; and they take the risk of bad weather at harvest time. This was a sensible method, and the Romans accepted it; in Cicero's day the tithe of Sicily was still being collected in accordance with the *lex Hieronica*. We learn from the Verrines that the governor could still be the cause of injustice, since he organised the auctions and disputes came to be settled by him, but the money did not go through his hands, and any other system would be likely to have given him greater opportunities.

It is when we come to the taxes of Asia that the picture begins to have an unpleasant look. The *lex Aquilia* of 129, which established the province, must have made provision for the collection of taxes, but what this was we do not know. Presumably it was either payment by the cities to the governor, or contracting in the province by private firms on the Sicilian model. We do know that Aquilius was dishonest and inefficient — he was prosecuted for extortion — and that the *lex Aquilia* was unsatisfactory. In 123 Gaius Gracchus made an important innovation. The taxes for the whole province, not of each state separately, were to be auctioned in Rome; like other state contracts, they were to be the responsibility of the censors. Clearly he considered that Aquilius' arrangement was working badly, but whether it was leading to extortion by Roman magistrates or by Asiatic collectors, or just to gross inefficiency we do not know; all we know of Gracchus suggests that he had good reason for dissatisfaction.[11] The result is well known. The business was now so large that only the wealthiest of companies could undertake it; it was no longer open to the small local firms (they may, of course, have been the villains of the piece; it may have been Asiatic corruption which aroused Gracchus' wrath; at Rome there could at least be less concealment). Since senators were not allowed in business this gave new opportunities to the equestrian *societates*, whose happy hunting grounds were to be the eastern provinces, first Asia, then Syria and others.[12] They came to hold a position similar to that of the big oil companies today, and their affairs were similarly mixed up with the foreign policy of the state. We have still to remember that these companies were relieving the state of a complicated burden, and that they had to recover their expenses and make a profit on their outlay; we must also remember that nobody likes being taxed, so that complaints are inevitable. Nevertheless, evidence is not lacking that their ideas of profit were on a grand scale.

Nor did their activities stop at collecting the taxes. If, as frequently happened, the provincials had not the necessary ready cash, the *publicani* were happy to lend it to them, at interest rates which in our day would be considered excessive; the provincials were not always prudent in their borrowing, and interest charges mounted up. The companies also acted as bankers for the state: it was not sensible to convey cash for the taxes of a province to Rome and then send it out again with the new governor. They therefore kept a working balance in the province, on which the state could draw for expenses on the spot, and only surplus cash was sent to Rome, or money to make up a deficit was sent out from the treasury. Like the modern banks, the *publicani* came to permeate the whole economy;[13] their overseas agents are men of whom we should like to hear much more than we do.

At the beginning of each five-year period, when the contract had been made at Rome, these agents descended upon the provincial communities to make arrangements for collection. Bargains were struck (*pactiones* is the word used for these), and it was at this time that the arbitration of the governor was most likely to be invoked; though it was never quite certain that a bargain approved by one governor would be counted valid by his successor.

The *publicani* were evidently involved in the abuses which Scaevola and Rutilius Rufus set out to cure in 95, as the violence of the equestrian reaction shows;[14] they made the exactions of Sulla in 84 their opportunity,[15] and when Lucullus twelve years later put a stop to their extortion they again had their revenge.[16] It is possible that when they supported Pompey in 66 it was in the expectation that he would open up to them a further profitable field in Syria — as in fact he did. And when, in Syria, Gabinius crossed swords with them, not even the support of Pompey himself could save him.[17] That the system was being abused was well known in Rome. Caesar did not apply it in the *Tres Galliae*, and even abolished the auction of the

Asiatic taxes, and Augustus set about creating, at long last, a civil service (which included men who had worked for the private companies before), able to do the detailed work of administration which the Republican state had been unable to do for itself.

Customs dues, *portoria*, were levied first at the ports of Italy, and then throughout the empire;[18] the object was revenue, not protection of local industries or agriculture. Again, our information is fragmentary and not very illuminating. In both Asia and Sicily, for instance, these dues were collected by *societates* headed by Roman equestrians, and when Cicero speaks of the Asiatic dues he seems to be assuming that the proceeds were sent to Rome; and when Verres evaded payment at Syracuse, Cicero describes it as a fraud practised on the shareholders of the Roman company.[19] The city of Termessus, which was within the province of Cilicia, was allowed to collect, and doubtless also to keep, its own transit dues (with the proviso that they should not be demanded from men on Roman public service, including *publicani*); but Termessus was being made a free city, and this was part of its exceptional privileges.[20] It is probable that the normal *portoria* of Cilicia were taken by the Romans. As the system was developed in the imperial period, the Romans collected dues as goods crossed the frontier of a province, or of a group of provinces, but allowed them to move, once within that frontier, without further payment. In the year 60, when the revenues from Pompey's conquests were flowing to Rome, *portoria* were abolished in Italy, where now no tax was levied except the 5 per cent tax on manumission.[21] During the fifties it is possible to say that the Romans were living on their empire.

Less serious, probably, in the amounts involved, but important in their effects on the minds of men, were the expenses of the Roman officials. The governor, though not paid, did receive from the Roman treasury a sum of money to cover the expenses of himself and his staff; and might also have the right to buy corn locally at a price fixed by the senate.[22] But there were certain things, including lodging for the night when on tour, which he could demand from the provincials among whom he moved. We may take it as certain that the scale of these allowances was generous. We need not rely on Cicero's attack on Piso's *vasarium*, which he says was eighteen million sesterces, adding that Piso did not even need to take it with him and therefore banked it at Rome; this may be misrepresentation. We can put aside the accounts of Verres the quaestor, since there was at that time a civil war on. We have more reliable evidence: Cicero was governor of Cilicia under nearly normal conditions, and he had been unusually scrupulous in paying for the things which he requisitioned; yet at the end of his year his surplus allowed him to give the new quaestor enough to last him a year and still leave a substantial sum over.[23]

That this should be so should cause us no great surprise, and there is no need to be cynical about it. In an aristocratic government where the holders of office are unpaid, yet have to keep up an imposing state, where they see that thanks to their public service their social inferiors are becoming richer, they take such steps as the morality of the time allows to pay themselves what they think they deserve. This is not confined to Romans: in 1773 the British House of Commons recorded that at the time of the deposing of Surajah

c

Dowlah, the Nabob of Bengal, Robert, Lord Clive had obtained rupees to the value of £234,000, and the story is told of how Sir Arthur Wellesley, the future Duke of Wellington, was offered — though he refused it — a bribe of £70,000 by the Nizam of Hyderabad. The Romans are not the only people of whom it could be said that 'with the increase of empire came also an increase of private wealth'.[24] The drawback of this system of unofficial payment is that the highest rewards go to the most unscrupulous. Of Roman governors, some lived strictly within the letter of the law, some lived rather more comfortably or made a modest profit on their 'expense accounts', while some set out to make all the money they could.[25] If Cicero is to be believed, the inhabitants of his province were amazed at his probity and delighted by his economy. Gaius Gracchus claimed that he lost money in his quaestorship. And there were others. But both Gracchus and Cicero would have the world believe that they were exceptional, and give the impression that the majority of governors were accustomed to embezzlement on a large scale. It was one of the merits of the *lex Julia* of 59 that it drastically limited the illicit profits of the nobility, stating in great detail what they were entitled to requisition.[26]

Nor were these expenses finished when the governor left. It was necessary to his prestige at Rome (and perhaps to his safety) that on his return he should be followed by deputations from the province praising his administration. This had to be done in style, of course, and might entail a considerable journey. It was often a strain on the local finances, especially if it had to be done every two or three years. Yet such was the need to keep in the good books of the Roman nobility that many cities which were not particularly wealthy were constrained to spend more than they could afford in this way. Apamea was bankrupt when Cicero found it honouring his predecessor; it was alleged as a disgrace to Verres that only one city of Sicily sent such a deputation in his honour.

Two more things should be added under this heading. One is the practice of granting official status to Roman individuals for the prosecution of their private business in the provinces. A senator with estates abroad was often appointed to a *libera legatio*, becoming a kind of ambassador without portfolio, which meant that he travelled at the public expense and was assisted in his business activities by the prestige attaching to the title of *legatus*; he might even be accompanied by lictors. This abuse of power, too, was curtailed by Caesar. Non-senators, if they had influence in high places, were often given the rank of *praefectus*, in effect a commission in the army, by a provincial governor, thus putting them also at an advantage in their dealings with the provincials. It was even known for such a *praefectus* to be given a body of troops with which to enforce his own private claims,[27] and this, even if it did not happen very often, was bound to be the cause of strong resentment. Again, it is Cicero's boast that he never gave the rank of *praefectus* to a business man, and though this seems an elementary matter to us, it evidently took some firmness to sustain this policy in the face of frequent requests from his friends.

Finally, there was the billeting of troops. In some countries and in some ages, it has been an advantage, both socially and economically, to become a garrison town. There is more social life, and more money is spent in the shops. In the time of the Roman emperors, the civilian centres which grew up around the great permanent camps prospered, and so did the whole neighbourhood. But the Republic did not build permanent fortresses; for the winter, if the military situation demanded, they kept the troops in their own winter quarters, probably none too comfortable, but if this was not necessary, they billeted them in private houses in provincial towns. This should have brought money into the town, since what they used should have been paid for. But evidently that did not happen; again and again we meet the complaint that billeting was a ruinous burden, which the cities will do almost anything to avoid; again, there is this gap between what Romans were entitled to take and what they actually did take.[28] One of the privileges granted to the city of Termessus was freedom from this imposition — freedom, that is, unless the senate specifically decreed otherwise.

There is, however, another blot on the picture, which, though it is not a part of the normal administration, should not be omitted from any survey of the finances of the empire. It was the Roman practice (and not one confined to Romans) to make wars pay for themselves. A commander was given a very free hand in the accumulation and distribution of booty, and in demanding supplies and other aid from the country in which he was campaigning. So long as these depredations take place outside the empire, like the scandalously profitable campaign of Manlius in Asia Minor in 189, they do not concern us directly. But commanders sometimes found it easier to plunder a province, which could not resist, rather than the enemy, who could; especially if it was a rich province. Sulla insisted on writing an indemnity into the treaty of Dardanus, as the price of his compact with Mithridates, but it was the rich province of Asia which paid the highest price: a huge indemnity for a war which they had not begun, and a lump sum of five years' taxes; and, added to that, the luxurious way in which they had to maintain Sulla's disgruntled troops through the winter.[29] The Asiatic cities had to have recourse to the moneylenders, incurring debts which were so ruinous that without Lucullus' help they might never have become solvent again.[30] Later, Cicero can claim it as an exceptional merit of Pompey that the allies regard him as less dangerous to them than to the enemy. There were too few limits to what the holder of an imperium could demand from the allies of Rome. In the civil wars, the luckless eastern provinces, rich and unwarlike, were ransacked, first by Pompey himself and then by Cassius, to finance struggles for power in which they had not the slightest interest.

In general we may conclude that the Roman government did not set out to make financial gain out of the provinces they ruled. The picture of worthless descendants of Romulus battening on the labours of industrious Spaniards and Asiatics is highly misleading.[31] Not until near the end of the Republican period did they make any substantial profit; and so long as they, and the Italians, did the bulk of the serious fighting on the frontiers they can claim to be entitled to some reward. If they are open to criticism it is because they did not adequately control the methods by which the taxes were collected and transmitted, and for too long allowed too much latitude to individuals. Too much of what the provincials paid found its way into private pockets. The Romans had never needed a complicated apparatus of collection for themselves, and the nobles were not sufficiently interested in public finance to appreciate the need of it in the provinces. This lack of organisation, the absence of expert auditing, put too great a strain on personal honesty. The senator's life was extravagant and unpaid; the opportunities of money-making and the pressures to help their friends were great; the dangers of defending the provincials from the tax collectors were notorious. Not all Roman governors could be as determined as Gaius Calpurnius Piso Frugi. Even so, in proportion to the wealth of the empire and the growth of prosperity which accompanied the *pax Romana*, it is possible that the average level of extortion was not nearly as high as we are sometimes tempted to believe. It was sudden exorbitant demands from ambitious proconsuls, to meet immediate military needs, which were so ruinous. Sulla and Cassius were the villains of the Asiatic scene.

V

THE EXECUTIVE

'PEACE, justice and low taxation.' We have seen in the preceding chapters how the Romans set themselves to achieve these three ideals of an imperial power, and we should by now have formed some idea of the magnitude of the task. It is time to consider who were the men they sent out to do the work, and how they were selected and controlled.

We can begin by saying what the Romans of the Republic did not do. They did not evolve a separate career for men who wanted to devote their lives to provincial administration. There was no colonial civil service, there were no career diplomats. The various activities of government were in their eyes indivisible, and it never occurred to them to separate off any one of them from the main stream of public life. Just as, at Rome, the same men were assumed to be capable of holding civilian and military power, so, in the empire, the men who governed at Rome could govern in the provinces.

When they made their first province, in Sicily, they sent there one of their annual praetors, and it was for provincial government that the number of praetors was increased from two to four. A praetor had just the right status; he could command troops and administer justice, and he was subordinate to the consuls. But as the empire grew, it did not seem right to them to go on increasing the number of praetors to meet the growing need; instead, they adapted a system which had already been evolved to meet military needs. When a consul (or praetor) was commanding in a war and his year of office expired, he ceased to be consul; but it might not be expedient to take him away from the war. The Romans therefore solved the problem by continuing his *imperium*, no longer as consul but as proconsul, while another consul reigned in Rome. For the purpose of the task assigned to him — and therefore perhaps in a limited area — the proconsul retained all the powers which he had had as consul, except that if conflict should arise he had to give way to the man who now held the office.[1] This system was applied to the normal government of the provinces. It gradually came to be an accepted rule that the Roman magistrates, consuls and praetors, remained in Italy during their year of office, and that they then, normally, went out for the next year or two to govern one of the provinces. Individuals sometimes preferred not to, and there was no compulsion, but the system demanded that the majority should shoulder the foreign burden. It has been thought that when Sulla increased the number of praetors to eight, he was calculating that as there were at that moment ten provinces and there would be ten holders of *imperium* available each year (the outgoing consuls and praetors), each province would receive a new governor each year. If so, his calculations were soon upset; before twenty years had elapsed the number of provinces had grown to thirteen, while a number of city magistrates preferred not to go to a province at all. As a result, two years seems to have been the normal term of provincial office, and three was not unknown.[2]

This system had results both good and bad. On the good side, it meant that the provinces had, for limited periods, their share of the best men in Rome, and did not have to be content with second best. Many men who would not have chosen to go to the provinces proved, when they were there, to be good governors. It also meant that these men, when they had returned to the capital, could draw on personal practical experience of the empire; the most notable reformers in this field, Pompey and Caesar, knew what they were about. If provincial affairs were neglected at Rome, it was not from ignorance on the part of the nobles. The senate, which was the recognised body for controlling foreign policy, might be expected, when the Sullan system of recruitment had had time to become established, to contain at any one time upwards of sixty men who had governed a province.[3] In addition, the great majority had served abroad as quaestors, and very many as *legati*.

But there were drawbacks. Some governors were men who would rather have been in Rome,[4] or who looked on their province as a means of making a name for themselves, to improve their chances of success in the forum. There was little sense of dedication, or tradition of service, in the proconsuls of the Republic. Moreover, the shortness of the term of office meant, it is true, that you could do less harm, but it also meant that you could do less good; in either case, much of what you did might soon be undone.

Unfortunately there was a more serious defect. Public life in Rome was expensive, provincial government could be made profitable. Apart from the normal senatorial extravagance, the rising young politician was likely to spend a great deal of money during his aedile-ship (when he was expected to give lavish games), when standing for the praetorship two years later, and especially when persuading the people to elect him to the consulship. To recoup himself — since he never received a salary — he too often relied on his tours of duty abroad. He had to come back with money as well as a reputation. And the connection was very close; a man who was elected in Rome could count on a pro-vince in eighteen months' time, and since unless he was elected there would be no province there was both the added incentive to secure success in the election and the prospect of acquiring the means to pay for it.[5] Verres is said to have paid his bribery agents three hundred thousand sesterces to help him to the praetorship,[6] and the Sicilians considered that they were being made to foot the bill. Apart from the notorious villains, it was probably normal for a governor to return to Rome richer than when he had set out.[7]

Election by the people, then, was the necessary first step. The next was taken by the senate. They heard deputations from their allies, especially in February, and then decided which of the provinces should receive new governors in the following year; the praetors in office, and until 123 also the consuls, then decided, probably by casting lots, how these provinces should be apportioned among them; the senate voted the money necessary for their expenses, judging in each case what the needs of the province were likely to be.[8]

Next, the governor's staff had to be selected. Most important were the legati — or legatus. Normally not more than three to each province, they were senators of some seniority, perhaps even senior to the governor himself. They were probably chosen by him in the first place, but their appointment had to be ratified by the senate. These men could be his best advisers, but apart from Caesar's marshals in Gaul, and a few like Rutilius Rufus in Asia, we hear little of their activities. Cicero's interest in Sicily extended no further than Verres, in Cilicia no further than himself. These legati had no imperium of their own, but the governor could delegate to them anything which he was entitled to do himself, and they acted in virtue of his imperium. Local assizes or the command of detached bodies of troops were their chief concern.[9]

Next in importance on the staff was the quaestor. Aged thirty, or a little more, he had done his military service and was just entering on a senatorial career. His primary task was financial, to keep the accounts, but this was seldom a full-time occupation, and we hear of quaestors holding assizes and even commanding troops, like the more senior legati. When Cicero left his consular province before the arrival of his successor, he eventually decided, after some hesitation, to give the charge of the province to his quaestor, which seems to us a remarkable delegation of important responsibility to a young man. Because of his inexperience, the quaestor was often regarded as being particularly under the personal care of the governor, and though they were supposed to be allocated to the various provinces by lot, we can see that friendships and family connections sometimes decided the choice.[10]

The legati and the quaestor were the official staff. To these it seems that we should add a few more individuals whom he might take with him, whose status was somewhere between public officials and private servants of his own.   They are his *comites*, but as they normally stayed around his house, and had not so many official duties delegated to them, they were colloquially known as his bodyguard, his *cohors*.[11]   As happens in many of these things, our most detailed description is in the Verrines;   there, however, though Cicero's invective in personal abuse is not yet at its height, his description of the cohors, 'which did more harm to Sicily than a hundred cohorts of runaway slaves',[12] may be as far from the truth as some of his later denunciations of Mark Antony.   All the same, it was obviously possible to have a good time as a hanger-on at headquarters, and to accept money for admitting men to the governor's presence and drawing his attention to individual requests.   There were likely to be some things which did not go through the official channels, and they could bring profit to the unofficial advisers.   The story of Pamphilus' cups, which is printed in Part Two, may well be true.

Apart from the army and its officers, these are the sum total of the administrators sent out to a Roman province: a proconsul; one or two legati of his own age (at the most, three); a young quaestor; a few assistants.   For the acts of all of them the proconsul was likely to be held responsible.   Since he could not be everywhere himself, he had to leave much to them, and his reputation in the province was to a large extent in their hands.   They might support him in honest dealing, or they might abuse their position behind his back; they might certainly be his confederates in crime; if the worst happened, he alone was likely to be prosecuted at Rome.[13]

The governor was a very powerful man.   But if his

staff were not good, or happened not to be congenial, he might also be a lonely one. Imposed for a year or two on an alien community,[14] with not much time for finding out how to be firm without being a tyrant, he could easily make mistakes. When Quintus Cicero was governing Asia, his elder brother wrote him some long letters of advice, from which we can learn some of the pitfalls which beset the path of the well-meaning governor. In particular, he might on his arrival make friendships with provincials which might prove embarrassing and hamper his impartial judgement; and he had to learn to be firm with the *publicani* without being unnecessarily rude. These pitfalls are doubtless familiar to colonial civil servants the world over; what strikes us in the Roman system as strange is that the governor had so little training or experience of these problems. Cicero had a year as quaestor in western Sicily at the age of thirty; twenty-four years later he was again officially abroad, this time as proconsul of a large and difficult province; he preferred Rome, and never expected to be a governor; as he says to Atticus, 'rem minime aptam meis moribus'. Yet he was a success. It is common to deride his vanity, easy to believe that he was too ready to be flattered by the praises of the Cilicians. But it is impossible to read his letters home without being convinced that they were written by a man who was honestly and competently doing the duty to which it had pleased the government to send him.

In the province, the governor was the only holder of an imperium; his duties of defence and jurisdiction gave him very wide powers, while his position as the only representative of the Roman people enabled him in fact to interfere in many things which were outside his proper sphere. When he gave an order, it had to be obeyed. The provincials might complain, they might point to a law which he was flouting, but if he insisted they had to do what he told them. His powers of punishing individuals and of bringing pressure to bear on communities was too great for them to resist. Restraint could not be imposed in the province; if there was to be any, it must come from Rome. We must now consider in more detail what control the home government exercised over its proconsuls. This is not the place to discuss the major decisions of foreign policy; the decisions to send first Lucullus and then Pompey to enlarge the empire in the east, or the decision not to send anyone to organise the affairs of Egypt. Some of these had administrative consequences, which we shall notice, but they belong in the main to the external history of the empire. What we are concerned with is the normal business which the governor had to transact.

First, as to positive policy; how did the Roman government get things done? They certainly gave the governor ample powers; how did they see that he did the right things? It is when we try to answer this question that we see most clearly the limitations of the Republican empire. The truth is that the Romans did not think of it as their duty to initiate policy in the administration of the empire — not by official state action, at least. They were not governing in that sense at all, and did not want to. The size of the staff they sent out makes that clear. Their aim was to interfere as little as possible, and then only when their own interests were concerned. The provincial communities planned their own affairs, while the Romans kept the peace and settled disputes.

Governors were senators, and had relations or friends who had served their term somewhere in the empire; they understood, in a general way, what was expected. Before they set out, they framed their edict, and this moment, if used properly, could be fruitful. There was expert advice available at Rome. They could go to their provinces full of good intentions. Once there, they were very largely cut off from home. Letters travelled slowly, and did not always arrive; people at Rome were busy about other things. It was nobody's business to watch their administration or to send advice or instructions. We can be sure that in Republican times there was nothing remotely resembling the letters which the emperor Trajan wrote to Pliny in Bithynia.[15]

Then, on the negative side, to prevent the governor from doing harm; what control did the central government have? The answer of course is 'not very much'. There was no right of appeal from proconsul to consul, no right of appeal to the populus Romanus, except for those who happened to be Roman citizens and if the case was important enough. There were no official channels by which injustice could be prevented. It is possible, however, to be too emphatic about this; the case of Sthenius, which we print, shows that it was sometimes possible to bring pressure to bear on a governor by agitating at Rome; but it also shows that the provincial by himself could do nothing. He had to secure the active goodwill of influential senators, who might write to the governor themselves,[16] or might even bring the case before the senate. The hearing of deputations from the provinces was a recognised part of senatorial business, and it enabled them to keep in touch with what was going on abroad. It became the custom, in fact, for the month of February to be set aside for this purpose, a convenient month because it was after that that they made their arrangements for future governors. It was not always easy to get a hearing, and expensive presents might have to be given. But if you did get a hearing, and your friends were influential, something might be done. For Sthenius, in fact, the senate came near to passing a decree which would have invalidated in advance the verdict which Verres was supposed to be going to pronounce against him. In that year (71), one of the consuls was *patronus Siciliae*, and it was thanks to him that the senate heard of the case.

It seems, too, that in the last years of the Republic a slightly simpler process was being evolved, which did not depend on a vote of the senate. Judicial decisions in the provinces had their validity from the *imperium* of the governor, and were therefore magisterial acts; but every act of a magistrate could be annulled by another magistrate of superior or equal *imperium*, and in the theory of the Roman constitution the *imperium* of the consuls was valid everywhere, being at least equal to that of a proconsul. It was therefore possible for a consul to intervene, if he wished, on behalf of a provincial. The provincial had no *right* to call in the consul, the governor had no obligation to delay the case while he did so, and in any event the consul could refuse to act — and probably would. Communications being what they were, the way was not easy, and we can hardly go so far as to list this among the processes of law under the Republic. But a start was made. The case of Mescinius (*ad fam.*, XIII. xxvi) is instructive: the consul had been approached in advance, by a man of influence, and had let the proconsul know that he was prepared to intervene; the governor might as well send the case to Rome in the first instance. This is *appello consulem*, not *provoco ad populum*; it is the beginning of *appellatio*; if the consul acts and the case goes to Rome, it is *revocatio Romae*. Again, we find that an institution which is thought of as imperial was a Republican invention.

We see now why it was so important for a provincial to have friends at Rome. And not only for individuals; communities might well want the same kind of protection. The result was that once a Roman noble became known in a province — even if he had not been well liked — he could be approached subsequently in this sort of matter, and would become a sort of unofficial advocate. His sons would be expected to inherit the position, and a body of fixed loyalties was created. M. Claudius Marcellus had captured Syracuse in the second Punic war, and terminated the revolt of Sicily; his family ever after that were patrons of the island, and in 95 they were consulted about the making of new regulations at Halaesa. This foreign extension of the client system was useful to the provincials as an insurance against injustice; it suited the Roman nobles, to whom it was a matter of prestige to have a large *clientela* and to have the reputation of being an effective *patronus*. It was the result of the lack of close control by the state: if there are no official channels, you turn to unofficial ones; the disadvantage is that your success then depends not on the justice of your cause so much as on the importance of your friends; when things are done by *gratia* they are not always the right things. The system naturally flourished, until in the end the great *principes* can count continents among their supporters, and to assess the resources of Pompey and Caesar in their political rivalry at Rome we need a map of the whole Roman world.

But it was when the governor returned to Rome that the provincials really had their chance. The moment he crossed the *pomoerium* his imperium fell from him, and he was no longer protected from action in the courts. In the early days of provincial complaints the senate had set up special tribunals (*quaestiones*) to hear them, as for the Spanish complaints of 171. In 149, by a law of the tribune Calpurnius Piso Frugi, a permanent court was established to try cases of extortion, the *quaestio perpetua de rebus repetundis*.[17] The composition of the court and the penalty were laid down by the law, and no further legislation was required to set the machinery in motion. If the governor was convicted, those who had been robbed had restitution made to them. The procedure was found to be a good one, and was adopted in courts subsequently established to try other crimes of public life.[18]

It was known to the provincials, then, that when their governor returned home there was a court established which would hear their complaints, and, if it convicted him, would order him to make restitution. Individuals could go to Rome, or communities could send deputations. Cicero describes this court as the only hope of the allies.[19] It was known also to the governor, who could take counter-measures; it was open to him to persuade cities in his province to send delegations to Rome to praise his administration. It was customary for such delegations to set off soon after the governor had himself left, and if there was any question of prosecution they would be powerful evidence on his side.

Cicero's predecessor in Cilicia had to face a prosecution, and was therefore very angry when Cicero prevented cities in the province from sending such testimonials. It was quoted against Verres that only one Sicilian city honoured him in this way.[20]

Here again, the provincials' chance of success was greatly increased if they could secure the services of a Roman of ability and influence to conduct the case. And now they came up against another of their difficulties: the most important men in Rome were senators, who were primarily concerned to advance their own careers; for this they needed alliances, not feuds; friends, not enemies. They were likely to do themselves harm by prosecuting a noble. It was not easy, under these circumstances, to persuade such a man to champion the cause of a distant community against one of his own kind. Cicero was indeed persuaded to represent the Sicilians, and did so with great ability and success, but within the year he was putting himself right with the nobility by defending Fonteius, governor of Transalpine Gaul, who was probably guilty.[21] Caesar prosecuted Dolabella and spoke for the Bithynians, and might well have done more had he not had so many calls on his energies; but then Caesar despised the ordinary senatorial intrigue, and was acquiring his own notoriety by defying them. When the Cilicians wanted to bring Appius Claudius to book, one of their chief difficulties was to find a good prosecutor; they had to be content with the young Dolabella, and Appius was acquitted. Moreover, unwary provincials were the most likely victims of the practice of *praevaricatio*.[22]

Having secured a prosecutor, the next thing was to persuade the jury to convict, which might be harder still. The exact nature of the obstacle varied with the composition of the jury.[23] Before the tribunate of Gracchus and in the ten years after the dictatorship of Sulla, it was the simple reluctance of senators to condemn one another; when the equestrians dominated the juries, the prospect was more varied: it was possible for a governor to be condemned, but it could be for the wrong reasons and it could be the wrong governor. On this one issue the equestrians felt as a body, and if a governor had offended the Roman business community, which included the tax-collecting firms, they were likely to get their own back in the extortion court. Unless, that is, the bribes offered by the defendant were sufficiently high; this other ugly feature of Roman public life also worked to the detriment of the allies. If the jury condemned, the provincials would get their restitution, but it might be because the governor had, in the main, protected their interests; while if he had been careful to keep on good terms with the class from which his future jury would be drawn, the wrongs which he had done to them would probably go unrequited. For the period of purely equestrian juries we have in fact not much evidence;[24] the Rutilius case is always quoted; the major scandals, before Gracchus and after Sulla, were unjust acquittals, achieved by a combination of bribery and senatorial fellow-feeling.

At the best, and leaving out of account the possibility of deliberate chicanery, the extortion court method suffered from two serious defects. On the one hand it was only a court of pecuniary restitution; unless the governor made an illicit profit which could be measured in money, no prosecution could be brought. There could be many kinds of injustice which were not covered at all.[25] On the other hand, it was too big and important. It called in question the entire reputation and career of a Roman noble. No court in Rome, however enlightened, would condemn a noble and terminate his career if his administration had been on the whole satisfactory. In such cases there was no machinery for righting the wrongs of individuals, however badly those individuals had suffered. And there was certainly no remedy for an honest mistake by the governor. Only when he had been pronounced guilty of extortion did the process of restitution begin. An action for assessment (the *litis aestimatio*) was then held, at which the jury decided, in detail, which of the charges was considered proven, and how much restitution was due for each. The convicted man had to pay the total sum to the quaestors, whose duty it then was to satisfy individual complainants. The process was also expensive: delegations to Rome, inducements to barristers, goodwill presents — the bill might be large. Only if there were many serious complaints would it be worth while.[26] There was need of a less spectacular review of ordinary administrative acts, and this need the Republic did not meet.[27] Nevertheless we must not unduly minimise the laws on this subject. Even if their enforcement was not easy, so that infringements were not often punished, they did lay down, especially after 59, what was legal and what was not. The mere fact that these things were on the statute book for all to see must have some effect. Most administrators have some respect for the law. And even if there is no great likelihood of being convicted, no one wants to be prosecuted; the prospect of having your shady dealings examined in open court is bound to act as a deterrent.

VI

AUGUSTAN EPILOGUE

It is time now to return to the question with which we began: is it true that the Roman Republic mismanaged its empire? We have touched on most of the charges which have been made, and have endeavoured to present a fair selection of the evidence. We are now in a position to collect the charges together and see what they amount to. We can also try to answer the other question: did morality really come in with Augustus? It will help us to answer both of these questions if we consider what he changed in the imperial system and what he left unchanged. He and his advisers made a careful study of the problem and tried hard over many years to find a solution. He had the great advantage that, once established, he did not need to spend his energies in preserving his position in the city; those who would have been his rivals were dead, or had learned that open opposition was useless. Assured, as long as his health permitted, of continuous power, he could turn his attention to each of the main problems of government, without the haste which characterised the annual tribunes of the Republic.[1] The Augustan reforms, both in what they changed and what they did not change, are a good contemporary commentary on the institutions of the Republic.

Let us begin with Augustus' military system. First, he accepted the existing composition of the armies, that the hard core should be the legions of Roman citizens, and that they should be supported by auxiliary forces provided by the *socii*. The size of an army was still measured in legions, and the day had not yet come when they were held in reserve while the allies do the fighting. He also accepted the necessity of keeping standing armies in most of the provinces. Long-term foreign service by Italians was the thing which held the empire together. What he did do was to abolish the emergency armies; these had been a great source of danger to the civilian government and of social and economic instability in Italy. All emergencies are now to be dealt with by the standing armies, which have therefore to be much larger. Instead of the fourteen permanent legions of the sixties, there are by the year 13 twenty-eight. Inevitably there will be in peacetime too many soldiers, in wartime too few. Nor was there a high degree of mobility: the shortages on the Rhine after the *clades Variana* were not made good by the idle legions of Syria. True, Italy was spared the unsettlement of mobilising and demobilising, and this helped in what was one of Augustus' greatest achievements, that of keeping the army out of politics. But it did not achieve it of itself; on the contrary, the standing armies themselves became a menace, if their commanders were disloyal. The secret lay rather in his choosing, and moving, of the army commanders.[2] The Republican senate had understood this too, but on occasions its hand had been forced by a law of the people; the military dangers had sprung from the *lex Vatinia* and the *lex Titia*. Augustus' control in these matters was unchallenged. No law made an unwelcome appointment, no appointment of his was vetoed by a tribune.

The Republican senate had lost control of its generals because it had lost control of their appointment.

Having found a way of keeping a large army in being and keeping it loyal, Augustus had more freedom for his own initiative in foreign policy. The Republic had fought its wars with reluctance, and its annexations had been spasmodic. Even Caesar had felt the need of a *casus belli* for the Gallic war. Augustus could plan to wage a continuous war over many years. The Republic had conquered Asia Minor and Gaul, and might have gone on, had there been provocation, to extend the province of Illyricum. But the cold-blooded advance to the Danube, the persistent 'rationalised aggression', had to wait until the senate no longer controlled affairs. We must not underrate the planning of senatorial policy, but it was by nature less radical and less adventurous. The senate could never have planned the invasion of Bohemia.[3] It is as if Augustus was the first Roman to sit down with a map of the world and decide how far the empire ought to go.[4] In his last instructions to his successor, he spoke of the *termini imperi*, the natural bounds of the empire.[5]

To turn to the civilian administration of the provinces; its main principles had been local autonomy with general control by senatorial governors; jurisdiction by edict; payment of taxes to Rome. These are, in the main, preserved. There are some changes, of course. Some of the smaller provincial districts, and before long some provinces, were governed by men who were not senators; so was Egypt, which was kept out of the main stream of provincial administration. In the more distant future, the great increase in the number of Roman citizens in the provinces, with their right of appeal, diminished the scope of the governor's jurisdiction. In taxation, the immunity of Italy was lessened; when the *aerarium militare* was established to pay the gratuities of demobilised soldiers, it was financed by a sales tax, paid by all, and a legacy duty paid only by Roman citizens. But this was not until A.D. 6, and in 17 the revenues of the new province of Cappadocia were used to reduce it from 1 to ½ per cent — reminiscent of 167 B.C. Judged by the scale of the empire, these changes were small, pragmatic and not immediate. It remains true that Augustus retained the chief characteristics of the system.

The faults which we have found have sprung mostly from insufficient control over the agents of government. This Augustus attempted to cure. He was himself proconsul of large provinces, in which all the governors were his deputies; they were under his orders, and he could recall them. So long as the emperor was vigilant and determined, it would be difficult to make private fortunes here by illicit means. In the other provinces there was at first no overt change at all. They were still governed by proconsuls appointed by the senate from the ranks of those who had held the city magistracies. They were controlled in the normal way, and could be tried for extortion on their return.[6] The procedure for extortion was changed, however. Senatorial dignity was enhanced by the growing practice of trying a senator in the senate, which made such a trial into a great occasion;[7] an occasion to be feared by the guilty. But since, as we saw in Chapter V, the very solemnity of prosecuting a senator sometimes made it more difficult for justice to be done to the humble provincial, an alternative process was made available; this was less formal and less expensive, and carried with it no penalty beyond simple restitution ; a reversion to the practice in force before the Calpurnian law. This might provide a more practical redress than the great impeachments. This new procedure was established by a decree of the senate, but the emperor was present, and was himself one of the proposers.[8]

There were two other important judicial changes affecting citizens resident in the provinces. The first is that the right of appeal to the people, the *provocatio ad populum*, becomes a right of appeal to the emperor. This must rank as one of the most unconstitutional things which Augustus did, and in view of the amount of work it was likely to entail he must have had strong reasons. The other was the further development of the recently evolved *appellatio*. We have seen that the consuls, by virtue of their *imperium*, could veto the judgements of a proconsul, and that a case might by this means be transferred to Rome; we have seen, too, that this would only happen if the consul made a statement well in advance of the trial. Augustus also had an adequate *imperium*, and had only to let it be known that he was prepared to use it. No legislation was required, and by the end of his reign the procedure was an established fact; eventually, but not at once, it will be possible to speak of the *right* of *appellatio*. These new uses of *appellatio* and *provocatio* acted as a check on the activities of governors, and enabled the emperors to appear as the champions of Romans abroad.[9]

Apart from these judicial developments, no change was made in the administration of the provinces still controlled by the senate. Nevertheless, things were different. For one thing, since the emperor has some

control over elections,[10] a senator could not bribe his
way into office and come to a province with that debt
to pay off. For another, his subsequent career was likely
to depend on the emperor, whose standards of honesty
therefore had to be satisfied. After 23 the emperor's
imperium was not only valid in his own provinces but
also in all the others, giving him the right, if he wished,
to send instructions to the governors of senatorial provinces. He made sparing use of this *maius imperium*,
a power for which there was little precedent,[11] but the
governors knew that it existed. The real difference in
all this is that instead of having to satisfy the senate,
composed of men who had been, or expected to be,
governors in their turn, and to escape the wrath of
equestrians, who also had a vested interest in dis-
honesty, the governor now had to satisfy the emperor,
whose standards of integrity and efficiency were much
higher. Add to this, that the senate in Rome was no
longer the originator of the policies of the state; as its
legislative activities became less important, some senators began to realise that the provinces could provide a
more satisfying career. A new attitude to the empire
begins to develop. The spirit, not the letter, of the
system changes. In time the new order will produce
its own faults, but in the meantime it went a long way to
curing the old ones.

In another very important respect Augustus was true
to the traditions of the Republic. We have already
seen evidence of the way the Romans thought about the
Greeks: respect for the ideas of classical Athens, which
every educated Roman from the mid-second century
onwards recognised as an important source of his
culture; contempt, almost, for the shifty cleverness,

the lack of *gravitas*, of the contemporary Greek-speaking east.[12] Although Pompey's conquests greatly increased the eastern part of the empire, there was no corresponding change in government or administration.[13] Oriental ideas are no more welcome at Rome after 62 than they had been before. In the civil war, Octavian had put himself on the side of this pro-western feeling, and had made capital out of the association of Antony with Cleopatra, the *fatale monstrum* of Horace's ode. The battle of Actium was represented by Vergil as a contest between Italy and barbarism.[14] When the civil war was over, there was no change in the *mores* of the empire. Italy was still dominant, and Augustus was no Alexander. When, with the passage of time, the provincials came to feel that they belonged securely to the empire, and the ties between them and the Romans became closer, when citizenship of Rome, and the right to sit in the Roman senate and hold office at Rome were gradually extended,[15] these extensions came first to the western provinces, whose culture was Latin, and only much later to the east. In his phil-hellenism Nero was ahead of his time.

But there was one direction in which Augustus made an alteration which eventually transformed the whole life of the empire: he created a civil service. Before his time, as we have seen, the Romans in a province who were officially in the public service numbered less than ten, and they were not all of them men who were accustomed to working what we should call office hours. Inevitably there were many things which the state was unable to do for itself, notably the very detailed work of a revenue department, for which it was necessary to hire private firms. Augustus decided that the executives of these firms, who were of equestrian status, could just as well serve the state, which would then be able to do much more of the detailed administration for itself. Included in this equestrian civil service were a few posts which the emperor dared not entrust to an independent-minded senator — such as the command of his new province of Egypt and of the only troops stationed in Italy — and a great many which he could not expect men of senatorial dignity to accept. His equestrian procurators could collect taxes, manage his own vast estates, govern small districts. In Rome, new possibilities of government are opened up. Administration can become a career for men who are not only clever and industrious, but also socially respectable. The rudiments of a Colonial Office were born. This brought changes to the Italian middle class, and naturally it was a long time before the process could be considered complete; in the meantime, since the work could not wait, the emperor's freedmen filled the gap.[16]

The effect on the empire was far-reaching. The private tax-collecting firms were doomed, though they might linger on for a time until the government was ready; equestrian *publicani*, making a profit on their tax contracts, were gradually replaced by equestrian procurators, salaried servants of the state. The citizen's right of *provocatio* no longer took him to the ignorant assemblies of urban Romans, but to the emperor's secretariat; the appeal was now to Caesar, who had the necessary staff to investigate complaints.[17] Much more complete records could be kept, and the way was open for a periodic census to be held in each province for the purpose of taxation.[18] More efficient planning of the imperial budget was not far away.[19] The emperor's procurators, operating for one purpose or another in most of the provinces, could send home reports from which the central government could form a picture of what was going on abroad.[20] The time was not far distant when a sudden calamity, such as an earthquake in a distant land, would be followed by financial assistance from the capital of the empire.[21] All this was naturally a gradual growth, but enough evidence exists that a start had been made long before the death of Augustus.[22]

The area of inefficiency was drastically diminished, and for two centuries the Mediterranean world prospered. In the famous judgement of Gibbon, 'If a man were called to fix the period in the history of the world during which the condition of the human race was most happy and prosperous, he would, without doubt, name that which elapsed from the death of Domitian to the accession of Commodus.'[23] But the balance between toleration and efficiency is a delicate one; for the efficient, the temptation to interfere with the inefficient is strong. When Pliny was sent to Bithynia the need was pressing, and he behaved with laborious caution, so that no harm was done.[24] Others might be less considerate. The empire had been built on local autonomy and local initiative; if central direction becomes too strong these things will die. Many things have been blamed, by many people, for the fall of the Roman empire: the barbarians, monks, too few soldiers, too many soldiers, slaves, the failure to industrialise. Whatever it was, in the attempt to stave off disaster, the central government imposed a rigid control which took from the empire the adaptability which is essential to health and survival. The history of the Roman empire prompts the melancholy reflection that good government is only an interval between too little government and too much.

The charges brought against the Republican empire are, in the main, three. First, that the civilian government failed to control its generals; but then, so did Nero. Three times the senate capitulated to an army commander; within the hundred years after Actium five emperors owed their elevation to soldiers. The emergency armies were a danger to the state; so were the standing armies, once the secret of empire was out.[25] The truth is that for armies to take over when the civilian government is in difficulties is a common occurrence the world over, and not many nations can claim to have been immune. We should rather praise the Romans for having avoided military rule for so long than blame them because they occasionally succumbed. Second, the control over provincial governors was inadequate; this charge must be admitted. Attempts were made to strengthen the extortion procedure, which was the chief safeguard, and many governors were brought to trial; but this did not prove a very effective deterrent, and not enough was done to prevent the injustices from occurring in the first place. It was too readily accepted by the nobility that the provinces were an opportunity for money-making, while the ultimate judges of a governor's behaviour were men who were themselves implicated, in one way or another, in the business of extortion. This is a charge against the Roman nobility which is not confined to provincial administration. Deep in their thinking was implanted the notion of the deference due to a man of pedigree. This feeling of superiority might prevent the governor from becoming involved in petty squabbles, at the expense of making him feel that his own conduct was above the law. Senators were not officially paid, and tended to regard themselves as the owners of the empire and not as its servants.[26] It was because it was founded on this attitude of mind that provincial exploitation was so difficult to prevent.

The third charge is that the system of collecting taxes by private companies was undesirable. This charge too we must probably accept. It is difficult to be quite certain, for lack of accurate figures, but it seems probable that the profits of the Roman equestrian *societates* were excessive; probable also that they were greater than the peculations of the imperial procurators who took their place, some of whom did not do so badly for themselves. But we must accept it with reservation; the alternative was a developed, expert, civil service, and if you have that, while you avoid one kind of evil, another is only just round the corner. In a diverse empire there are great advantages in a central government which cannot do too much; many temptations are thereby avoided. Once the Romans started collecting their own taxes in the provinces, there was no halting the growth of bureaucracy, especially as the first results were so obviously beneficial. It is a choice between two worlds, in which not all the virtues are on the side of the superior organisation.

Leaving aside the faults of administration, which the emperors endeavoured, with some success, to cure, the general accusation remains that the Romans of the Republic regarded the empire as a source of profit to

themselves. On this subject it is not easy to be fair; it
it not sensible to set up an impossibly high standard
and then blame the Romans for not being a nation of
missionaries. Roman foreign policy was directed to
furthering the interests of Rome; the same is true of
any other nation, and it is no use quarrelling with that.
On the other hand, it does sometimes seem that they
acted with a narrower selfishness than is proper for an
imperial power. But that the official tax structure was
in principle inequitable is far from certain. True, when
there was money to spare, it was Italy which was
relieved of taxation, while the provincials continued to
pay; but the taxes paid by them were not higher than
was normal in the Mediterranean world, and only when
the administration was iniquitous did they seriously
interfere with the growth of prosperity. The Romans
were continually at war; accurate budgeting was
difficult; they exacted the normally acceptable taxation, spent a great deal of it abroad, and when there
was a surplus brought it back to Rome; having the
surplus, they used it to finance their bread and circuses.[27]
About these, we have seen reason to think that the
fulminations of the moralists are unreasonable and un-
imaginative; the government could not forbid Romans
to live in Rome, and the mother city of a world-wide
empire could hardly be expected to allow its own
citizens to starve in its streets. After a successful war,
the treasury might be full,[28] but normally there is little
evidence of extravagant expenditure from public funds.
The private wealth of Romans did increase, but in view
of the general prosperity of the Mediterranean world
and the higher standards of taste and material posses-
sions which came with the opening up of Greece and the

D

east, anything else would have been surprising. The antique ideal hymned by Horace;

> Privatus illis census erat brevis,
> commune magnum[29]

only shows how some Romans liked to think of their forbears; even if it had ever been true, it had no practical relevance to the age of expanding horizons and flourishing commerce. Nor can we expect that the men who made this prosperity possible should themselves live the Spartan life. Hortensius openly admitted that the imperial people were entitled to their reward, and the growth of private fortunes was defended in the Tiberian senate by Asinius Gallus.[30] The defence was a reasonable one. The age of Fabricius was over long before, and even the frugal Tiberius would not legislate for its return. We must admit, however, that the methods by which some of these fortunes were made were unsavoury, and that some of them were founded on provincial plunder. And not plunder of money only: Verres was not the first to indulge a taste for the acquisition of works of art. The Hellenist Aemilius Paullus had begun it; the greatest of the Republican collectors was the philistine Mummius.[31]

The provincial *civitas* paid taxes to Rome, which, if only they were honestly collected, were not excessive; it supplied troops to the imperial armies;[32] it lost the right to an independent foreign policy, and was compelled to accept the position of a client; all its affairs became municipal affairs — the same downgrading as that which under the emperors diminished the importance of the *senatus populusque Romanus* itself. Most surely, they lost the right to make war. But they had little else to complain about. There were no hordes of Roman officials inquiring into the private affairs of their subjects, because a counterpart to Roman selfishness was Roman toleration, based on a lack of interest. It did not occur to them to pry into the private affairs of their subjects, unless it was necessary for their own security.[33] There was also no danger to the provincials of a sudden attack by their neighbours from beyond the hills or down the valley. It was not only under the emperors that the Romans 'imposed the custom of peace'. A less exciting life, perhaps, but more civilised, and certainly more prosperous materially. To these benefits we must add the jurisdiction of the Roman governor. We do not need to claim that this was always perfect — we have seen too many examples of how it could be perverted — and we cannot deny that the need for it was less great in some provinces than in others. But in many parts of the Roman empire it was a great improvement on the methods which the natives had evolved for themselves.

These solid benefits the allies enjoyed, and they owed them to Roman governors and Roman legions. If it had not been for Roman citizens serving abroad for years at a time, the struggle of tribe against tribe and faction against faction would have had no end. When all the faults have been added up and all the exceptions allowed for, we can safely say that the Romans gave good value for money. We must also emphasise that the empire was built, solidly and laboriously, by the Roman Republic; it was not the creation of the emperors. Nor did the Republic fall because it was incapable of administering the empire. The empire, by calling for large armies and enterprising generals, provided the weapon with which the Republic destroyed itself, but, even after twenty years of civil wars, it did not disintegrate. For all its faults, Augustus inherited a going concern.

The solid achievement of the Republican empire does not always receive the credit which it deserves. This is due, partly at least, to a failure of propaganda. The image which the senate projected into the minds of the provincials was one of power and majesty, but without benevolence. Senators moved about the empire like kings, and were treated with fear and respect; Rome was strong beyond compare. But its rulers were busy about their own affairs, and if you had a grievance it was not easy to find anyone to pay attention. There was little active feeling of goodwill. The senate had what we called in Chapter II a practical man's idea of empire, with its limitations as well as its virtues. Augustus saw this too, and in his propaganda, and that of his successors, there is an emphasis on personal care and positive action; 'so that it may be clear to all those who live in the provinces how much care I and the senate take that no one of our subjects is wrongfully hurt or robbed'.[34] The allies are to be made conscious of the benevolence as well as of the power of Rome; a surer bond of loyalty will be forged. It was easier for the emperors: especially in the eastern half of the empire, men had long been accustomed to owing loyalty to the person of a king, whether in Egypt, Syria, Asia or Macedonia. It was less easy to feel the same way about a senate. A king's head can be put on coins[35], his statue set up in the market-place. Some eastern peoples found no difficulty in believing that the king was a god, or at least a relation of the gods.

Though the west was less impressed,[36] in the most vocal part of the empire the new propaganda was embarrassingly successful.[37]

This notion of the Man-God is to our way of thinking unhealthy as well as blasphemous, the product of superstition and megalomania. We shall not rank emperor-worship as a virtue of the empire; though we shall admit that as expressed by Tiberius it could be salutary and even inspiring. But granted that it existed, the early emperors turned it to good account. In a polytheistic world, temples to 'Rome and Augustus' probably did little religious harm, while the official organisation of the cult made it emotionally more innocuous. It served also another purpose. Previously, as we have said, it had been the practice for the Roman governor of a province to deal separately with each of its many *civitates*; there were no natives who could speak for the province as a whole. Augustus saw that this policy of *divide et impera* was negative and emotionally barren. It had been necessary in the days when Rome was weak, but there was now no danger in allowing the provincials to come together, provided that the occasion was one which would encourage loyalty and not disaffection. The formal worship of the emperor provided just such an occasion, and in the *concilium* which was based on it the provincials at last had some way of making their corporate feelings known.

Literature, too, was pressed into service, and the day was not far distant when the schoolboy of the Latin west would be absorbing suitable sentiments along with his poetry lesson,

Imperium sine fine dedi. . . .

Vergil grew up in the time of the Republic; he was already twenty-five when Julius died, nearing forty when peace and order were restored in Italy. But the Aeneid is a child of the empire, and breathes a new spirit. Not that the spread of civilisation by Romans was anything new; but added to that is the fact that in some of the best minds in Rome there is now some feeling of a mission:[38]

Tu regere imperio. . . .

What is more, in many of the important centres of the empire there were visible monuments of the new age. Not only the network of roads — everyone knew that they existed for Roman troops — but buildings which were impressive and useful. To us the Pont du Gard is a magnificent monument; to the people of Nemausus it was also a welcome amenity. Hadrian built the wind-swept defences of Northumberland; he also completed the Olympieion. From the forum of Timgad to the altar of Cologne, wherever men assembled to make important decisions, they found before their eyes this combination of power and beneficence. They might be forgiven for thinking that such an empire must last for ever.

In propaganda the Romans of the Republic were deficient; they dealt in hard facts and did not see the need for fine words. Thus they left the field wide open to their traducers. With posterity they have not been much more fortunate. Even the ambiguity of the word 'empire' has worked against them, since it encourages us to associate the foreign dominions with the rule of the emperors, and to forget how many of the essentials already existed by the time Augustus began to reign.

Our sources of information are biased against them too; abroad, the generations who are being compelled to become subjects are naturally hostile — the feelings of unity and gratitude are slow of growth.[39] At home, the picture is dominated by the extortion court. We hear of regulations when they are broken, not when they are kept. Provincial government had its heroes as well as its villains, but it is Verres, not Scaevola or Piso Frugi, who fills a whole volume of the Oxford Classical Texts. In the words of a wartime Royal Commission on the women's services, 'Virtue has no gossip-value'.

PART TWO
TEXTS

I
THE GROWTH OF THE EMPIRE

Livy, XXXIII. 32–34

32 Isthmiorum statum ludicrum aderat, semper quidem
et alias frequens cum propter spectaculi studium in-
situm genti, quo certamina omnis generis artium
viriumque et pernicitatis visuntur, tum quia propter
opportunitatem loci per duo diversa maria omnium
rerum usus ministrantis humano generi, concilium
Asiae Graeciaeque is mercatus erat: tum vero non ad
solitos modo usus undique convenerant, sed exspectatione erecti, qui deinde status futurus Graeciae, quae
sua fortuna esset, alii alia non taciti solum opinabantur
sed sermonibus etiam ferebant Romanos facturos: vix
cuiquam persuadebatur Graecia omni cessuros. ad
spectaculum consederant; et praeco cum tubicine, ut
mos est, in mediam aream, unde solemni carmine
ludicrum indici solet, processit, et tuba silentio facto
ita pronuntiat, "senatus Romanus et T. Quinctius
imperator Philippo rege Macedonibusque devictis
liberos, immunes suis legibus esse iubet Corinthios
Phocenses Locrensesque omnis et insulam Euboeam et
Magnetas, Thessalos, Perrhaebos, Achaeos Phthiotas."
percensuerat omnis gentis, quae sub dicione Philippi
regis fuerant. audita voce praeconis maius gaudium
fuit, quam quod universum homines acciperent. vix
satis credere se quisque audisse, et alii alios intueri,

mirabundi velut ad somnii vanam speciem: quod ad
quemque pertinebat, suarum aurium fidei minimum
credentes, proximos interrogabant. revocatus praeco,
cum unusquisque non audire modo sed videre libertatis
suae nuntium averet, iterum pronuntiavit eadem. tum
ab certo iam gaudio tantus cum clamore plausus est
ortus totiensque repetitus, ut facile appareret nihil
omnium bonorum multitudini gratius quam libertatem
esse. ludicrum deinde ita raptim peractum est, ut
nullius nec animi nec oculi spectaculo intenti essent:
adeo unum gaudium praeoccupaverat omnium aliarum
sensum voluptatium.

33　　ludis vero dimissis cursu prope omnes tendere ad
imperatorem Romanum, ut ruente turba in unum adire,
contingere dextram cupientium, coronas lemniscosque
iacientium, haud procul periculo fuerit. sed erat trium
ferme et triginta annorum: et cum robur iuventae, tum
gaudium ex tam insigni gloria et fructus vires suppedi-
tabat. nec praesens tantummodo effusa est laetitia,
sed per multos dies gratis et cogitationibus et sermonibus renovata: esse aliquam in terris gentem, quae sua
impensa, suo labore ac periculo bella gerat pro libertate
aliorum; nec hoc finitimis aut propinquae vicinitatis
hominibus aut terris continenti iunctis praestet: sed
maria traiciat, ne quod toto orbe terrarum iniustum
imperium sit, ubique ius fas lex potentissima sint. una
voce praeconis liberatas omnis Graeciae atque Asiae
urbes. hoc spe concipere audacis animi fuisse, ad
effectum adducere et virtutis et fortunae ingentis.

34　　Secundum Isthmia Quinctius et decem legati legationes
regum gentiumque audivere. primi omnium regis
Antiochi vocati legati sunt. iis eadem fere, quae
Romae egerant, verba sine fide rerum iactantibus nihil

iam perplexe ut ante, cum dubiae res incolumi Philippo
erant, sed aperte denuntiatum, ut excederet Asiae
urbibus, quae Philippi aut Ptolemaei regum fuissent,
abstineret liberis civitatibus, neu umquam lacesseret
armis: et in pace et in libertate esse debere omnis
ubique Graecas urbes. ante omnia denuntiatum, ne in
Europam aut ipse transiret aut copias traiceret.
dimissis regis legatis conventus civitatum gentiumque
est haberi coeptus; eoque maturius peragebatur, quod
decreto decem legatorum civitates nominatim pro-
nuntiabantur. Orestis — Macedonum ea gens est — ,
quod primi ab rege defecissent, suae leges redditae.
Magnetes et Perrhaebi et Dolopes liberi quoque pro-
nuntiati. Thessalorum genti praeter libertatem con-
cessam Achaei Phthiotae dati, Thebis Phthioticis et
Pharsalo excepta. Aetolos de Pharsalo et Leucade
postulantes, ut ex foedere sibi restituerentur, ad
senatum reiecerunt. Phocenses Locrensesque, sicut
ante fuerant, adiecta decreti auctoritate iis contri-
buerunt. Corinthus et Triphylia et Heraea — Pelopon-
nesi et ipsa urbs est — reddita Achaeis. Oreum et
Eretriam decem legati Eumeni regi, Attali filio, dabant.
dissentiente Quinctio ea una res in arbitrium senatus
reiecta est: senatus libertatem his civitatibus dedit.

Caesar, *de bello Gallico*, VII. 32–33.

32. Caesar Avarici compluris dies commoratus summamque ibi copiam frumenti et reliqui commeatus
2 nactus exercitum ex labore atque inopia reficit. Iam
prope hieme confecta, cum ipso anni tempore ad
gerendum bellum vocaretur et ad hostem proficisci
constituisset, sive eum ex paludibus silvisque elicere

sive obsidione premere posset, legati ad eum principes
Aeduorum veniunt oratum ut maxime necessario tem-
3 pore civitati subveniat: summo esse in periculo rem,
quod, cum singuli magistratus antiquitus creari atque
regiam potestatem annum obtinere consuessent, duo
magistratum gerant et se uterque eorum legibus
4 creatum esse dicat. Horum esse alterum Convictolitavem, florentem et inlustrem adulescentem; alterum
Cotum, antiquissima familia natum atque ipsum
hominem summae potentiae et magnae cognationis,
cuius frater Valetiacus proximo anno eundem magis-
5 tratum gesserit. Civitatem esse omnem in armis;
divisum senatum, divisum populum, suas cuiusque
6 eorum clientelas. Quod si diutius alatur controversia,
fore uti pars cum parte civitatis confligat. Id ne
accidat, positum in eius diligentia atque auctoritate.

33. Caesar, etsi a bello atque hoste discedere detrimen-
tosum esse existimabat, tamen non ignorans quanta ex
dissensionibus incommoda oriri consuessent, ne tanta
et tam coniuncta populo Romano civitas, quam ipse
semper aluisset omnibusque rebus ornasset, ad vim
atque arma descenderet atque ea pars quae minus sibi
2 confideret auxilia a Vercingetorige arcesseret, huic rei
praevertendum existimavit et, quod legibus Aeduorum
eis qui summum magistratum obtinerent excedere ex
finibus non liceret, ne quid de iure aut de legibus eorum
deminuisse videretur, ipse in Aeduos proficisci statuit
senatumque omnem et quos inter controversia esset ad
3 se Decetiam evocavit. Cum prope omnis civitas eo
convenisset, docereturque paucis clam convocatis alio
loco, alio tempore atque oportuerit fratrem a fratre
renuntiatum, cum leges duo ex una familia vivo utroque
non solum magistratus creari vetarent sed etiam in

senatu esse prohiberent, Cotum imperium deponere coegit; Convictolitavem, qui per sacerdotes more civitatis intermissis magistratibus esset creatus, potestatem obtinere iussit.

Cicero, *II in Verrem*, II. 122–127.

122 Halaesini pro multis ac magnis suis maiorumque suorum in rem publicam nostram meritis atque beneficiis suo iure nuper, L. Licinio Q. Mucio consulibus, cum haberent inter se controversias de senatu cooptando, leges ab senatu nostro petiverunt. Decrevit senatus honorifico senatus consulto ut iis C. Claudius Appi filius Pulcher praetor de senatu cooptando leges conscriberet. C. Claudius, adhibitis omnibus Marcellis qui tum erant de eorum sententia leges Halaesinis dedit, in quibus multa sanxit de aetate hominum, ne qui minor xxx annis natus, de quaestu, quem qui fecisset ne legeretur, de censu, de ceteris rebus: quae omnia ante istum praetorem et nostrorum magistratuum auctoritate et Halaesinorum summa voluntate valuerunt. Ab isto et praeco, qui voluit, illum ordinem pretio mercatus est, et pueri annorum senum septenumque denum senatorium nomen nundinati sunt; et quod Halaesini, antiquissimi et fidelissimi socii atque amici, Romae impetrarant, ut apud se ne suffragiis quidem fieri liceret, id pretio ut fieri posset effecit.

123 Agrigentini de senatu cooptando Scipionis leges antiquas habent, in quibus et illa eadem sancta sunt et hoc amplius: cum Agrigentinorum duo genera sint, unum veterum, alterum colonorum quos T. Manlius praetor ex senatus consulto de oppidis Siculorum deduxit Agrigentum, cautum est in Scipionis legibus ne

plures essent in senatu ex colonorum numero quam ex
vetere Agrigentinorum. Iste, qui omnia iura pretio
exaequasset omniumque rerum dilectum atque discrimen pecunia sustulisset, non modo illa quae erant
aetatis ordinis quaestusque permiscuit, sed etiam in his
duobus generibus civium novorum veterumque tur-
124bavit. Nam cum esset ex vetere numero quidam
senator demortuus, et cum ex utroque genere par
numerus reliquus esset, veterem cooptari necesse erat
legibus, ut is amplior numerus esset. Quae cum ita se
res haberet, tamen ad istum emptum venerunt illum
locum senatorium non solum veteres, verum etiam novi.
Fit ut pretio novus vincat litterasque a praetore adferat
Agrigentum. Agrigentini ad istum legatos mittunt
qui eum leges doceant consuetudinemque omnium
annorum demonstrent, ut iste intellegeret ei se illum
locum vendidisse cui ne commercium quidem esse
oporteret; quorum oratione iste, cum pretium iam
125accepisset, ne tantulum quidem commotus est. Idem
fecit Heracleae. Nam eo quoque colonos P. Rupilius
deduxit, legesque similis de cooptando senatu et de
numero veterum ac novorum dedit. Ibi non solum iste
ut apud ceteros pecuniam accepit, sed etiam genera
veterum ac novorum numerumque permiscuit. Nolite
exspectare dum omnis obeam oratione mea civitates:
hoc uno complector omnia, neminem isto praetore
senatorem fieri potuisse nisi qui isti pecuniam dedisset.
126 Hoc idem transfero in magistratus, curationes, sacer-
dotia; quibus in rebus non solum hominum iura, sed
etiam deorum immortalium religiones omnis repudiavit.
Syracusis lex est de religione, quae in annos singulos
Iovis sacerdotem sortito capi iubeat, quod apud illos
127amplissimum sacerdotium putatur: cum suffragiis tres

ex tribus generibus creati sunt, res revocatur ad sortem. Perfecerat iste imperio ut pro suffragio Theomnastus, familiaris suus, in tribus illis renuntiaretur: in sorte, cui imperare non potuerat, exspectabant homines quidnam acturus esset. Homo, id quod erat facillimum, primo vetat sortiri: iubet extra sortem Theomnastum renuntiari. Negant id Syracusani per religiones sacrorum ullo modo fieri posse, fas denique negant esse. Iubet iste sibi legem recitari. Recitatur; in qua scriptum erat ut, quot essent renuntiati, tot in hydriam sortes conicerentur; cuium nomen exisset, ut is haberet id sacerdotium. Iste homo ingeniosus et peracutus, 'Optime,' inquit, 'nempe scriptum ita est, QVOT RENVNTIATI ERVNT. Quot ergo, inquit, sunt renuntiati?' Respondent, 'Tres.' 'Numquid igitur oportet nisi tres sortis conici, unam educi?' 'Nihil.' Conici iubet tres, in quibus omnibus esset inscriptum nomen Theomnasti. Fit clamor maximus, cum id universis indignum ac nefarium videretur. Ita Iovis illud sacerdotium amplissimum per hanc rationem Theomnasto datur.

Extracts from the *Lex Antonia de Termessibus.*

I de Termesi(bus) Pisid(is) mai(oribus). — | . . . C. Antonius, M(arci) f(ilius), Cn. Corne | . . . C. Fundanius, C. f., tr. pl., de s(enatus) s(ententia) plebem *ioure rogaverunt plebesque ioure scivit in* . . . . . *a. d.* . . . . . . *Tribus* . . . . *principium fuit: pro Tribu* | preimus scivit.— |

(1) Quei Thermeses maiores Peisidae fuerunt, queique | eorum legibus Thermesium maior*u*m Pisidarum | ante k. April., quae fuerunt L. Gellio Cn. Lentulo cos., | Thermeses maiores Pisidae factei sunt,

queique ‖ ab ieis prognati sunt erunt, iei omnes |
postereique eorum Thermeses maiores Peisidae | leiberi
amicei socieique populi Romani sunto, | eique legibus
sueis ita utunto, itaque ieis | omnibus sueis legibus
Thermensis maioribus ‖ Pisideis utei liceto, quod
advorsus hanc legem | non fiat.— |

(3) Quae Thermensorum m*aioru*m Pisidarum publica |
preivatave praeter loca agros aedificia sunt | fueruntve
ante bellum Mitridatis, quod preimum ‖ factum est,
quodque earum rerum iei antea | habuerunt possederunt
usei fructeive sunt, | quod eius ipsei sua voluntate ab
se non abalienarunt, | ea omnia Termensium maiorum
Pisidarum utei sunt | fuerunt, ita sunto, itemque ieis
ea omnia ‖ habere possidere uutei frueique liceto.— |

(5) Nei quis magistratus prove magistratu legatus
ne*ive* | quis alius meilites in oppidum Thermesum
maiorum | Pisidarum agrumue Thermensium maiorum |
Pisidarum hiemandi caussa introducito, neive ‖ facito,
quo quis eo meilites introducat quove ibei | meilites
hiement, nisei senatus nominatim, utei Thermesum |
maiorum Pisidarum in hibernacula meilites | deducan-
tur, decreverit; neive quis magistratus | prove magis-
tratu legatus neive quis alius facito ‖ neive inperato,
quo quid magis iei dent praebeant | ab ieisve auferatur,
nisei quod e*o*s ex lege Porcia | dare praebere oportet
oportebit.— |

(7) Quam legem portorieis terrestribus mari-
tumeisque | Termenses maiores Phisidae capiundeis
intra suos | fineis deixserint, ea lex ieis portorieis

capiundeis | esto, dum nei quid portori ab ieis capiatur, quei publica ‖ populi Romani vectigalia redempta habebunt; quos | per eorum fineis publicani ex eo vectigali transportabunt ‖ *fructus eorum portorium Thermenses maiores Pisidae ne petunto neve capiunto.*

II

DEFENCE

Cicero, *ad familiares*, III. iii.

M. CICERO S. D. AP. PULCRO

1. A. d. XI. Kalendas Iunias Brundisium cum venis,
sem, Q. Fab*ius Vergili*anus, legatus tuus, mihi praesto
fuit eaque me ex tuis mandatis monuit quae non mihi
ad quem pertinebant, sed universo senatui venerant in
mentem, praesidio firmiore opus esse ad istam provinciam. Censebant enim omnes fere ut in Italia supple-
mentum meis et Bibuli legionibus scriberetur. Id cum
Sulpicius consul passurum se negaret, multa nos quidem
questi sumus, sed tantus consensus senatus fuit ut
mature proficisceremur, parendum ut fuerit: itaque
fecimus. Nunc, quod a te petii litteris iis, quas Romae
tabellariis tuis dedi, velim tibi curae sit ut, quae succes-
sori coniunctissimo et amicissimo commodare potest is
qui provinciam tradit, ut ea pro nostra consociatissima
voluntate cura ac diligentia tua complectare, ut omnes
intellegant nec me benevolentiori cuiquam succedere
nec te amiciori potuisse provinciam tradere. 2. Ex iis
litteris, quarum ad me exemplum misisti, quas in
senatu recitari voluisti, sic intellexeram, permultos a te
milites esse dimissos, sed mihi Fabius idem demonstravit
te id cogitasse facere, sed, cum ipse a te discederet,
integrum militum numerum fuisse. Id si ita est, per-
gratum mihi feceris si istas exiguas copias quas habuisti

quam minime imminueris: qua de re senatus consulta
quae facta sunt ad te missa esse arbitror. Equidem pro
eo quanti te facio quidquid feceris approbabo, sed te
quoque confido ea facturum quae mihi intelleges maxime esse accommodata. Ego C. Pomptinum legatum
meum Brundisi exspectabam eumque ante Kalendas
Iunias Brundisium venturum arbitrabar. Qui cum
venerit, quae primum navigandi nobis facultas data
erit utemur.

Cicero, *ad familiares*, XV. ii.

M. TULLIUS M. F. CICERO PROCOS
S. D. COS. PR. TR. PL. SENATUI

1. S. V. V. B. E. E. Q. V. Cum pridie Kalend. Sext.
in provinciam venissem neque maturius propter
itinerum et navigationum difficultatem venire potuissem, maxime convenire officio meo reique publicae
conducere putavi parare ea quae ad exercitum quaeque
ad rem militarem pertinerent. Quae cum essent a me
cura magis et diligentia quam facultate et copia constituta, nuntiique et litterae de bello a Parthis in provinciam Syriam illato cotidie fere adferrentur, iter mihi
faciendum per Lycaoniam et per Isauros et per Cappadociam arbitratus sum. Erat enim magna suspicio
Parthos, si ex Syria egredi atque irrumpere in meam
provinciam conarentur, iter eos per Cappadociam, quod
ea maxime pateret, esse facturos. 2. Itaque cum exercitu
per Cappadociae partem eam quae cum Cilicia continens
est iter feci castraque ad Cybistra, quod oppidum est ad
montem Taurum, locavi, ut Artavasdes, rex Armenius,
quocumque animo esset, sciret non procul a suis finibus
exercitum populi Romani esse et Deiotarum, fidelissi-

mum regem atque amicissimum rei publicae nostrae,
maxime coniunctum haberem, cuius et consilio et
opibus adiuvari posset res publica. 3. Quo cum in loco
castra haberem equitatumque in Ciliciam misissem, ut
et meus adventus iis civitatibus quae in ea parte essent
nuntiatus firmiores animos omnium faceret et ego
mature quid ageretur in Syria scire possem, tempus eius
tridui, quod in iis castris morabar, in magno officio et
necessario mihi ponendum putavi. 4. Cum enim vestra
auctoritas intercessisset ut ego regem Ariobarzanem
Eusebem et Philorhomaeum tuerer eiusque regis
salutem et incolumitatem regnumque defenderem, regi
regnoque praesidio essem, adiunxissetisque salutem
eius regis populo senatuique magnae curae esse, quod
nullo umquam de rege decretum esset a nostro ordine,
existimavi me iudicium vestrum ad regem deferre debere eique praesidium meum et fidem et diligentiam
polliceri, ut, quoniam salus ipsius, incolumitas regni
mihi commendata esset a vobis, diceret si quid vellet.
5. Quae cum essem in consilio meo cum rege locutus,
initio ille orationis suae vobis maximas, ut debuit,
deinde etiam mihi gratias egit, quod ei permagnum et
perhonorificum videbatur senatui p. q. R. tantae curae
esse salutem suam, meque tantam diligentiam adhibere
ut et mea fides et commendationis vestrae auctoritas
perspici posset. Atque ille primo, quod mihi maximae
laetitiae fuit, ita mecum locutus est, ut nullas insidias
neque vitae suae neque regno diceret se aut intellegere
fieri aut etiam suspicari. Cum ego ei gratulatus essem
idque me gaudere dixissem, et tamen adulescentem
essem cohortatus ut recordaretur casum illum interitus
paterni et vigilanter se tueretur atque admonitu senatus
consuleret saluti suae, tum a me discessit in oppidum

Cybistra. 6. Postero autem die cum Ariarathe, fratre
suo, et cum paternis amicis maioribus natu ad me in
castra venit perturbatusque et flens, cum idem et frater
faceret et amici, meam fidem, vestram commendation-
em implorare coepit. Cum admirarer quid accidisset
novi, dixit ad se indicia manifestarum insidiarum esse
delata, quae essent ante adventum meum occultata,
quod ii qui ei patefacere possent propter metum reti-
cuissent: eo autem tempore spe mei praesidi compluris
ea quae scirent audacter ad se detulisse; in his aman-
tissimum sui, summa pietate praeditum fratrem dicere
(ea quae is quoque me audiente dicebat) se sollicitatum
esse ut regnare vellet: id vivo fratre suo accipere non
potuisse: se tamen ante illud tempus eam rem numquam in medium propter periculi metum protulisse.
Quae cum esset locutus, monui regem ut omnem diligentiam ad se conservandum adhiberet, amicosque in
patris eius atque avi iudicio probatos hortatus sum,
regis sui vitam docti casu acerbissimo patris eius omni
cura custodiaque defenderent. 7. Cum rex a me equitatum cohortisque de exercitu meo postularet, etsi intel-
legebam vestro senatus consulto non modo posse me id
facere sed etiam debere, tamen, cum res publica postularet propter cotidianos ex Syria nuntios ut quam
primum exercitum ad Ciliciae finis adducerem, cumque
mihi rex patefactis iam insidiis non egere exercitu
p. R. sed posse suis opibus defendere videretur, illum
cohortatus sum ut in sua vita conservanda primum
regnare disceret: a quibus perspexisset sibi insidias
paratas, in eos uteretur iure regio: poena adficeret eos
quos necesse esset, reliquos metu liberaret; praesidio
exercitus mei ad eorum qui in culpa essent timorem
potius quam ad contentionem uteretur: fore autem

ut omnes, quoniam senatus consultum nossent, intellegerent me regi, si opus esset, ex auctoritate vestra praesidio futurum. 8. Ita confirmato illo ex eo loco castra movi, iter in Ciliciam facere institui: cum hac opinione e Cappadocia discederem, ut consilio vestro, casu incredibili ac paene divino regem, quem vos honorificentissime appellassetis nullo postulante quemque meae fidei commendassetis et cuius salutem magnae vobis curae esse decressetis, meus adventus praesentibus insidiis liberarit. Quod ad vos a me scribi non alienum putavi, *ut* intellegeretis ex iis quae paene acciderunt, vos multo ante ne ea acciderent providisse, eoque vos studiosius feci certiores, quod in rege Ariobarzane ea mihi signa videor virtutis, ingeni, fidei benevolentiaeque erga vos perspexisse ut non sine causa tantam curam in eius vos salutem diligentiamque videamini contulisse.

Cicero, *ad familiares*, XV. iv. 7–11 (Cicero to Cato)

7. Interea cognovi multorum litteris atque nuntiis magnas Parthorum copias *atque* Arabum ad oppidum Antiocheam accessisse magnumque eorum equitatum, qui in Ciliciam transisset, ab equitum meorum turmis et a cohorte praetoria, quae erat Epiphaneae praesidi causa, occidione occisum. Qua re cum viderem a Cappadocia Parthorum copias aversas non longe a finibus esse Ciliciae, quam potui maximis itineribus ad Amanum exercitum duxi. Quo ut veni, hostem ab Antiochea recessisse, Bibulum Antiocheae esse cognovi: Deiotarum confestim iam ad me venientem cum magno et firmo equitatu et peditatu et cum omnibus suis copiis certiorem feci non videri esse causam cur abesset a regno meque ad eum, si quid novi forte accidis-

set, statim litteras nuntiosque missurum esse. 8.
Cumque eo animo venissem, ut utrique provinciae, si
ita tempus ferret, subvenirem, tum id, quod iam ante
statueram vehementer interesse utriusque provinciae,
pacare Amanum et perpetuum hostem ex eo monte
tollere, agere perrexi. Cumque me discedere ab eo
monte simulassem et alias partis Ciliciae petere abes-
semque ab Amano iter unius diei et castra apud
Epiphaneam fecissem, a. d. IIII Idus Oct. cum adves-
perasceret, expedito exercitu ita noctu iter feci, ut a. d.
III Idus Oct. cum lucisceret, in Amanum ascenderem
distributisque cohortibus et auxiliis, cum aliis Q. frater
legatus mecum simul, aliis C. Pomptinus legatus, reliquis M. Anneius et L. Tullius legati praeessent,
plerosque nec opinantis oppressimus, qui occisi cap-
tique sunt interclusi fuga. Eranam autem, quae fuit
non vici instar sed urbis, quod erat Amani caput,
itemque Sepyram et Commorim, acriter et diu repug-
nantis, Pomptino illam partem Amani tenente, ex
antelucano tempore usque ad horam diei decimam,
magna multitudine hostium occisa, cepimus castellaque
vi capta complura incendimus. 9. His rebus ita gestis
castra in radicibus Amani habuimus apud Aras
Alexandri quadriduum et in reliquiis Amani delendis
agrisque vastandis, quae pars eius montis meae provinciae est, id tempus omne consumpsimus. 10. Confectis his rebus ad oppidum Eleutherocilicum Pindenissum exercitum abduxi: quod cum esset altissimo et
munitissimo loco ab iisque incoleretur qui ne regibus
quidem umquam paruissent, cum et fugitivos reciperent
et Parthorum adventum acerrime exspectarent, ad
existimationem imperi pertinere arbitratus sum com-
primere eorum audaciam, quo facilius etiam ceterorum

animi, qui alieni essent ab imperio nostro, frangerentur. Vallo et fossa circumdedi, sex castellis castrisque maximis saepsi, aggere, viniis, turribus oppugnavi, ususque tormentis multis, multis sagittariis, magno labore meo, sine ulla molestia sumptuve sociorum, septimo quinquagensimo die rem confeci ut omnibus partibus urbis disturbatis aut incensis compulsi in potestatem meam pervenirent. His erant finitimi pari scelere et audacia Tebarani; ab iis Pindenisso capto obsides accepi: exercitum in hiberna dimisi. Quintum fratrem negotio praeposui ut in vicis aut captis aut male pacatis exercitus collocaretur. 11. Nunc velim sic tibi persuadeas, si de iis rebus ad senatum relatum sit, me existimaturum summam mihi laudem tributam si tu honorem meum sententia tua comprobaris; idque, etsi talibus de rebus gravissimos homines et rogare solere et rogari scio, tamen admonendum potius te a me quam rogandum puto. Tu es enim is qui me tuis sententiis saepissime ornasti, qui oratione, qui praedicatione, qui summis laudibus in senatu, in contionibus ad caelum extulisti, cuius ego semper tanta esse verborum pondera putavi ut uno verbo tuo cum mea laude coniuncto omnia adsequi me arbitrarer. Te denique memini, cum cuidam clarissimo atque optimo viro supplicationem non decerneres, dicere te decreturum, si referretur ob eas res quas is consul in urbe gessisset. Tu idem mihi supplicationem decrevisti togato, non ut multis re publica bene gesta sed ut nemini re publica conservata.

III

ADMINISTRATION OF JUSTICE

Cicero, *ad Atticum*, VI. i. 15

15. De Bibuli edicto nihil novi praeter illam exceptionem, de qua tu ad me scripseras, 'nimis gravi
praeiudicio in ordinem nostrum'. Ego tamen habeo
ἰσοδυναμοῦσαν sed tectiorem, ex Q. Muci P. f. edicto
Asiatico, EXTRA QUAM SI ITA NEGOTIUM GESTUM EST
UT EO STARI NON OPORTEAT EX FIDE BONA, multaque
sum secutus Scaevolae, in iis illud in quo sibi libertatem
censent Graeci datam, ut Graeci inter se disceptent suis
legibus. Breve autem edictum est propter hanc meam
διαίρεσιν, quod duobus generibus edicendum putavi:
quorum unum est provinciale in quo est de rationibus
civitatum, de aere alieno, de usura, de syngraphis, in
eodem omnia de publicanis; alterum, quod sine edicto
satis commode transigi non potest, de hereditatum
possessionibus, de bonis possidendis vendendis, magis-
tris faciendis, quae ex edicto et postulari et fieri solent;
tertium de reliquo iure dicundo ἄγραφον reliqui. Dixi
me de eo genere mea decreta ad edicta urbana accommo-
daturum, itaque curo et satis facio adhuc omnibus.
Graeci vero exsultant quod peregrinis iudicibus utuntur.
Nugatoribus quidem, inquies. Quid refert? Tamen se
αὐτονομίαν adeptos putant.

Cicero, *ad Atticum*, V. xxi. 9.

9. Idibus Februariis, quo die has litteras dedi, forum
institueram agere Laodiceae Cibyraticum et Apameense,
ex Idibus Mart. ibidem Synnadense, Pamphylium —
tum Phemio dispiciam κέρας — Lycaonium, Isauricum:
ex Idibus Maiis in Ciliciam, ut ibi Iunius consumatur,
velim tranquille a Parthis. Quinctilis, si erit ut
volumus, in itinere est per provinciam redeuntibus
consumendus. Venimus enim *in* provinciam Laodi-
ceam Sulpicio et Marcello consulibus, pridie Kal.
Sextilis. Inde nos oportet decedere a. d. III. Kal. Sext.
Primum contendam a Quinto fratre ut se praefici
patiatur, quod et illo et me invitissimo fiet. Sed aliter
honeste fieri non potest, praesertim cum virum optimum
Pomptinum ne nunc quidem retinere possim. Rapit
enim hominem Postumius Romam, fortasse etiam
Postumia.

Cicero, *II in Verrem*, II. 30–42, 62, 68–75.

30   Cum hos sibi quaestus constituisset magnos atque
uberes ex his causis quas ipse instituerat cum consilio,
hoc est cum sua cohorte, cognoscere, tum illud infinitum
genus invenerat ad innumerabilem pecuniam corripien-
dam. Dubium nemini est quin omnes omnium pecuniae
positae sint in eorum potestate qui iudicia dant, et
eorum qui iudicant, quin nemo vestrum possit aedis
suas, nemo fundum, nemo bona patria obtinere, si, cum
haec a quopiam vestrum petita sint, praetor improbus,
cui nemo intercedere possit, det quem velit iudicem,
31   iudex nequam et levis quod praetor iusserit iudicet. Si

vero illud quoque accedit, ut praetor in ea verba
iudicium det ut vel L. Octavius Balbus iudex, homo et
iuris et offici peritissimus, non possit aliter iudicare, —
si iudicium sit eius modi

L. OCTAVIVS IVDEX ESTO. SI PARET FVNDVM
CAPENATEM, QVO DE AGITVR, EX IVRE QVIRITIVM P.
SERVILI ESSE, NEQVE IS FVNDVS Q. CATVLO RESTITVETVR,
non necesse erit L. Octavio iudici cogere P. Servilium
Q. Catulo fundum restituere, aut condemnare eum quem
non oporteat? Eius modi totum ius praetorium, omnis
res iudiciaria fuit in Sicilia per triennium Verre praetore.
Decreta eius modi, SI NON ACCIPIT QVOD TE DEBERE
DICIS, ACCVSES; SI PETIT, DVCAS: C. Fuficium duci
iussit petitorem, L. Suettium, L. Racilium. Iudicia eius
modi: qui cives Romani erant *iudicabant* si Siculi essent,
cum Siculos eorum legibus dari oporteret, qui Siculi, si
32 cives Romani essent. Verum ut totum genus amplecta-
mini iudiciorum, prius iura Siculorum, deinde istius
instituta cognoscite.

Siculi hoc iure sunt ut, quod civis cum cive agat,
domi certet suis legibus, quod Siculus cum Siculo non
eiusdem civitatis, ut de eo praetor iudices ex P. Rupili
decreto, quod is de decem legatorum sententia statuit,
quam illi legem Rupiliam vocant, sortiatur. Quod
privatus a populo petit aut populus a privato, senatus
ex aliqua civitate qui iudicet datur, cum alternae
civitates reiectae sunt; quod civis Romanus a Siculo
petit, Siculus iudex, quod Siculus a civi Romano, civis
Romanus datur; ceterarum rerum selecti iudices ex
conventu civium Romanorum proponi solent. Inter
aratores et decumanos lege frumentaria, quam Hieroni-
33 cam appellant, iudicia fiunt. Haec omnia isto praetore
non modo perturbata, sed plane et Siculis et civibus

Romanis erepta sunt. Primum suae leges: quod civis cum civi ageret, aut eum iudicem quem commodum erat, — praeconem, haruspicem, medicum suum, — dabat, aut si legibus erat iudicium constitutum et ad civem suum iudicem venerant, libere civi iudicare non licebat. Edictum enim hominis cognoscite, quo edicto omnia iudicia redegerat in suam potestatem, SI QVI PERPERAM IVDICASSET, SE COGNITVRVM; CVM COGNOSSET, ANIMADVERSVRVM. Idque cum faciebat, nemo dubitabat quin, cum iudex alium de suo iudicio putaret iudicaturum seque in eo capitis periculum aditurum, voluntatem spectaret eius quem statim de capite suo

34 putaret iudicaturum. Selecti ex conventu aut propositi ex negotiatoribus iudices nulli: haec copia, quam dico, iudicum cohors non Q. Scaevolae, qui tamen de cohorte sua dare non solebat, sed C. Verris. Cuius modi cohortem putatis hoc principe fuisse? Sicubi videtis edictum, SI QVI PERPERAM IVDICARIT SENATVS, eum quoque ostendam, si quando sit datus, coactu istius quod non senserit iudicasse. Ex lege Rupilia sortitio nulla, nisi cum nihil intererat istius; lege Hieronica iudicia plurimarum controversiarum sublata uno nomine omnia; de conventu ac negotiatoribus nulli iudices. Quantam potestatem habuerit videtis, quas res gesserit cognoscite.

35 Heraclius est Hieronis filius Syracusanus, homo in primis domi suae nobilis et ante hunc praetorem vel pecuniosissimus Syracusanorum, nunc nulla alia calamitate nisi istius avaritia atque iniuria pauperrimus. Huic hereditas ad HS facile triciens venit testamento propinqui sui Heraclii, plena domus caelati argenti optimi multaeque stragulae vestis pretiosorumque mancipiorum; quibus in rebus istius cupiditates et

insanias quis ignorat? Erat in sermone res, magnam
Heraclio pecuniam relictam; non solum Heraclium
divitem, sed etiam ornatum supellectile, argento, veste,
36 mancipiis futurum. Audit haec etiam Verres, et primo
illo suo leniore artificio Heraclium adgredi conatur, ut
eum roget inspicienda, quae non reddat. Deinde a
quibusdam Syracusanis admonetur, — hi autem quidam
erant adfines istius, quorum iste uxores numquam
alienas existimavit, Cleomenes et Aeschrio, qui quantum apud istum et quam turpi de causa potuerint ex
reliquis criminibus intellegetis: hi, ut dico, hominem
admonent rem esse praeclaram, refertam omnibus rebus,
ipsum autem Heraclium hominem esse maiorem natu,
non promptissimum; eum praeter Marcellos patronum,
quem suo iure adire aut appellare posset, habere
neminem; esse in eo testamento quo ille heres esset
scriptus, ut statuas in palaestra deberet ponere.
'Faciemus ut palaestritae negent ex testamento esse
positas, petant hereditatem, quod eam palaestrae
37 commissam esse dicant.' Placuit ratio Verri; nam hoc
animo providebat, cum tanta hereditas in controversiam
venisset iudicioque peteretur, fieri non posse ut sine
praeda ipse discederet. Adprobat consilium; auctor
est ut quam primum agere incipiant, hominemque id
aetatis minime litigiosum quam tumultuosissime adori-
antur. Scribitur Heraclio dica. Primo mirantur
omnes improbitatem calumniae; deinde qui istum
nossent partim suspicabantur, partim plane videbant
adiectum esse oculum hereditati. Interea dies advenit
quo die sese ex instituto ac lege Rupilia dicas sortiturum
Syracusis iste edixerat. Paratus ad hanc dicam sor-
tiendam venerat. Tum eum docet Heraclius non posse
eo die sortiri, quod lex Rupilia vetaret diebus xxx

sortiri dicam quibus scripta esset. Dies xxx nondum
fuerant. Sperabat Heraclius, si illum diem effugisset,
ante alteram sortitionem Q. Arrium, quem provincia
38 tum maxime exspectabat, successurum. Iste omnibus
dicis diem distulit, et eam diem constituit ut hanc
Heraclii dicam sortiri post dies triginta ex lege posset.
Posteaquam ea dies venit, iste incipit simulare se velle
sortiri. Heraclius cum advocatis adit et postulat ut
sibi cum palaestritis, hoc est cum populo Syracusano,
aequo iure disceptare liceat. Adversarii postulant ut
in eam rem iudices dentur, ex iis civitatibus quae in id
forum convenirent electi, qui Verri viderentur: Heraclius contra, ut iudices ex lege Rupilia dentur, ut ab
institutis superiorum, ab auctoritate senatus, ab iure
39 omnium Siculorum ne recedatur. Quid ego istius in
iure dicundo libidinem et scelera demonstrem? quis
vestrum non in urbana iuris dictione cognovit? quis
umquam isto praetore Chelidone invita lege agere
potuit? Non istum, ut non neminem, provincia cor-
rupit; idem fuit qui Romae. Cum id quod omnes
intellegebant diceret Heraclius, ius esse certum Siculis
inter se quo iure certarent, legem esse Rupiliam quam
P. Rupilius consul de decem legatorum sententia
dedisset, hanc omnis semper in Sicilia consules prae-
toresque servasse, negavit se e lege Rupilia sortiturum:
quinque iudices, quos commodum ipsi fuit, dedit.
40 Quid hoc homine facias? quod supplicium dignum
libidine eius invenias? Praescriptum tibi cum esset,
homo deterrime et impudentissime, quem ad modum
iudices inter Siculos dares, cum imperatoris populi
Romani auctoritas, legatorum decem, summorum
hominum, dignitas, senatus consultum intercederet,
quo senatus consulto P. Rupilius de decem legatorum

sententia leges in Sicilia constituerat, cum omnes ante
te praetorem Rupilias leges et in ceteris rebus et in
iudiciis maxime servassent, tu ausus es pro nihilo prae
tua praeda tot res sanctissimas ducere? tibi nulla lex
fuit, nulla religio, nullus existimationis pudor, nullus
iudici metus? nullius apud te gravis auctoritas, nullum
41 exemplum quod sequi velles? Verum, ut institui
dicere, quinque iudicibus nulla lege, nullo instituto,
nulla reiectione, nulla sorte ex libidine istius datis, non
qui causam cognoscerent, sed qui quod imperatum esset
iudicarent, eo die nihil actum est; adesse iubentur
postridie. Heraclius interea, cum omnis insidias for-
tunis suis a praetore fieri videret, capit consilium de
amicorum et propinquorum sententia non adesse ad
iudicium; itaque illa nocte Syracusis profugit. Iste
postridie mane, cum multo maturius quam umquam
antea surrexisset, iudices citari iubet. Vbi comperit
Heraclium non adesse, cogere incipit eos ut absentem
Heraclium condemnent. Illi eum commonefaciunt ut,
si sibi videatur, utatur instituto suo nec cogat ante
horam decimam de absente secundum praesentem
42 iudicare: impetrant. Interea sane perturbatus et ipse
et eius amici et consiliarii moleste ferre coeperunt
Heraclium profugisse; putabant absentis damnationem,
praesertim tantae pecuniae, multo invidiosiorem fore
quam si praesens damnatus esset. Eo accedebat quod
iudices e lege Rupilia dati non erant; multo etiam rem
turpiorem fore et iniquiorem visum iri intellegebant.
Itaque hoc dum corrigere vult, apertior eius cupiditas
improbitasque facta est. Nam illis quinque iudicibus
uti se negat; iubet, id quod initio lege Rupilia fieri
oportuerat, citari Heraclium et eos qui dicam scrip-
serant; ait se iudices ex lege velle sortiri. Quod ab eo

E

pridie, cum multis lacrimis cum oraret atque obsecraret,
Heraclius impetrare non potuerat, id ei postridie venit
in mentem, ex lege Rupilia sortiri dicas oportere.
Educit ex urna tris; his ut absentem Heraclium condemnent imperat; itaque condemnant.

62   Hic nunc de miseria Siculorum, iudices, audite.
Et Heraclius ille Syracusanus et hic Bidinus Epicrates
expulsi bonis omnibus Romam venerunt; sordidati,
maxima barba et capillo, Romae biennium prope
fuerunt. Cum L. Metellus in provinciam profectus est,
tum isti bene commendati cum Metello una proficis-
cuntur. Metellus, simul ac venit Syracusas, utrumque
rescidit, et de Epicrate et de Heraclio. In utriusque
bonis nihil erat quod restitui posset, nisi si quid moveri
loco non potuerat.

68   Iam vero in rerum capitalium quaestionibus quid
ego unam quamque rem colligam et causam? Ex
multis similibus ea sumam quae maxime improbitate
excellere videbuntur. Sopater quidam fuit Halicyensis,
homo domi suae cum primis locuples atque honestus;
is ab inimicis suis apud C. Sacerdotem praetorem rei
capitalis cum accusatus esset, facile eo iudicio est
liberatus. Huic eidem Sopatro idem inimici ad C.
Verrem, cum is Sacerdoti successisset, eiusdem rei
nomen detulerunt. Res Sopatro facilis videbatur, et
quod erat innocens et quod Sacerdotis iudicium im-
probare istum ausurum non arbitrabatur. Citatur reus;
causa agitur Syracusis; crimina tractantur ab accusatore ea quae erant antea non solum defensione, verum

69 etiam iudicio dissoluta. Causam Sopatri defendebat Q. Minucius, eques Romanus in primis splendidus atque honestus, vobisque, iudices, non ignotus. Nihil erat in causa quod metuendum aut omnino quod dubitandum videretur. Interea istius libertus et accensus Timarchides, qui est, id quod ex plurimus testibus priore actione didicistis, rerum huiusce modi omnium transactor et administer, ad Sopatrum venit; monet hominem ne nimis iudicio Sacerdotis et causae suae confidat; accusatores inimicosque eius habere in animo pecuniam praetori dare; praetorem tamen ob salutem malle accipere, et simul malle, si fieri posset, rem iudicatam non rescindere. Sopater, cum hoc illi improvisum atque inopinatum accidisset, commotus est sane neque in praesentia Timarchidi quid responderet habuit, nisi se consideraturum quid sibi esset faciendum, et simul ostendit se in summa difficultate esse nummaria. Post ad amicos rettulit; qui cum ei fuissent auctores redimendae salutis, ad Timarchidem venit. Expositis suis difficultatibus hominem ad HS LXXX

70 perducit, eamque ei pecuniam numerat. Posteaquam ad causam dicendam ventum est, tum vero sine metu sine cura omnes erant qui Sopatrum defendebant. Crimen nullum erat, res erat iudicata, Verres nummos acceperat: quis posset dubitare quidnam esset futurum? Res illo die non peroratur, iudicium dimittitur. Iterum ad Sopatrum Timarchides venit, ait accusatores eius multo maiorem pecuniam praetori polliceri quam quantam hic dedisset; proinde, si saperet, videret [quid sibi esset faciendum]. Homo, quamquam erat et Siculus et reus, hoc est et iure iniquo et tempore adverso, ferre tamen atque audire diutius Timarchidem non potuit. 'Facite,' inquit, 'quod libet; daturus non sum amplius.'

Idemque hoc amicis eius et defensoribus videbatur atque eo etiam magis quod iste, quoquo modo se in ea quaestione praebebat, tamen in consilio habebat homines honestos e conventu Syracusano, qui Sacerdoti quoque in consilio fuerant tum cum est idem hic Sopater absolutus. Hoc rationis habebant, facere eos nullo modo posse ut eodem crimine eisdem testibus Sopatrum condemnarent idem homines qui antea absolvissent. Itaque 71 hac una spe ad iudicium venitur. Quo posteaquam est ventum, cum in consilium frequentes convenissent idem qui solebant, et hac una spe tota defensio Sopatri niteretur, consili frequentia et dignitate, et quod erant, ut dixi, idem qui antea Sopatrum eodem illo crimine liberarant, cognoscite hominis apertam ac non modo non ratione, sed ne dissimulatione quidem tectam improbitatem et audaciam. M. Petilium, equitem Romanum, quem habebat in consilio, iubet operam dare, quod rei privatae iudex esset. Petilius recusabat, quod suos amicos, quos sibi in consilio esse vellet, ipse Verres retineret in consilio. Iste homo liberalis negat se quemquam retinere eorum qui Petilio vellent adesse. Itaque discedunt omnes; nam ceteri quoque impetrant ne retineantur; qui se velle dicebant alterutri eorum qui tum illud iudicium habebant adesse. Itaque iste 72 solus cum sua cohorte nequissima relinquitur. Non dubitabat Minucius, qui Sopatrum defendebat, quin iste, quoniam consilium dimisisset, illo die rem illam quaesiturus non esset, cum repente iubetur dicere. Respondet, 'Ad quos?' 'Ad me,' inquit, 'si tibi idoneus videor qui de homine Siculo ac Graeculo iudicem.' 'Idoneus es,' inquit, 'sed pervellem adessent ii qui adfuerant antea causamque cognorant.' 'Dic,' inquit; 'illi adesse non possunt.' 'Nam hercule,' inquit Minu-

cius, 'me quoque Petilius ut sibi in consilio adessem
73 rogavit', et simul a subselliis abire coepit. Iste iratus
hominem verbis vehementioribus prosequitur, atque ei
gravius etiam minari coepit quod in se tantum crimen
invidiamque conflaret. Minucius, qui Syracusis sic
negotiaretur ut sui iuris dignitatisque meminisset, et
qui sciret se ita in provincia rem augere oportere ut ne
quid de libertate deperderet, homini quae visa sunt, et
quae tempus illud tulit et causa, respondit, causam
sese dimisso atque ablegato consilio defensurum negavit.
Itaque a subselliis discessit, idemque hoc praeter Siculos
74 ceteri Sopatri amici advocatique fecerunt. Iste quamquam est incredibili importunitate et audacia, tamen
subito solus destitutus pertimuit et conturbatus est;
quid ageret, quo se verteret nesciebat. Si dimisisset eo
tempore quaestionem, post, illis adhibitis in consilium
quos ablegarat, absolutum iri Sopatrum videbat; sin
autem hominem miserum atque innocentem ita con-
demnasset, cum ipse praetor sine consilio, reus autem
sine patrono atque advocatis fuisset, iudiciumque C.
Sacerdotis rescidisset, invidiam se sustinere tantam
non posse arbitrabatur. Itaque aestuabat dubitatione,
versabat se utramque in partem non solum mente,
verum etiam corpore, ut omnes qui aderant intellegere
possent in animo eius metum cum cupiditate pugnare.
Erat hominum conventus maximus, summum silentium,
summa exspectatio quonam esset eius cupiditas erup-
tura; crebro se accensus demittebat ad aurem Tim-
75 archides. Tum iste aliquando 'Age dic!' inquit. Reus
orare atque obsecrare ut cum consilio cognosceret. Tum
repente iste testis citari iubet; dicit unus et alter
breviter; nihil interrogatur; praeco DIXISSE pronuntiat. Iste, quasi metueret ne Petilius privato illo

iudicio transacto aut prolato cum ceteris in consilium
reverteretur, ita properans de sella exsilit, hominem
innocentem a C. Sacerdote absolutum indicta causa de
sententia scribae medici haruspicisque condemnat.

Cicero, *II in Verrem*, III. 25–28.

25   Primum edictum, iudices, audite praeclarum: Quantum decumanus edidisset aratorem sibi decumae dare
oportere, ut tantum arator decumano dare cogeretur.
Quo modo? Quantum poposcerit Apronius, dato. Quid
est hoc? utrum praetoris institutum in socios an in
hostis victos insani edictum atque imperium tyranni?
Ego tantundem dabo quantum ille poposcerit? poscet
omne quantum exaravero. Quid omne? plus immo
etiam, inquit, si volet. Quid tum? quid censes? Aut
dabis aut contra edictum fecisse damnabere. Per deos
26 immortalis, quid est hoc? veri enim simile non est. Sic
mihi persuadeo, iudices, tametsi omnia in istum hominem convenire putetis, tamen hoc vobis falsum videri.
Ego enim, cum hoc tota Sicilia diceret, tamen adfirmare
non auderem, si haec edicta non ex ipsius tabulis
totidem verbis recitare possem, sicuti faciam. Da,
quaeso, scribae, recitet ex codice professionem. Recita.
EDICTVM DE PROFESSIONE. Negat me recitare totum;
nam id significare nutu videtur. Quid praetereo? an
illud, ubi caves tamen Siculis et miseros respicis aratores?
dicis enim te in decumanum, si plus abstulerit quam
debitum sit, in octuplum iudicium daturum. Nihil
mihi placet praetermitti; recita hoc quoque quod
postulat totum. Recita. EDICTVM DE IVDICIO IN
OCTVPLVM. Iudicio ut arator decumanum persequatur?
Miserum atque iniquum! Ex agro homines traducis in

forum, ab aratro ad subsellia, ab usu rerum rusticarum
27 ad insolitam litem atque iudicium? Cum omnibus in
aliis vectigalibus, Asiae Macedoniae Hispaniae Galliae
Africae Sardiniae, ipsius Italiae quae vectigalia sunt —
cum in his, inquam, rebus omnibus publicanus petitor
ac pignerator, non ereptor neque possessor soleat esse,
tu de optimo, de iustissimo, de honestissimo genere
hominum, hoc est de aratoribus, ea iura constituebas
quae omnibus aliis essent contraria? Vtrum est aequius,
decumanum petere an aratorem repetere? iudicium
integra re an perdita fieri? eum qui manu quaesierit, an
eum qui digito sit licitus possidere? Quid? qui singulis
iugis arant, qui ab opere ipsi non recedunt, — quo in
numero magnus ante te praetorem numerus ac magna
multitudo Siculorum fuit, — quid facient cum dederint
Apronio quod poposcerit? relinquent arationes, relinquent Larem familiarem suum? venient Syracusas, ut te
praetore videlicet aequo iure Apronium, delicias ac vitam
28 tuam, iudicio recuperatorio persequantur? Verum esto:
reperietur aliqui fortis et experiens arator, qui, cum
tantum dederit decumano quantum ille deberi dixerit,
iudicio repetat et poenam octupli persequatur: exspecto
vim edicti, severitatem praetoris: faveo aratori, cupio
octupli damnari Apronium. Quid tandem postulat
arator? nihil nisi ex edicto iudicium in octuplum. Quid
Apronius? non recusat. Quid praetor? iubet recuperatores reicere. 'Decurias scribamus.' Quas decurias? 'de
cohorte mea reicies,' inquit. 'Quid? ista cohors quorum
hominum est?' Volusi haruspicis et Corneli medici
et horum canum quos tribunal meum vides lambere;
nam de conventu nullum umquam iudicem nec re-
cuperatorem dedit; iniquos decumanis aiebat omnis
esse qui ullam agri glebam possiderent. Veniendum

erat ad eos contra Apronium qui nondum Aproniani
convivi crapulam exhalassent. O praeclarum et com-
memorandum iudicium! o severum edictum! o tutum
perfugium aratorum!

Cicero, *II in Verrem*, V. 160–163.

160 Gavius hic quem dico, Consanus, cum in illo numero
civium Romanorum ab isto in vincla coniectus esset et
nescio qua ratione clam e lautumiis profugisset Messa-
namque venisset, qui tam prope iam Italiam et moenia
Reginorum, civium Romanorum, videret et ex illo metu
mortis ac tenebris quasi luce libertatis et odore aliquo
legum recreatus revixisset, loqui Messanae et queri
coepit se civem Romanum in vincla coniectum, sibi
recta iter esse Romam, Verri se praesto advenienti
futurum. Non intellegebat miser nihil interesse utrum
haec Messanae an apud istum in praetorio loqueretur;
nam, ut antea vos docui, hanc sibi iste urbem delegerat
quam haberet adiutricem scelerum, furtorum recep-
tricem, flagitiorum omnium consciam. Itaque ad magistratum Mamertinum statim deducitur Gavius, eoque
ipso die casu Messanam Verres venit. Res ad eum
defertur, esse civem Romanum qui se Syracusis in
lautumiis fuisse quereretur; quem iam ingredientem
in navem et Verri nimis atrociter minitantem ab se
retractum esse et adservatum, ut ipse in eum statueret
161 quod videretur. Agit hominibus gratias et eorum beni-
volentiam erga se diligentiamque conlaudat. Ipse
inflammatus scelere et furore in forum venit; ardebant
oculi, toto ex ore crudelitas eminebat. Exspectabant
omnes quo tandem progressurus aut quidnam acturus
esset, cum repente hominem proripi atque in foro medio

nudari ac deligari et virgas expediri iubet. Clamabat
ille miser se civem esse Romanum, municipem Con-
sanum; meruisse cum L. Raecio, splendidissimo equite
Romano, qui Panhormi negotiaretur, ex quo haec
Verres scire posset. Tum iste, se comperisse eum
speculandi causa in Siciliam a ducibus fugitivorum esse
missum; cuius rei neque index neque vestigium aliquod
neque suspicio cuiquam esset ulla; deinde iubet undique
162 hominem vehementissime verberari. Caedebatur virgis
in medio foro Messanae civis Romanus, iudices, cum
interea nullus gemitus, nulla vox alia illius miseri inter
dolorem crepitumque plagarum audiebatur nisi haec,
'Civis Romanus sum.' Hac se commemoratione civitatis
omnia verbera depulsurum cruciatumque a corpore
deiecturum arbitrabatur; is non modo hoc non per-
fecit, ut virgarum vim deprecaretur, sed cum imploraret
saepius usurparetque nomen civitatis, crux, — crux,
inquam, — infelici et aerumnoso, qui numquam istam
pestem viderat, comparabatur.

163 O nomen dulce libertatis! o ius eximium nostrae civitatis! o lex Porcia legesque Semproniae! o graviter desiderata et aliquando reddita plebi Romanae tribunicia
potestas! Hucine tandem haec omnia reciderunt ut
civis Romanus in provincia populi Romani, in oppido
foederatorum, ab eo qui beneficio populi Romani fascis
et securis haberet deligatus in foro virgis caederetur?

Cicero, *ad Atticum*, V. xxi. 10–12, VI. i. 3–4.

10. Habes consilia nostra. Nunc cognosce de Bruto.
Familiaris habet Brutus tuus quosdam creditores
Salaminorum ex Cypro M. Scaptium et P. Matinium,
quos mihi maiorem in modum commendavit. Mati-

nium non novi, Scaptius ad me in castra venit. Pollicitus sum curaturum me Bruti causa ut ei Salamini pecuniam solverent. Egit gratias: praefecturam petivit. Negavi me cuiquam negotianti dare (quod idem tibi ostenderam. Cn. Pompeio petenti probaram institutum meum; quid dicam Torquato de M. Laenio tuo, multis aliis?); sin praefectus vellet esse syngraphae causa, me curaturum ut exigeret. Gratias egit: discessit. Appius noster turmas aliquot equitum dederat huic Scaptio, per quas Salaminos coerceret, et eundem habuerat praefectum. Vexabat Salaminos. Ego equites ex Cypro decedere iussi. Moleste tulit Scaptius. 11. Quid multa? Ut ei fidem meam praestarem, cum ad me Salamini Tarsum venissent et una Scaptius, imperavi ut pecuniam solverent. Multa de syngrapha, de Scapti iniuriis. Negavi me audire. Hortatus sum, petivi etiam pro meis in civitatem beneficiis ut negotium conficerent: denique dixi me coacturum. Homines non modo non recusare sed etiam hoc dicere, se a me solvere: quod enim praetori dare consuessent quoniam ego non acceperam, se a me quodam modo dare, atque etiam minus esse aliquanto in Scapti nomine quam in vectigali praetorio. Collaudavi homines. 'Recte,' inquit Scaptius, 'sed subducamus summam.' Interim, cum ego in edicto translaticio centesimas me observaturum haberem cum anatocismo anniversario, ille ex syngrapha postulabat quaternas. 'Quid ais?' inquam, 'possumne contra meum edictum?' At ille profert senatus consultum Lentulo Philippoque consulibus, UT QUI CILICIAM OBTINERET IUS EX ILLA SYNGRAPHA DICERET. 12. Cohorrui primo: etenim erat interitus civitatis. Reperio duo senatus consulta iisdem consulibus de eadem syngrapha. Salamini cum Romae versuram facere vellent, non poterant, quod lex Gabinia vetabat. Tum iis Bruti familiares, freti gratia Bruti, dare volebant quaternis, si sibi senatus consulto caveretur. Fit gratia Bruti senatus consultum, UT NEVE SALAMINIS NEVE QUI EIS DEDISSET FRAUDI ESSET. Pecuniam numerarunt. At postea venit in mentem feneratoribus nihil se iuvare illud S. C. quod ex syngrapha ius dici lex Gabinia vetaret. Tum fit S. C., UT EX EA SYNGRAPHA *IUS DICERETUR: non ut alio iure ea syngrapha* esset quam ceterae, sed ut eodem. Cum haec disseruissem, seducit me Scaptius: ait se nihil contra dicere, sed illos putare talenta CC. se debere: ea se velle accipere, debere autem illos paullo minus, rogat ut eos ad CC. perducam. 'Optime,' inquam. Voco illos ad me, remoto Scaptio. 'Quid vos? quantum,' inquam, 'debetis?' Respondent, CVI. Refero ad Scaptium. Homo clamare. 'Quid? opus est' inquam [quam] 'rationes conferatis.' Adsidunt, subducunt, *ad* nummum convenit. Illi se numerare velle, urgere ut acciperet. Scaptius me rursus seducit: rogat ut rem sic relinquam. Dedi veniam homini impudenter petenti. Graecis querentibus, ut in fano deponerent postulantibus, non concessi. Clamare omnes qui aderant, *alii* nihil impudentius Scaptio qui centesimis cum anatocismo contentus non esset: alii, nihil stultius. Mihi autem impudens magis quam stultus videbatur. Nam aut bono nomine centesimis contentus erat aut non bono quaternas centesimas sperabat.

VI. i. 3. Nunc venio ad Brutum quem ego omni studio te auctore sum complexus, quem etiam amare coeperam; sed ilico me revocavi ne te offenderem. Noli enim putare me quidquam maluisse quam ut mandatis satis facerem, nec ulla de re plus laborasse. Mandatorum autem mihi libellum dedit, iisdemque de rebus tu mecum egeras. Omnia sum diligentissime persecutus. Primum ab Ariobarzane sic contendi ut talenta quae mihi pollicebatur illi daret. Quoad mecum rex fuit, perbono loco res erat: post a Pompei procuratoribus sescentis premi coeptus est. Pompeius autem cum ob ceteras causas plus potest unus quam ceteri omnes, tum quod putatur ad bellum Parthicum esse venturus. Ei tamen sic nunc solvitur: tricesimo quoque die talenta Attica xxxiii et hoc ex tributis: nec id satis efficitur in usuram menstruam. Sed Gnaeus noster clementer id fert: sorte caret, usura nec ea solida contentus est. Alii neque solvit cuiquam nec potest solvere. Nullum enim aerarium, nullum vectigal habet. Appi instituto tributa imperat. Ea vix in fenus Pompei quod satis sit efficiunt. Amici regis duo tresve perdivites sunt, sed ii suum tam diligenter tenent quam ego aut tu. Equidem non desino tamen per litteras rogare, suadere, accusare regem. 4. Deiotarus etiam mihi narravit se ad eum legatos misisse de re Bruti: eos sibi responsum rettulisse illum non habere. Et mehercule ego ita iudico, nihil illo regno spoliatius, nihil rege egentius. Itaque aut tutela cogito me abdicare aut, ut pro Glabrione Scaevola, fenus et impendium recusare. Ego tamen quas per te Bruto promiseram praefecturas M. Scaptio, L. Gavio, qui in regno rem Bruti procurabant, detuli. Nec enim in provincia mea negotiabantur. Tu autem meministi nos sic agere ut quot vellet praefecturas sumeret, dum ne negotiatori. Itaque duas ei praeterea dederam. Sed ii quibus petierat de provincia decesserant.

IV

TAXATION AND FINANCE

Cicero, *II in Verrem*, III. 11–15, 18–20, 147–148, 163,
188–197

Neminem vestrum praeterit, iudices, omnem utilitatem opportunitatemque provinciae Siciliae, quae ad
commoda populi Romani adiuncta sit, consistere in re
frumentaria maxime; nam ceteris rebus adiuvamur ex
12 illa provincia, hac vero alimur ac sustinemur. Ea causa
tripertita, iudices, erit in accusatione; primum enim
de decumano, deinde de empto dicemus frumento,
postremo de aestimato.

Inter Siciliam ceterasque provincias, iudices, in
agrorum vectigalium ratione hoc interest, quod ceteris
aut impositum vectigal est certum, quod stipendiarium
dicitur, ut Hispanis et plerisque Poenorum quasi vic-
toriae praemium ac poena belli, aut censoria locatio
constituta est, ut Asiae lege Sempronia: Siciliae
civitates sic in amicitiam fidemque accepimus ut eodem
iure essent quo fuissent, eadem condicione populo
13 Romano parerent qua suis antea paruissent. Per
paucae Siciliae civitates sunt bello a maioribus nostris
subactae; quarum ager cum esset publicus populi
Romani factus, tamen illis est redditus; is ager a
censoribus locari solet. Foederatae civitates duae sunt,
quarum decumae venire non soleant, Mamertina et
Tauromenitana, quinque praeterea sine foedere immunes [civitates] ac liberae, Centuripina, Halaesina,

Segestana, Halicyensis, Panhormitana; praeterea omnis
ager Siciliae civitatum decumanus est, itemque ante
imperium populi Romani ipsorum Siculorum voluntate
14 et institutis fuit. Videte nunc maiorum sapientiam,
qui cum Siciliam tam opportunum subsidium belli
atque pacis ad rem publicam adiunxissent, tanta cura
Siculos tueri ac retinere voluerunt ut non modo eorum
agris vectigal novum nullum imponerent, sed ne legem
quidem venditionis decumarum neve vendundi aut
tempus aut locum commutarent, ut certo tempore
anni, ut ibidem in Sicilia, denique ut lege Hieronica
venderent. Voluerunt eos in suis rebus ipsos interesse,
eorumque animos non modo lege nova sed ne nomine
15 quidem legis novo commoveri. Itaque decumas lege
Hieronica semper vendundas censuerunt, ut iis iucun-
dior esset muneris illius functio, si eius regis qui
Siculis carissimus fuit non solum instituta commutato
imperio, verum etiam nomen maneret. Hoc iure ante
Verrem praetorem Siculi semper usi sunt: hic primus
instituta omnium, consuetudinem a maioribus traditam,
condicionem amicitiae, ius societatis convellere et
commutare ausus est.

18   L. Octavio et C. Cottae consulibus senatus permisit
ut vini et olei decumas et frugum minutarum, quas ante
quaestores in Sicilia vendere consuessent, Romae venderent, legemque his rebus quam ipsis videretur
dicerent. Cum locatio fieret, publicani postularunt
quasdem res ut ad legem adderent neque tamen a
ceteris censoriis legibus recederent. Contra dixit is qui
casu tum Romae fuit, tuus hospes, Verres, — hospes,

inquam, et familiaris tuus, — Sthenius hic Thermitanus.
Consules causam cognorunt; cum viros primarios atque
amplissimos civitatis multos in consilium advocassent,
de consili sententia pronuntiarunt se lege Hieronica
19 vendituros. Itane vero? Prudentissimi viri summa
auctoritate praediti, quibus senatus legum dicendarum
in locandis vectigalibus omnem potestatem permiserat
populusque Romanus idem iusserat, Siculo uno recusante cum amplificatione vectigalium nomen Hiero-
nicae legis mutare noluerunt: tu, homo minimi consili,
nullius auctoritatis, iniussu populi ac senatus, tota
Sicilia recusante, cum maximo detrimento atque adeo
exitio vectigalium totam Hieronicam legem sustulisti?
20 At quam legem corrigit, iudices, atque adeo totam
tollit! Acutissime ac diligentissime scriptam, quae lex
omnibus custodiis subiectum aratorem decumano tradi-
dit, ut neque in segetibus neque in areis neque in horreis
neque in amovendo neque in exportando frumento
grano uno posset arator sine maxima poena fraudare
decumanum. Scripta lex ita diligenter est ut eum
scripsisse appareat qui alia vectigalia non haberet, ita
acute ut Siculum, ita severe ut tyrannum; qua lege
Siculis tamen arare expediret; nam ita diligenter constituta sunt iura decumano ut tamen ab invito aratore
plus decuma non possit auferri.

147 Decumas agri Leontini magno dicis te vendidisse.
Ostendi iam illud initio, non existimandum magno
vendidisse eum qui verbo decumas vendiderit, re et
condicione et lege et edicto et licentia decumanorum
decumas aratoribus nullas reliquas fecerit. Etiam illud

ostendi, vendidisse alios magno decumas agri Leontini
ceterorumque agrorum, et lege Hieronica vendidisse et
pluris etiam quam te vendidisse, nec aratorem quemquam esse questum; nec enim fuit quod quisquam
queri posset, cum lege aequissime scripta venderent,
neque illud umquam aratoris interfuit, quanti decumae
venirent. Non enim ita est ut, si magno venierint, plus
arator debeat, si parvo, minus; ut frumenta nata sunt,
ita decumae veneunt; aratoris autem interest ita se
frumenta habere ut decumae quam plurimo venire
possint; dum arator ne plus decuma det, expedit ei
148decumam esse quam maximam. Verum hoc, ut opinor,
esse vis caput defensionis tuae, magno te decumas vendidisse, atque aliorum quidem agrorum pro portione
magno decumas vendidisse, agri vero Leontini, qui
plurimum efficit, tritici mod. CCXVI. Si doceo pluris
aliquanto potuisse te vendere, neque iis voluisse
addicere qui contra Apronium licerentur, et Apronio
multo minoris quam aliis potueris vendere tradidisse, —
si hoc doceo, poteritne te ipse Alba, tuus antiquissimus
non solum amicus verum etiam amator, absolvere?

163 Sequitur ut de frumento empto vos, iudices, doceam,
maximo atque impudentissimo furto; de quo dum
certa et pauca et magna dicam breviter, attendite.
Frumentum emere in Sicilia debuit Verres ex senatus
consulto et ex lege Terentia et Cassia frumentaria.
Emundi duo genera fuerunt, unum decumanum, alterum quod praeterea civitatibus aequaliter esset distri-
butum; illius decumani tantum quantum ex primis
decumis fuisset, huius imperati in annos singulos tritici

mod. DCCC; pretium autem constitutum decumano in modios singulos HS III, imperato HS III s. Ita in frumentum imperatum HS duodetriciens in annos singulos Verri decernebatur quod aratoribus solveret, in alteras decumas fere ad nonagiens. Sic per triennium ad hanc frumenti emptionem Siciliensem prope centiens et viciens erogatum est.

188 Dictum, iudices, est de decumano frumento, dictum de empto, extremum reliquum est de aestimato; quod cum magnitudine pecuniae tum iniuriae genere quemvis debet commovere, tum vero eo magis quod ad hoc crimen non ingeniosa aliqua defensio sed improbissima confessio comparatur. Nam cum ex senatus consulto et ex legibus frumentum in cellam ei sumere liceret idque frumentum senatus ita aestimasset, quaternis HS tritici modium, binis hordei, iste *hordei* numero ad summam tritici adiecto tritici modios singulos cum aratoribus denariis ternis aestimavit. Non est in hoc crimen, Hortensi, ne forte ad hoc meditere, multos saepe viros bonos et fortis et innocentis cum aratoribus et cum civitatibus frumentum, in cellam quod sumi oporteret, aestimasse et pecuniam pro frumento abstulisse. Scio quid soleat fieri, scio quid liceat; nihil quod antea fuerit in consuetudine bonorum nunc in 189istius facto reprehenditur; hoc reprehendo, quod, cum in Sicilia HS binis tritici modius esset, ut istius epistula ad te missa declarat, summum HS ternis, id quod et testimoniis omnium et tabulis aratorum planum factum antea est, tum iste pro tritici modiis singulis ternos ab

aratoribus denarios exegit; hoc crimen est, ut intellegas
non ex aestimatione neque ex ternis denariis pendere
crimen, sed ex coniunctione annonae atque aestimationis.

Etenim haec aestimatio nata est initio, iudices, non
ex praetorum aut consulum, sed ex civitatum et
aratorum commodo. Nemo enim fuit initio tam impudens qui, cum frumentum deberetur, pecuniam
posceret. Certe hoc ab aratore primum est profectum,
aut ab ea civitate cui imperabatur; cum aut frumentum
vendidisset aut servare vellet aut in eum locum quo
imperabatur portare nollet, petivit in benefici loco et
gratiae ut sibi pro frumento quanti frumentum esset
dare liceret. Ex huiusce modi principio atque ex
liberalitate et accommodatione magistratuum con-
190suetudo aestimationis introducta est. Secuti sunt
avariores magistratus, qui tamen in avaritia sua non
solum viam quaestus invenerunt, verum etiam exitum
ac rationem defensionis. Instituerunt semper in ultima
ac difficillima ad portandum loca frumentum imperare,
ut vecturae difficultate ad quam vellent aestimationem
pervenirent. In hoc genere facilior est existimatio
quam reprehensio, ideo quod eum qui hoc facit avarum
possumus existimare, crimen in eo constituere non
tam facile possumus, quod videtur concedendum
magistratibus nostris esse ut iis quo loco velint frumentum accipere liceat. Itaque hoc est quod multi
fortasse fecerunt, sed ita multi ut ii quos innocentis-
simos meminimus aut audivimus non fecerint.

191 Quaero nunc abs te, Hortensi, cum utrisne tandem
istius factum collaturus es? Cum iis, credo, qui benignitate adducti per beneficium et gratiam civitatibus
concesserunt ut nummos pro frumento darent. Ita

credo petisse ab isto aratores ut, cum HS ternis tritici modium vendere non possent, pro singulis modiis ternos denarios dare liceret. An quoniam hoc non audes dicere, illuc confugies, vecturae difficultate adductus ternos denarios dare maluisse? Cuius vecturae? quo ex loco in quem locum ne portarent? Philomelio Ephesum? Video quid inter annonam interesse soleat, video quot dierum via sit, video Philomeliensibus expedire, quanti Ephesi sit frumentum, dare potius in Phrygia quam Ephesum portare aut ad emendum 192frumentum Ephesum pecuniam et legatos mittere. In Sicilia vero quid eius modi est? Henna mediterranea est maxime. Coge ut ad aquam tibi, id quod summi iuris est, frumentum Hennenses admetiantur vel Phintiam vel Halaesam vel Catinam, loca inter se maxime diversa: eodem die quo iusseris deportabunt. Tametsi ne vectura quidem est opus. Nam totus quaestus hic, iudices, aestimationis ex annonae natus est varietate. Hoc enim magistratus in provincia adsequi potest, ut ibi accipiat ubi est carissimum. Ideo valet ista ratio aestimationis in Asia, valet in Hispania, valet in iis provinciis in quibus unum pretium frumento esse non solet: in Sicilia vero quid cuiusquam intererat quo loco daret? neque enim portandum erat, et, quo quisque vehere iussus esset, ibi tantidem frumentum emeret 193quanti domi vendidisset. Quam ob rem, si vis, Hortensi, docere aliquid ab isto simile in aestimatione atque a ceteris esse factum, doceas oportebit aliquo in loco Siciliae praetore Verre ternis denariis tritici modium fuisse.

Vide quam tibi defensionem patefecerim, quam iniquam in socios, quam remotam ab utilitate rei publicae, quam seiunctam a voluntate ac sententia legis.

Tu, cum tibi ego frumentum in meis agris atque in mea
civitate, denique cum in iis locis in quibus es, versaris,
rem geris, provinciam administras, paratus sim dare,
angulum mihi aliquem eligas provinciae reconditum ac
derelictum? iubeas ibi me metiri quo portare non ex-
194pediat, ubi emere non possim?   Improbum facinus,
iudices, non ferendum, nemini lege concessum, sed
fortasse adhuc in nullo etiam vindicatum! Tamen ego
hoc, quod ferri nego posse, Verri, iudices, concedo et
largior. Si ullo in loco eius provinciae frumentum tanti
fuit quanti iste aestimavit, hoc crimen in istum reum
valere oportere non arbitror. Verum enim vero, cum
esset HS binis aut etiam ternis quibusvis in locis provinciae, duodenos sestertios exegisti. Si mihi tecum
neque de annona neque de aestimatione tua potest esse
controversia, quid sedes, quid exspectas, quid defendis?
utrum tibi pecuniae coactae conciliatae videntur adversus leges, adversus rem publicam cum maxima
sociorum iniuria, an vero id recte, ordine, e re publica,
sine cuiusquam iniuria factum esse defendis?

195 Cum tibi senatus ex aerario pecuniam prompsisset et
singulos tibi denarios adnumerasset quos tu pro
singulis modiis aratoribus solveres, quid facere debuisti?
Si quod L. Piso ille Frugi, qui legem de pecuniis repetundis primus tulit, cum emisses quanti esset, quod
superaret pecuniae rettulisses; si ut ambitiosi homines
aut benigni, cum pluris senatus aestimasset quam
quanti esset annona, ex senatus aestimatione, non ex
annonae ratione solvisses; sin, ut plerique faciunt, in
quo erat aliqui quaestus, sed is honestus atque concessus, frumentum, quoniam vilius erat, ne emisses,
sumpsisses id nummorum quod tibi senatus cellae
nomine concesserat.

Hoc vero quid est? quam habet rationem non quaero aequitatis, sed ipsius improbitatis atque impudentiae? Neque enim est fere quicquam quod homines palam facere audeant in magistratu quamvis improbe, quin eius facti si non bonam, at aliquam rationem adferre 196soleant. Hoc quid est? Venit praetor; frumentum, inquit, me abs te emere oportet. Optime. Modium denario. Benigne ac liberaliter: nam ego ternis HS non possum vendere. Mihi frumentum non opus est, nummos volo. Nam sperabam, inquit arator, me ad denarios perventurum; sed, si ita necesse est, quanti frumentum sit considera. Video esse binis HS. Quid ergo a me tibi nummorum dari potest, cum senatus tibi quaternos HS dederit? Quid poscit? Attendite et, vos quaeso, simul, iudices, aequitatem praetoris attendite. 197Quaternos HS, quos mihi senatus decrevit et ex aerario dedit, ego habebo et in cistam transferam de fisco. Quid postea? quid? Pro singulis modiis, quos tibi impero, tu mihi octonos HS dato. Qua ratione? Quid quaeris rationem? non tantam rationem res habet quantam utilitatem atque praedam. Dic, dic, inquit ille, planius. Senatus te voluit mihi nummos, me tibi frumentum dare: tu eos nummos quos mihi senatus dare voluit ipse habebis; a me, cui singulos denarios a te dari oportuit, binos auferes et huic praedae ac direptioni cellae nomen impones?

Livy, XXXII. 27, 2.

Eadem aestate equites ducenti et elephanti decem et tritici modium ducenta milia ab rege Masinissa ad exercitum qui in Graecia erat pervenerunt. item ex Sicilia Sardiniaque magni commeatus et vestimenta exercitui missa. Siciliam M. Marcellus, Sardiniam M. Porcius Cato obtinebat, sanctus et innocens, asperior tamen in fenore coercendo habitus. fugatique ex insula feneratores, et sumptus, quos in cultum praetorum socii facere soliti erant, circumcisi aut sublati.

Cicero, *ad Atticum*, V. xvi.

1. Etsi in ipso itinere et via discedebant publicanorum tabellarii et eramus in cursu, tamen surripiendum aliquid putavi spati ne me immemorem mandati tui putares. Itaque subsedi in ipsa via, dum haec, quae longiorem desiderant orationem, summatim tibi perscriberem. 2. Maxima exspectatione in perditam et plane eversam in perpetuum provinciam nos venisse scito pridie Kal. Sextilis, moratos triduum Laodiceae, triduum Apameae, totidem dies Synnade. Audivimus nihil aliud nisi imperata ἐπικεφάλια solvere non posse: ὠνὰς omnium venditas: civitatum gemitus, ploratus: monstra quaedam non hominis, sed ferae nescio cuius immanis. Quid quaeris? taedet omnino eos vitae. 3. Levantur tamen miserae civitates quod nullus fit sumptus in nos neque in legatos neque in quaestorem neque in quemquam. Scito non modo nos foenum aut quod e lege Iulia dari solet non accipere sed ne ligna quidem, nec praeter quattuor lectos et tectum quemquam accipere quidquam, multis locis ne tectum quidem et in tabernaculo manere plerumque. Itaque incredibilem in modum concursus fiunt ex agris, ex vicis, ex domibus, ex omnibus. Mehercule etiam adventu nostro reviviscunt iustitia, abstinentia, clementia tui Ciceronis; ita[que] opiniones omnium superavit. 4. Appius, ut

audivit nos venire, in ultimam provinciam se coniecit
Tarsum usque: ibi forum agit. De Partho silentium
est, sed tamen concisos equites nostros a barbaris
nuntiabant ii qui veniebant. Bibulus ne cogitabat
quidem etiam nunc in provinciam suam accedere. Id
autem facere ob eam causam dicebant quod tardius
vellet decedere. Nos in castra properabamus, quae
aberant tridui.

ad familiares, III. viii. 1–5.

M. CICERO S. D. AP. PULCRO.

1. Etsi, quantum ex tuis litteris intellegere potui,
videbam te hanc epistulam, cum ad urbem esses, esse
lecturum refrigerato iam levissimo sermone hominum
provincialium, tamen, cum tu tam multis verbis ad
me de improborum oratione scripsisses, faciendum mihi
putavi ut tuis litteris brevi responderem. 2. Sed prima
duo capita epistulae tuae tacita mihi quodam modo
relinquenda sunt: nihil enim habent quod definitum sit
aut certum, nisi me vultu et taciturnitate significasse
tibi non esse amicum, idque pro tribunali cum aliquid
ageretur et non nullis in conviviis intellegi potuisse.
Hoc totum nihil esse possum intellegere: sed cum sit
nihil, ne quid dicatur quidem intellego. Illud quidem
scio, meos multos et illustris et ex superiore et ex aequo
loco sermones habitos cum tua summa laude et cum
magna sollicitudine et significatione nostrae familiari-
tatis ad te vere potuisse deferri. Nam quod ad legatos
attinet, quid a me fieri potuit aut elegantius aut iustius
quam ut sumptus egentissimarum civitatum minuerem
sine ulla imminutione dignitatis tuae, praesertim ipsis

civitatibus postulantibus? Nam mihi totum genus legationum tuo nomine proficiscentium notum non erat. Apameae cum essem, multarum civitatum principes ad me detulerunt sumptus decerni legatis nimis magnos, cum solvendo civitates non essent. 3. Hic ego multa simul cogitavi. Primum te, hominem non solum sapientem verum etiam, ut nunc loquimur, urbanum, non arbitrabar genere isto legationum delectari, idque me arbitror Synnadis pro tribunali multis verbis disputavisse: primum Appium Claudium senatui populoque Romano non Midaeensium testimonio — in ea enim civitate mentio facta est — sed sua sponte esse laudatum: deinde me ita vidisse accidere multis ut eorum causa legationes Romam venirent, sed iis legationibus non meminisse ullum tempus laudandi aut locum dari: studia mihi eorum placere quod in te bene merito grati essent, consilium totum videri minime necessarium; si autem vellent declarare in eo officium suum, laudaturum me, si qui suo sumptu functus esset officio, concessurum, si legitimo, non permissurum, si infinito. Quid enim reprehendi potest? nisi quod addis visum esse quibusdam edictum meum quasi consulto ad istas legationes impediendas esse accommodatum. Iam non tantum mihi videntur iniuriam facere ii qui haec disputant quam si cuius aures ad hanc disputationem patent. 4. Romae composui edictum: nihil addidi nisi quod publicani me rogarunt, cum Samum ad me venissent, ut de tuo edicto totidem verbis transferrem in meum. Diligentissime scriptum caput est quod pertinet ad minuendos sumptus civitatum: quo in capite sunt quaedam nova salutaria civitatibus, quibus ego magno opere delector: hoc vero, ex quo suspicio nata est me exquisisse aliquid in quo te

offenderem, tralaticium est. Neque enim eram tam
desipiens ut privatae rei causa legari putarem, qui et
tibi non privato et pro re non privata sua sed publica,
non in privato sed in publico orbis terrae consilio, id
est in senatu, ut gratias agerent, mittebantur. Neque
cum edixi ne quis iniussu meo proficisceretur, exclusi
eos qui me in castra et qui trans Taurum persequi non
possent. Nam id est maxime in tuis literis inridendum:
quid enim erat quod me persequerentur in castra
Taurumve transirent, cum ego Laodicea usque ad
Iconium iter ita fecerim ut me omnium illarum dioecesium quae cis Taurum sunt omniumque earum
civitatum magistratus legationesque convenirent? 5.
Nisi forte postea coeperunt legare quam ego Taurum
transgressus sum: quod certe non ita est. Cum enim
Laodiceae, cum Apameae, cum Synnadis, cum Philo-
meli, cum Iconi essem, quibus in oppidis omnibus
commoratus sum, omnes iam istius generis legationes
erant constitutae. Atque hoc tamen te scire volo, me
de isto sumptu legationum aut minuendo aut remit-
tendo decrevisse nihil nisi quod principes civitatum a
me postulassent, ne in venditionem tributorum et illam
acerbissimam exactionem, quam tu non ignoras, capitum atque ostiorum inducerentur sumptus minime
necessarii. Ego autem cum hoc suscepissem, non solum
iustitia sed etiam misericordia adductus, ut levarem
miseriis perditas civitates et perditas maxime per
magistratus suos, non potui in illo sumptu non necessario neglegens esse. Tu, *si* istius modi sermones ad te
delati de me sunt, non debuisti credere: si autem hoc
genere delectaris, ut quae tibi in mentem veniant aliis
attribuas, genus sermonis inducis in amicitiam minime
liberale.

ad Atticum, V. xxi. 6–8.

6. Ego aestivis confectis Quintum fratrem hibernis et
Ciliciae praefeci; Q. Volusium, tui Tiberi generum,
certum hominem sed mirifice etiam abstinentem, misi
in Cyprum ut ibi pauculos dies esset, ne cives Romani
pauci qui illic negotiantur ius sibi dictum negarent:
nam evocari ex insula Cyprios non licet. 7. Ipse in
Asiam profectus sum Tarso Nonis Ianuariis, non mehercule dici potest qua admiratione Ciliciae civitatum
maximeque Tarsensium. Postea vero quam Taurum
transgressus sum, mirifica exspectatio Asiae nostrarum
dioecesium, quae sex mensibus imperi mei nullas meas
acceperat litteras, numquam hospitem viderat. Illud
autem tempus quotannis ante me fuerat in hoc quaestu:
civitates locupletes, ne in hiberna milites reciperent,
magnas pecunias dabant: Cyprii talenta Attica CC, qua
ex insula — non ὑπερβολικῶς sed verissime loquor —
nummus nullus me obtinente erogabitur. Ob haec
beneficia, quibus illi obstupescunt, nullos honores mihi
nisi verborum decerni sino: statuas, fana, τέθριππα
prohibeo, nec sum in ulla re alia molestus civitatibus,
sed fortasse tibi qui haec praedicem de me. Perfer, si
me amas; tu enim me haec facere voluisti. 8. Iter
igitur ita per Asiam feci ut etiam fames, qua nihil
miserius est, quae tum erat in hac mea Asia — messis
enim nulla fuerat — mihi optanda fuerit. Quacumque
iter feci, nulla vi, nullo iudicio, nulla contumelia,
auctoritate et cohortatione perfeci ut et Graeci et cives
Romani qui frumentum compresserant magnum numerum populis pollicerentur.

ad Atticum, VI. i. 16.

16. De publicanis quid agam videris quaerere. Habeo in deliciis, obsequor, verbis laudo, orno: efficio ne cui molesti sint. Τὸ παραδοξότατον, usuras eorum quas pactionibus ascripserant servavit etiam Servilius. Ego sic: diem statuo satis laxam, quam ante si solverint, dico me centesimas ducturum: si non solverint, ex pactione. Itaque et Graeci solvunt tolerabili fenore et publicanis res est gratissima, si illa iam habent pleno modio, verborum honorem, invitationem crebram. Quid plura? Sunt omnes ita mihi familiares ut se quisque maxime putet.

ad familiares, II. xvii. 1–5.

M. CICERO IMP. S. D. CN. SALLUSTIO PROQUAEST.

1. Litteras a te mihi stator tuus reddidit Tarsi a. d. XVI. Kalend. Sextilis. His ego ordine, ut videris velle, respondebo. De successore meo nihil audivi ne*que* quemquam fore arbitror. Quin ad diem decedam nulla causa est, praesertim sublato metu Parthico. Commoraturum me nusquam sane arbitror: Rhodum Ciceronum causa puerorum accessurum puto, neque id tamen certum. Ad urbem volo quam primum venire, sed tamen iter meum rei publicae et rerum urbanarum ratio gubernabit. Successor tuus non potest ita maturare, ullo modo ut tu me in Asia possis convenire. 2. De rationibus referendis non erat incommodum te nullam referre, quam tibi scribis a Bibulo fieri potestatem: sed id vix mihi videris per legem Iuliam facere

posse, quam Bibulus certa quadam ratione non servat, tibi magno opere servandam censeo. 3. Quod scribis Apamea praesidium deduci non oportuisse, videbam item ceteros existimare, molesteque ferebam de ea re minus commodos sermones malevolorum fuisse. Parthi transierint necne praeter te video dubitare neminem. Itaque omnia praesidia, quae magna et firma paraveram, commotus hominum non dubio sermone dimisi. 4. Rationes mei quaestoris nec verum fuit me tibi mittere nec tum erant confectae: eas nos Apameae deponere cogitabamus. De praeda mea praeter quaestores urbanos, id est populum Romanum, terruncium nec attigit nec tacturus est quisquam. Laodiceae me praedes accepturum arbitror omnis pecuniae publicae, ut et mihi et populo cautum sit sine vecturae periculo. Quod scribis ad me de drachmum cccꟛꟛꟛ, nihil est quod in isto genere cuiquam possim commodare; omnis enim pecunia ita tractatur ut praeda a praefectis, quae autem mihi attributa est a quaestore curetur. 5. Quod quaeris quid existimem de legionibus quae decretae sunt in Syriam, antea dubitabam venturaene essent: nunc mihi non est dubium quin, si antea auditum erit otium esse in Syria, venturae non sint. Marium quidem successorem tarde video esse venturum, propterea quod senatus ita decrevit ut cum legionibus iret.

ad Atticum, VII. i. 6.

6. Quam non est facilis virtus! quam vero difficilis eius diuturna simulatio! Cum enim hoc rectum et gloriosum putarem, ex annuo sumptu, qui mihi de-

cretus esset, me C. Caelio quaestori relinquere annuum,
referre in aerarium ad HS. cɔ, ingemuit nostra cohors,
omne illud putans distribui sibi oportere, ut ego amicior
invenirer Phrygum et Cilicum aerariis quam nostro.
Sed me non moverunt. Nam et mea laus apud me
plurimum valuit: nec tamen quidquam honorifice in
quemquam fieri potuit quod praetermiserim.

ad familiares, XII. xxi.

CICERO CORNIFICIO

C. Anicius, familiaris meus, vir omnibus rebus
ornatus, negotiorum suorum causa legatus est in
Africam legatione libera: eum velim rebus omnibus
adiuves operamque des ut quam commodissime sua
negotia conficiat; in primisque, quod ei carissimum est,
dignitatem eius tibi commendo, idque a te peto, quod
ipse in provincia facere sum solitus non rogatus, ut
omnibus senatoribus lictores darem; quod idem
acceperam et id cognoveram a summis viris factitatum.
Hoc igitur, mi Cornifici, facies ceterisque rebus omnibus
eius dignitati reique, si me amas, consules: erit id mihi
gratissimum. Da operam ut valeas.

ad familiares, XIII. ix.

CICERO CRASSIPEDI S.

1. Quamquam tibi praesens commendavi ut potui
diligentissime socios Bithyniae, teque cum mea com-
mendatione tum etiam tua sponte intellexi cupere ei

societati quibuscumque rebus posses commodare,
tamen, cum ii quorum res agitur magni sua interesse
arbitrarentur me etiam per litteras declarare tibi qua
essem erga ipsos voluntate, non dubitavi haec ad te
scribere. 2. Volo enim te existimare me, cum universo
ordini publicanorum semper libentissime tribuerim,
idque magnis eius ordinis erga me meritis facere de-
buerim, tum in primis amicum esse huic Bithynicae
societati: quae societas ordine ipso et hominum genere
pars est maxima civitatis (constat enim ex ceteris
societatibus), et casu permulti sunt in ea societate valde
mihi familiares in primisque is cuius praecipuum
officium agitur hoc tempore, P. Rupilius P. F. Men.,
qui est magister in ea societate. 3. Quae cum ita sint,
in maiorem modum a te peto Cn. Pupium, qui est in
operis eius societatis, omnibus tuis officiis atque omni
liberalitate tueare curesque ut eius operae, quod tibi
facile factu est, quam gratissimae sint sociis, remque et
utilitatem sociorum (cuius rei quantam potestatem
quaestor habeat non sum ignarus) per te quam maxime
defensam et auctam velis. Id cum mihi gratissimum
feceris tum illud tibi expertus promitto et spondeo, te
socios Bithyniae, si iis commodaris, memores esse et
gratos cogniturum.

ad familiares, V. xx. 1–2, 7–9.

CICERO RUFO

1. Quo*quo* modo potuissem, te convenissem, si eo
quo constitueras venire voluisses. Qua re etsi mei commodi causa commovere me noluisti, tamen ita existimes
velim me antelaturum fuisse, si ad me misisses, volun-

tatem tuam commodo meo. Ad ea quae scripsisti com-
modius equidem possem de singulis ad te rebus scribere,
si M. Tullius, scriba meus, adesset: a quo mihi explora-
tum est in rationibus dumtaxat referendis — de ceteris
rebus adfirmare non possum — nihil eum fecisse scientem quod esset contra aut rem aut existimationem
tuam: dein, si rationum referendarum ius vetus et mos
antiquus maneret, me relaturum rationes, nisi tecum
pro coniunctione nostrae necessitudinis contulissem
confecissemque, non fuisse. 2. Quod igitur fecissem ad
urbem, si consuetudo pristina maneret, id, quoniam
lege Iulia relinquere rationes in provincia necesse erat
easdemque totidem verbis referre ad aerarium, feci in
provincia; neque ita feci ut te ad meum arbitrium
adducerem, sed tribui tibi tantum quantum me tribuisse
numquam me paenitebit: totum enim scribam meum,
quem tibi video nunc esse suspectum, tibi tradidi: tu
ei M. Mindium fratrem tuum adiunxisti. Rationes
confectae me absente sunt tecum, ad quas ego nihil
adhibui praeter lectionem: ita accepi librum a meo
servo scriba ut eundem acceperim a fratre tuo. Si
honos is fuit, maiorem tibi habere non potui: si fides,
maiorem tibi habui quam paene ipsi mihi: si provi-
dendum fuit ne quid aliter ac tibi et honestum et utile
esset referretur, non habui cui potius id negoti darem
quam *cui* dedi. Illud quidem certe factum est, quod
lex iubebat, ut apud duas civitates, Laodiceensem et
Apameensem, quae nobis maxime videbantur, quoniam
ita necesse erat, rationes confectas collatasque de-
poneremus. Itaque huic loco primum respondeo, me,
quamquam iustis de causis rationes deferre properarim,
tamen te exspectaturum fuisse, nisi in provincia relictas
rationes pro *re*latis haberem.

7. Quod scribis de beneficiis, scito a me et tribunos militaris et praefectos et contubernalis dumtaxat meos delatos esse. In quo quidem me ratio fefellit: liberum enim mihi tempus ad eos deferendos existimabam dari: postea certior sum factus triginta diebus deferri necesse esse quibus rationes rettulissem. Sane moleste tuli non illa beneficia tuae potius ambitioni reservata esse quam meae, qui ambitione nihil uterer. De centurionibus tamen et de tribunorum militarium contubernalibus res est in integro: genus enim horum beneficiorum definitum lege non erat. 8. Reliquum est de HS centum milibus, de quibus memini mihi a te Myrina litteras esse adlatas, non mei errati, sed tui: in quo peccatum videbatur esse, si modo erat, fratris tui et Tulli. Sed cum id corrigi non posset, quod iam depositis rationibus ex provincia decessimus, credo me quidem tibi pro animi mei voluntate proque ea spe facultatum quam tum habebamus quam humanissime potuerim rescripsisse. Sed neque tum me humanitate litterarum mearum obligatum puto neque me tuam hodie epistulam de HS centum sic accepisse ut ii accipiunt quibus epistulae per haec tempora molestae sunt. 9. Simul illud cogitare debes, me omnem pecuniam, quae ad me salvis legibus pervenisset, Ephesi apud publicanos deposuisse: id fuisse HS |xxii|: eam omnem pecuniam Pompeium abstulisse. Quod ego sive aequo animo sive iniquo fero, tu de HS centum aequo animo ferre debes et existimare eo minus ad te vel de tuis cibariis vel de mea liberalitate pervenisse. Quod si mihi expensa ista HS centum tulisses, tamen, quae tua est suavitas quique in me amor, nolles a me hoc tempore aestimationem accipere: nam numeratum si cuperem, non erat. Sed haec iocatum me putato, ut ego te existimo. Ego tamen,

cum Tullius rure redierit, mittam eum ad te, si quid ad
rem putabis pertinere. Hanc epistulam cur conscindi
velim causa nulla est.

F

V

THE EXECUTIVE

Cicero, *ad Quintum fratrem*, I. i. 15–16, 32–36; ii. 10–11.

V. 15. In provincia vero ipsa si quem es nactus qui in tuam familiaritatem penitus intrarit, qui nobis ante fuerit ignotus, huic quantum credendum sit vide; non quin possint multi esse provinciales viri boni, sed hoc sperare licet, iudicare periculosum est. Multis enim simulationum involucris tegitur et quasi velis quibusdam obtenditur unius cuiusque natura: frons, oculi, vultus persaepe mentiuntur, oratio vero saepissime. Quam ob rem qui potes reperire ex eo genere hominum qui pecuniae cupiditate adducti careant iis rebus omnibus a quibus nos divulsi esse non possumus, te autem, alienum hominem, ament ex animo ac non sui commodi causa simulent? Mihi quidem permagnum videtur, praesertim si iidem homines privatum non fere quemquam, praetores semper omnis amant. Quo ex genere si quem forte tui cognosti amantiorem — fieri enim potuit — quam temporis, hunc vero ad tuum numerum libenter ascribito: sin autem id non perspicies, nullum genus erit in familiaritate cavendum magis, propterea quod et omnis vias pecuniae norunt et omnia pecuniae causa faciunt et, quicum victuri non sunt, eius existimationi consulere non curant. 16. Atque etiam e Graecis ipsis diligenter cavendae sunt quaedam familiaritates praeter hominum perpaucorum si qui sunt vetere Graecia digni. Sic vero fallaces sunt per-

multi et leves et diuturna servitute ad nimiam adsenta-
tionem eruditi. Quos ego universos adhiberi liberaliter,
optimum quemque hospitio amicitiaque coniungi dico
oportere: nimiae familiaritates eorum neque tam
fideles sunt — non enim audent adversari nostris volun-
tatibus — et invident non nostris solum verum etiam
suis.

XI. 32. Atqui huic tuae voluntati ac diligentiae
difficultatem magnam adferunt publicani: quibus si
adversamur, ordinem de nobis optime meritum et per
nos cum re publica coniunctum et a nobis et a re publica
diiungemus: sin autem omnibus in rebus obsequemur,
funditus eos perire patiemur quorum non modo saluti
sed etiam commodis consulere debemus. Haec est
una, si vere cogitare volumus, in toto imperio tuo
difficultas. Nam esse abstinentem, continere omnis
cupiditates, suos coërcere, iuris aequabilem tenere
rationem, facilem se in rebus cognoscendis, in hominibus
audiendis admittendisque praebere, praeclarum magis
est quam difficile. Non est enim positum in labore
aliquo sed in quadam inductione animi et voluntate.
33. Illa causa publicanorum quantam acerbitatem
adferat sociis intelleximus ex civibus qui nuper in
portoriis Italiae tollendis non tam de portorio quam de
non nullis iniuriis portitorum querebantur. Qua re non
ignoro quid sociis accidat in ultimis terris, cum audierim
in Italia querelas civium. Hic te ita versari ut et publicanis satis facias, praesertim publicis male redemptis,
et socios perire non sinas divinae cuiusdam virtutis esse
videtur, id est, tuae. Ac primum Graecis id quod acer-
bissimum est, quod sunt vectigales, non ita acerbum
videri debet, propterea quod sine imperio populi

Romani suis institutis per se ipsi ita fuerunt. Nomen autem publicani aspernari non possunt, qui pendere ipsi vectigal sine publicano non potuerint quod iis aequaliter Sulla discripserat. Non esse autem leniores in exigendis vectigalibus Graecos quam nostros publicanos hinc intellegi potest quod Caunii nuper omnesque ex insulis quae erant a Sulla Rhodiis attributae confugerunt ad senatum, nobis ut potius vectigal quam Rhodiis penderent. Qua re nomen publicani neque ii debent horrere qui semper vectigales fuerunt, neque ii aspernari qui per se pendere vectigal non potuerunt, neque ii recusare qui postulaverunt. 34. Simul et illud Asia cogitet, nullam ab se neque belli externi neque domesticarum discordiarum calamitatem afuturam fuisse, si hoc imperio non teneretur. Id autem imperium cum retineri sine vectigalibus nullo modo possit, aequo animo parte aliqua suorum fructuum pacem sibi sempiternam redimat atque otium.

XII. 35. Quod si genus ipsum et nomen publicani non iniquo animo sustinebunt, poterunt iis consilio et prudentia tua reliqua videri mitiora. Possunt in pactionibus faciendis non legem spectare censoriam sed potius commoditatem conficiendi negoti et liberationem molestiae. Potes etiam tu id facere, quod et fecisti egregie et facis, ut commemores quanta sit in publicanis dignitas, quantum nos illi ordini debeamus, ut remoto imperio ac vi potestatis et fascium publicanos cum Graecis gratia atque auctoritate coniungas et ab iis de quibus optime tu meritus es et qui tibi omnia debent hoc petas ut facilitate sua nos eam necessitudinem quae est nobis cum publicanis obtinere et conservare patiantur. 36. Sed quid ego te haec hortor quae tu non modo facere potes tua sponte sine cuiusquam praeceptis sed etiam magna iam ex parte perfecisti? Non enim desistunt nobis agere cotidie gratias honestissimae et maximae societates, quod quidem mihi idcirco iucundius est quod idem faciunt Graeci. Difficile est autem ea quae commodis, utilitate et prope natura diversa sunt voluntate coniungere. At ea quidem quae supra scripta sunt non ut te instituerem scripsi — neque enim prudentia tua cuiusquam praecepta desiderat — sed me in scribendo commemoratio tuae virtutis delectavit: quamquam in his litteris longior fui quam aut vellem aut quam me putavi fore.

ii. 10. Sed tempore ipso de epistulis: nam cum hanc paginam tenerem, L. Flavius, praetor designatus, ad me venit, homo mihi valde familiaris. Is mihi, te ad procuratores suos litteras misisse quae mihi visae sunt iniquissimae, ne quid de bonis quae L. Octavi Nasonis fuissent, cui L. Flavius heres est, deminuerent ante quam C. Fundanio pecuniam solvissent, itemque misisse ad Apollonidensis, ne de bonis quae Octavi fuissent deminui paterentur prius quam Fundanio debitum solutum esset. Haec mihi veri similia non videntur: sunt enim a prudentia tua remotissima. Ne deminuat heres? Quid si infitiatur? Quid si omnino non debet? Quid? praetor solet iudicare deberi? Quid? ego Fundanio non cupio? non amicus sum? non misericordia moveor? Nemo magis: sed via iuris eius modi est quibusdam in rebus ut nihil sit loci gratiae. Atque ita mihi dicebat Flavius scriptum in ea epistula quam tuam esse dicebat, te aut quasi amicis tuis gratias acturum aut quasi inimicis incommodaturum. 11. Quid multa? ferebat graviter, id vehementer mecum querebatur

orabatque ut ad te quam diligentissime scriberem:
quod facio et te prorsus vehementer etiam atque etiam
rogo ut et procuratoribus Flavi remittas de deminuendo
et Apollonidensibus ne quid praescribas quod contra
Flavium sit amplius. Et Flavi causa et scilicet Pompei
facies omnia. Nolo me dius fidius ex tua iniuria in
illum tibi liberalem me videri, sed [et] te oro ut tu ipse
auctoritatem et monumentum aliquod decreti aut
litterarum tuarum relinquas quod sit ad Flavi rem et ad
causam accommodatum. Fert enim graviter homo et
mei observantissimus et sui iuris dignitatisque retinens
se apud te neque amicitia nec iure valuisse, et, ut
opinor, Flavi aliquando rem et Pompeius et Caesar tibi
commendarunt et ipse ad te scripserat Flavius et ego
certe. Qua re si ulla res est quam tibi me petente
faciendam putes, haec ea sit. Si me amas, cura,
elabora, perfice ut Flavius et tibi et mihi quam maximas
gratias agat. Hoc te ita rogo ut maiore studio rogare
non possim.

Cicero, *II in Verrem*, IV. 32.

32   Verum mehercule hoc, iudices, dicam. Memini
Pamphilum Lilybitanum, amicum et hospitem meum,
nobilem hominem, mihi narrare, cum iste ab sese
hydriam Boethi manu factam praeclaro opere et grandi
pondere per potestatem abstulisset, se sane tristem et
conturbatum domum revertisse, quod vas eius modi,
quod sibi a patre et a maioribus esset relictum, quo
solitus esset uti ad festos dies, ad hospitum adventus, a
se esset ablatum. 'Cum sederem,' inquit, 'domi tristis,
accurrit Venerius; iubet me scyphos sigillatos ad
praetorem statim adferre. Permotus sum,' inquit;

'binos habebam; iubeo promi utrosque, ne quid
plus mali nasceretur, et mecum ad praetoris domum
ferri. Eo cum venio, praetor quiescebat; fratres illi
Cibyratae inambulabant. Qui me ubi viderunt, "Vbi
sunt, Pamphile," inquiunt, "scyphi?" Ostendo tristis;
laudant. Incipio queri me nihil habiturum quod
alicuius esset preti si etiam scyphi essent ablati. Tum
illi, ubi me conturbatum vident, "Quid vis nobis dare
ut isti abs te ne auferantur?" Ne multa, HS mille me,'
inquit, 'poposcerunt; dixi me daturum. Vocat interea
praetor, poscit scyphos.' Tum illos coepisse praetori
dicere putasse se, id quod audissent, alicuius preti
scyphos esse Pamphili; luteum negotium esse, non
dignum quod in suo argento Verres haberet. Ait ille
idem sibi videri. Ita Pamphilus scyphos optimos aufert.

Cicero, *II in Verrem*, II. 83–85, 88–101.

83   Sthenius est, hic qui nobis adsidet, Thermitanus,
antea multis propter summam virtutem summamque
nobilitatem, nunc propter suam calamitatem atque
istius insignem iniuriam omnibus notus. Huius hospitio Verres cum esset usus, et cum apud eum non solum
Thermis saepenumero fuisset, sed etiam habitasset,
omnia domo eius abstulit quae paulo magis animum
cuiuspiam aut oculos possent commovere. Etenim
Sthenius ab adulescentia paulo studiosius haec compararat: supellectilem ex aere elegantiorem et Deliacam
et Corinthiam, tabulas pictas, etiam argenti bene facti,
prout Thermitani hominis facultates ferebant, satis.
Quae cum esset in Asia adulescens studiose, ut dixi,
compararat, non tam suae delectationis causa quam ad

invitationes adventusque nostrorum hominum, [suorum]
84 amicorum atque hospitum. Quae posteaquam iste
omnia abstulit, alia rogando, alia poscendo, alia
sumendo, ferebat Sthenius ut poterat; angebatur
animi necessario quod domum eius exornatam et in-
structam fere iam iste reddiderat nudam atque inanem;
verum tamen dolorem suum nemini impertiebat;
praetoris iniurias tacite, hospitis placide ferendas arbi-
85 trabatur. Interea iste cupiditate illa sua nota atque
apud omnis pervagata, cum signa quaedam pulcherrima
atque antiquissima Thermis in publico posita vidisset,
adamavit; a Sthenio petere coepit ut ad ea tollenda
operam suam profiteretur seque adiuvaret. Sthenius
vero non solum negavit, sed etiam ostendit fieri id
nullo modo posse ut signa antiquissima, monumenta
P. Africani, ex oppido Thermitanorum incolumi illa
civitate imperioque populi Romani tollerentur.

88   Haec cum iste posceret agereturque ea res in senatu,
Sthenius vehementissime restitit multaque, ut in primis
Siculorum in dicendo copiosus est, commemoravit:
urbem relinquere Thermitanis esse honestius quam pati
tolli ex urbe monumenta maiorum, spolia hostium,
beneficia clarissimi viri, indicia societatis populi
Romani atque amicitiae. Commoti animi sunt omnium;
repertus est nemo quin mori diceret satius esse. Itaque
hoc adhuc oppidum Verres invenit prope solum in orbe
terrarum unde nihil eius modi rerum de publico per vim,
nihil occulte, nihil imperio, nihil gratia, nihil pretio
posset auferre. Verum hasce eius cupiditates exponam
89 alio loco; nunc ad Sthenium revertar. Iratus iste
vehementer Sthenio atque incensus hospitium ei re-

nuntiat, domo eius emigrat atque adeo exit; nam iam
ante emigrarat. Eum autem statim inimicissimi Stheni
domum suam invitant, ut animum eius in Sthenium
inflammarent ementiendo aliquid et criminando. Hi
autem erant inimici Agathinus, homo nobilis, et Doro-
theus, qui habebat in matrimonio Callidamam, Agathini
eius filiam; de qua iste audierat, itaque ad generum
Agathini migrare maluit. Vna nox intercesserat cum
iste Dorotheum sic diligebat ut diceres omnia inter eos
esse communia, Agathinum ita observabat ut aliquem
adfinem atque propinquum; contemnere etiam signum
illud Himerae iam videbatur, quod eum multo magis
90 figura et liniamenta hospitae delectabant. Itaque
hortari homines coepit ut aliquid Sthenio periculi
crearent criminisque confingerent. Dicebant se illi
nihil habere quod dicerent. Tum iste iis aperte ostendit
et confirmavit eos in Sthenium quidquid vellent, simul
atque ad se detulissent, probaturos. Itaque illi non
procrastinant, Sthenium statim educunt, aiunt ab eo
litteras publicas esse corruptas. Sthenius postulat ut,
cum secum sui cives agant de litteris publicis corruptis,
eiusque rei legibus Thermitanorum actio sit, senatusque
et populus Romanus Thermitanis, quod semper in
amicitia fideque mansissent, urbem agros legesque suas
reddidisset Publiusque Rupilius postea leges ita Siculis
ex senatus consulto de x legatorum sententia dedisset ut
cives inter sese legibus suis agerent, idemque hoc
haberet Verres ipse in edicto: ut de his omnibus causis
91 se ad leges reiceret. Iste homo omnium aequissimus
atque a cupiditate remotissimus se cogniturum esse
confirmat; paratum ad causam dicendam venire hora
nona iubet. Non erat obscurum quid homo improbus
ac nefarius cogitaret; neque enim ipse satis occultarat,

nec mulier tacere potuerat. Intellectum est id istum agere ut, cum Sthenium sine ullo argumento ac sine teste damnasset, tum homo nefarius de homine nobili atque id aetatis suoque hospite virgis supplicium crudelissime sumeret. Quod cum esset perspicuum, de amicorum hospitumque suorum sententia Thermis Sthenius Romam profugit: hiemi fluctibusque sese committere maluit quam non istam communem

92 Siculorum tempestatem calamitatemque vitaret. Iste homo certus et diligens ad horam nonam praesto est, Sthenium citari iubet. Quem posteaquam videt non adesse, dolore ardere atque iracundia furere coepit, Venerios domum Stheni mittere, equis circum agros eius villasque dimittere. Itaque dum exspectat quidnam sibi certi adferatur, ante horam tertiam noctis de foro non discedit. Postridie mane descendit; Agathinum ad se vocat; iubet eum de litteris publicis in absentem Sthenium dicere. Erat eius modi causa ut ille ne sine adversario quidem apud inimicum iudicem reperire

93 posset quid diceret; itaque tantum verbo posuit, Sacerdote praetore Sthenium litteras publicas corrupisse. Vix ille hoc dixerat cum iste pronuntiat STHENIVM LITTERAS PVBLICAS CORRVPISSE VIDERI; et hoc praeterea addit homo Venerius novo modo nullo exemplo, OB EAM REM HS D VENERI ERYCINAE DE STHENI BONIS SE EXACTVRVM, bonaque eius statim coepit vendere; et vendidisset, si tantulum morae

94 fuisset quo minus ei pecunia illa numeraretur. Ea posteaquam numerata est, contentus hac iniquitate iste non fuit; palam de sella ac tribunali pronuntiat, SI QVIS ABSENTEM STHENIVM REI CAPITALIS REVM FACERE VELLET, SESE EIVS NOMEN RECEPTVRVM, et simul ut ad causam accederet nomenque deferret, Agathinum,

novum adfinem atque hospitem, coepit hortari. Tum ille clare omnibus audientibus se id non esse facturum, neque se usque eo Sthenio esse inimicum ut eum rei capitalis adfinem esse diceret. Hic tum repente Pacilius quidam, homo egens et levis, accedit; ait, si liceret, absentis nomen deferre se velle. Iste vero et licere et fieri solere, et se recepturum; itaque defertur; edicit statim ut Kalendis Decembribus adsit Sthenius
95 Syracusis. Hic qui Romam pervenisset, satisque felici- ter anni iam adverso tempore navigasset, omniaque habuisset aequiora et placabiliora quam animum praetoris atque hospitis, rem ad amicos suos detulit, quae, ut erat acerba atque indigna, sic videbatur omnibus.

Itaque in senatu continuo Cn. Lentulus et L. Gellius consules faciunt mentionem placere statui, si patribus conscriptis videretur, ne absentes homines in provinciis rei fierent rerum capitalium; causam Stheni totam et istius crudelitatem et iniquitatem senatum docent. Aderat in senatu Verres pater istius, et flens unum quemque senatorum rogabat ut filio suo parceret; neque tamen multum proficiebat; erat enim summa voluntas senatus. Itaque sententiae dicebantur: CVM STHENIVS ABSENS REVS FACTVS ESSET, DE ABSENTE IVDICIVM NVLLVM FIERI PLACERE, ET, SI QVOD ESSET
96 FACTVM, ID RATVM ESSE NON PLACERE. Eo die transigi nihil potuit, quod et id temporis erat et ille pater istius invenerat homines qui dicendo tempus consumerent. Postea senex Verres defensores atque hospites omnis Stheni convenit, rogat eos atque orat ne oppugnent filium suum, de Sthenio ne laborent; confirmat iis curaturum se esse ne quid ei per filium suum noceretur; se homines certos eius rei causa in Siciliam et terra et

mari esse missurum. Et erat spatium dierum fere xxx
ante Kalendas Decembris, quo die iste ut Syracusis
97 Sthenius adesset edixerat. Commoventur amici Stheni;
sperant fore ut patris litteris nuntiisque filius ab illo
furore revocetur. In senatu postea causa non agitur.
Veniunt ad istum domestici nuntii litterasque a patre
adferunt ante Kalendas Decembris, cum isti etiam tum
de Sthenio in integro tota res esset, eodemque ei tempore de eadem re litterae complures a multis eius amicis
ac necessariis adferuntur. Hic iste, qui prae cupiditate
neque offici sui neque periculi neque pietatis neque
humanitatis rationem habuisset umquam, neque in eo
quod monebatur auctoritatem patris neque in eo quod
rogabatur voluntatem anteponendam putavit libid-
ini suae, mane Kalendis Decembribus, ut edixerat,
98 Sthenium citari iubet. Si abs te istam rem parens tuus
alicuius amici rogatu benignitate aut ambitione adductus petisset, gravissima tamen apud te voluntas patris
esse debuisset; cum vero abs te tui capitis causa peteret
hominesque certos domo misisset, hique eo tempore
ad te venissent cum tibi in integro tota res esset,
ne tum quidem te potuit si non pietatis, at salutis
tuae ratio ad officium sanitatemque reducere? Citat
reum; non respondit; citat accusatorem; (attendite,
quaeso, iudices, quanto opere istius amentiae fortuna
ipsa adversata sit, et simul videte qui Stheni causam
casus adiuverit); citatus accusator, M. Pacilius, nescio
99 quo casu non respondit, non adfuit. Si praesens
Sthenius reus esset factus, si manifesto in maleficio
teneretur, tamen, cum accusator non adesset, Sthenium
condemnari non oporteret. Etenim si posset reus
absente accusatore damnari, non ego a Vibone Veliam
parvulo navigio inter fugitivorum ac praedonum ac tua

tela venissem, quo tempore omnis illa mea festinatio fuit
cum periculo capitis, ob eam causam ne tu ex reis
eximerere si ego ad diem non adfuissem. Quod igitur
tibi erat in tuo iudicio optatissimum, me cum citatus
essem non adesse, cur Sthenio non putasti prodesse
oportere, cum eius accusator non adfuisset? Itaque
fecit ut exitus principio simillimus reperiretur: quem
absentem reum fecerat, eum absente accusatore condemnat.

100 Nuntiabatur illi primis illis temporibus, id quod pater
quoque ad eum pluribus verbis scripserat, agitatam rem
esse in senatu; etiam in contione tribunum plebis de
causa Stheni, M. Palicanum, esse questum; postremo
me ipsum apud hoc collegium tribunorum plebis, cum
eorum omnium edicto non liceret Romae quemquam
esse qui rei capitalis condemnatus esset, egisse causam
Stheni, et, cum ita rem exposuissem quem ad modum
nunc apud vos, docuissemque hanc damnationem duci
non oportere, x tribunos plebis hoc statuisse, idque de
omnium sententia pronuntiatum esse, NON VIDERI
STHENIVM IMPEDIRI EDICTO QVO MINVS EI ROMAE
101LICERET ESSE. Cum haec ad istum adferrentur, pertimuit aliquando et commotus est; vertit stilum in
tabulis suis, quo facto causam omnem evertit suam;
nihil enim sibi reliqui fecit quod defendi aliqua ratione
posset. Nam si ita defenderet, 'Recipi nomen absentis
licet; hoc fieri in provincia nulla lex vetat,' mala et
improba defensione, verum aliqua tamen uti videretur;
postremo illo desperatissimo perfugio uti posset, se
imprudentem fecisse, existimasse id licere. Quamquam
haec perditissima defensio est, tamen aliquid dici
videretur. Tollit ex tabulis id quod erat, et facit coram
esse delatum.

Livy, XLIII. 2.

Hispaniae deinde utriusque legati aliquot populorum in senatum introducti. ii de magistratuum Romanorum avaritia superbiaque conquesti, nixi genibus ab senatu petierunt ne se socios foedius spoliari vexarique quam hostes patiantur. cum et alia indigna quererentur, manifestum autem esset pecunias captas, L. Canuleio praetori, qui Hispaniam sortitus erat, negotium datum est ut in singulos, a quibus Hispani pecunias repeterent, quinos reciperatores ex ordine senatorio daret, patronosque quos vellent sumendi potestatem faceret. vocatis in curiam legatis recitatum est senatus consultum, iussique nominare patronos quattuor nominaverunt. M. Porcium Catonem, P. Cornelium Cn. F. Scipionem, L. Aemilium L. F. Paulum, C. Sulpicium Gallum. cum M. Titinio primum, qui praetor A. Manlio M. Junio consulibus in citeriore Hispania fuerat, reciperatores sumpserunt. bis ampliatus, tertio absolutus est reus. dissensio inter duarum provinciarum legatos est orta: citerioris Hispaniae populi M. Catonem et Scipionem, ulterioris L. Paulum et Gallum Sulpicium patronos sumpserunt. ad reciperatores adducti a citerioribus populis P. Furius Philus, ab ulterioribus M. Matienus: ille Sp. Postumio Q. Mucio consulibus triennio ante, hic biennio prius, L. Postumio M. Popillio consulibus praetor fuerat. gravissimis criminibus accusati ambo ampliatique: cum dicenda de integro causa esset, excusati exsilii causa solum vertisse. Furius Praeneste, Matienus Tibur exsulatum abierunt. fama erat prohiberi a patronis nobiles ac potentes compellare; auxitque eam suspicionem Canuleius praetor, quod

omissa ea re dilectum habere instituit, dein repente in
provinciam abiit, ne plures ab Hispanis vexarentur. ita
praeteritis silentio oblitteratis, in futurum consultum
tamen ab senatu Hispanis, quod impetrarunt, ne
frumenti aestimationem magistratus Romanus haberet,
neve cogeret vicesimas vendere Hispanos quanti ipse
vellet, et ne praefecti in oppida sua ad pecunias
cogendas imponerentur.

Extracts from the *Lex Acilia Repetundarum*

Quoi ceivi Romano sociumve nominisve Latini ex-
terarumve nationum, quoive in arbitratu dicione
2 potestate amicitiave *populi Romani*, . . 65 | 215 . .
*ab eo quei dic(tator), co(n)s(ul), pr(aetor), mag(ister)
eq(uitum), cens(or), aid(ilis), tr(ibunus) pl(ebei), q(uaestor),
IIIvir cap(italis), IIIvir a(gris) d(andis) a(dsignandis),
tribunus mi*l(itum) l(egionibus) IIII primis aliqua
earum fuerit, queive filius eorum quoius erit, (*queive*)
quoius(*ve*) pater senator siet, in annos singolos pequniae
3 quod siet amp*lius HS . . . n(ummum)* . . 102 | 215 . .
*pro inperio prove potestate ipsei regive populove suo,
parentive suo, queive in potestate manu mancipio suo
parentisve sui siet fuerit quo*ive ipse parensve suos
filiusve suos heres siet, ablatum captum coactum con-
ciliatum aversumve siet: de ea re eius petitio nomi-
nisque delatio esto, *pr(aetoris) quaestio esto, ioudicium
ioudicatio leitisque aestumatio, queiquomque ioudicium
ex h. l. erunt, eorum hace lege esto.*

De patroneis dandeis. — *Quei ex h.* l. pequniam petet
nomenque detuler*it*, quoius eorum ex h. l. ante k. Sept.
petitio erit, sei eis volet sibei patronos in eam rem

10 darei, pr(aetor), ad quem *nomen detulerit* . . 102 | 47 . .
patronos civeis Romanos ingenuos ei dato, dum neiquem
eorum det sciens d(olo) m(alo), quoiei is, *quoius nomen
delatum erit,* . . 110 . . *gener socer vitricus privignusve siet.*

De CDLvireis quot annis *legundis. — Praetor, quei*
16 *post h. l. rogatam ex h. l. ioudex factus erit* . . 102 | 27 . . *is
in diebus X proxumeis, quibus qui*sque eorum eum
mag(istratum) coiperit, facito utei CDLviros ita legat,
quei ha*ce in civitate HS $\overline{CCCC}$ n. plurisve census siet* . .
99 . . *d*um nequem eorum legat, quei tr. pl., q., IIIvir
cap., tr. mil. l. IIII primis aliqua earum, IIIvir a. d. a.
siet fueritve, queive in senatu siet fueritve, queive
17 merce*de conductus depugnavit* . . 112 | 26 . . *queive
quaestione ioudicioque puplico condemnatus siet quod
circa eum in senatum legei non liceat, queive minor annis
XXX maiorve a*nnos LX gnatus siet, queive in urbe
Romae propiusve urbem Roma*m p(assus) M domicilium
non habeat* . . 99 . . *queive eius mag(istratus), quei s(upra)
s(criptus) e(st) pater frater filiusve siet,* queive eius quei
in senatu siet fueritve pater frater filiusve siet, queive
trans mare erit. —

Quos legerit, eos patrem tribum cognomenque *in-*
dice*t. — Quei ex h. l. in eu*m *annum quaeret, is die n. n.
ex quo legerit, eorum, quei ex h. l. CDLvirei in eum*
18 *annum lectei erunt* (102 | 27) *ea nomina omnia in tabula,
in albo, atramento scriptos, p*at*rem tribu*m cognomenque
tributimque discriptos, habeto, eosque propositos suo
mag*istratu, ubei de plano recte legei possitur, habeto* . .
85 . . *Sei quis describere volet, pr(aetor) permittito,
potestatem*que scribundi, quei volet, facito. Pr(aetor)
quei legerit, is eos, quos ex h. l. *CDLv*iros legeri*t,* facito
in conctione recite*n*tur.

De reis quo modo iudicetur. — Ubi duae partes iudicum, quei ader*unt, causam sibi liquere deixerint* . . III . .
*pr(aetor), quei de ea re quaeret, utei eis iudice*s, quei
50 iudicare negarint, semovant*ur, facito* . . 170 | 45 . . rem
agito. Tum praetor quom soueis viatoribus apparitori-
busque nei de i*udicio iudex discedat facito* . . 108 . .
sitellamque latam digitos n. n. altam digitos x̄x̄, quo
51 ioudices sorticolas conieciant *apponi facito* . . 170 | 37 . .
*quoius*que iudicis is praetor sorticolam unam buxeam
longam digitos IIII, la*tam digitos n. n. ab utraque parte
ceratam* . . 108 . . *in qua sorticola ex altera parti litera A
perscripta siet, ex alte*ra parti C, in manu palam dato,
a*b eoque iudice alteram, utram is volet, induci iubeto* . .
52 170 | 32 . . *Iudex sortem accipito alteram literam inducito,
alteram servato* eamque sortem ex hac lege apertam
bracioque aperto lit*teram digiteis opertam pala*m *ad
eam sitellam deferto* . . 106 . . *sortem populo ostendito*
i*temque in eos ceteros singilatim iu*dices versus ostendito,
itaque eam sortem in eam sitellam coniecito.*

De leitibus aestumandeis. — *Quei ex* hac*e* lege condemnatus erit, ab eo quod quisque petet, quoius ex
hace lege peti*tio erit, praetor, quei eam rem quaesierit, per
eos iudices, quei eam rem ioudicaverint, leites aestumari*
59 *iubeto* . . 244 | 8 . . *quod ante h. l. rogatam consilio pro-
babitur captum coactum ab*latum avorsum conciliatumve esse, ea*s res omnis simpli, ceteras res omnis,
quo*d post hance legem rogatam co*nsilio probabit*ur
captum coactum ablatum avorsum conciliatumve esse,
dupli; idque ad qua*estorem, quoi aerarium provincia
obvenerit, quantum siet quoiusque nomine ea lis aestumata,
facito deferatur.* —

Extract from Speech of C. Gracchus *apud censores*, 124 B.C.

Versatus sum in provincia, quomodo ex usu vestro existimabam esse, non quomodo ambitioni meae conducere arbitrabar. . . . Ita versatus sum in provincia, uti nemo posset vere dicere, assem aut eo plus in muneribus me accepisse, aut mea opera quemquam sumptum fecisse. . . . Itaque, Quirites, cum Romam profectus sum, zonas, quas plenas argenti extuli, eas ex provincia inanes retuli. alii vini amphoras, quas plenas tulerunt, eas argento repletas domum reportaverunt.

VI
AUGUSTAN EPILOGUE

VI

AUGUSTAN EPILOGUE

Extracts from the *Edicts of Augustus in Cyrene*.

I

αὐτοκράτωρ Καῖσαρ Σεβαστὸς ἀρχιερεὺς δημαρχικῆς |
ἐξουσίας ἑπτακαιδέκατον αὐτοκράτωρ τεσσερασκαιδέκατον
| λέγει· | ἐπειδὴ τοὺς πάντας εὑρίσκω Ῥωμαίους ἐν τῆι
5 περὶ Κυρήνην ‖ ἐπαρχήαι πέντε καὶ δέκα καὶ διακοσίους ἐκ
πάσης ἡλικίας | δισχειλίων καὶ πεντακοσίων διναρίων ἢ
μείζω τίμησιν ἔχοντας, | ἐξ ὧν εἰσιν οἱ κριταί, καὶ ἐν
αὐτοῖς τούτοις εἶναί τινας συνωμοσίας | αἱ πρεσβῆαι τῶν ἐκ
τῆς ἐπαρχήας πόλεων ἀπωδύραντο τὰς ἐπιβαρού|σας τοὺς
Ἕλληνας ἐν ταῖς θανατηφόροις δίκαις, τῶν αὐτῶν ἐμ
10 μέρει κα‖τηγορούντων καὶ μαρτυρούντων ἀλλήλοις, κἀγὼ
δὲ αὐτὸς ἔγνωκα ἀ|ναιτίους τινὰς τῶι τρόπῳ τούτῳ κατα-
βεβαρημένους καὶ ἐς τὴν ἐσχά|την ἠγμένους τιμωρίαν,
ἄχρι ἂν ἡ σύγκλητος βουλεύσηται περὶ τούτου | ἢ ἐγὼ
αὐτὸς ἄμεινον εὕρω τι, δοκοῦσί μοι καλῶς καὶ προση-
κόντως ποιήσειν | οἱ τὴν Κρητικὴν καὶ Κυρηναικὴν ἐπαρ-
15 χήαν καθέξοντες προτιθέντες ἐν τῆι κατὰ ‖ Κυρήνην
ἐπαρχήαι τὸν ἴσον ἀριθμὸν Ἑλλήνων κριτῶν ἐκ τῶν
μεγίστων τιμημά|των ὅσον καὶ Ῥωμαίων, μηδένα νεώτερον
πέντε καὶ εἴκοσι ἐτῶν, μήτε Ῥωμαῖον μή|τε Ἕλληνα,
μηδὲ ἔλασ‹σ›ον ἔχοντα τίμημα καὶ οὐσίαν, ἄν γε εὐπορία
τοιούτων ἀν|θρώπων ἦι, δειναρίων ἑπτακισχειλίων καὶ
πεντακοσίων, ἢ ἂν τούτωι τῶι τρόπωι | μὴ δύνηται συμ-
πληροῦσθαι ὁ ἀριθμὸς τῶν ὀφειλόντων προτίθεσθαι κριτῶν,

VI

AUGUSTAN EPILOGUE

I

A decree of the Emperor Caesar Augustus, High Priest, Holder of the Tribunician Power for the seventeenth time, Saluted as Imperator fourteen times: Since I find that all the Romans in the province of Cyrene, of all ages, who are rated at two thousand five hundred denarii or more, and from whom the jurymen are drawn, number two hundred and fifteen, and since delegations from the cities of the province have complained that even among these there are some conspiracies which bear hardly on the Greeks in capital cases, the same men alternately making accusations and supporting one another by giving evidence, and since I myself also know that some innocent men have been brought to ruin by this means and have suffered the severest of penalties, therefore, until the senate shall debate the matter or I myself shall find a better solution, I think that the governors of the province of Crete and Cyrene will do what is right and fitting if they publish, in the Cyrenaean district of the province, a list of the same number of Greek jurymen of the highest property qualification as of Roman, none of them, Roman or Greek, being less than twenty-five years of age, nor, if there are enough of such men, having a smaller property qualification than seven thousand five hundred denarii; or, if by this means it is impossible to complete the number of jurymen who must be enrolled,

20 τοὺς ‖ τὸ ἥμισυ καὶ μὴ ἔλασ‹σ›ον τούτου τοῦ τιμ‹ήμ›ατος
ἔχοντας προτιθέτωσαν κριτὰς ἐν | τοῖς θανατηφόροις τῶν
Ἑλλήνων κριτηρίοις. ἐὰν δὲ Ἕλλην κρινόμε|νος, πρὸ
μιᾶς ἡμέρας ἢ τὸν κατήγορον ἄρξασθαι λέγειν, δοθείσης
ἐξου|σίας αὐτῷ πότερον ἅπαντας βούλεται κριτὰς αὐτῶι
Ῥωμαίους εἶναι ἢ τοὺς | ἡμίσους Ἕλληνας, ἔληται τοὺς
25 ἡμίσεις Ἕλληνας, τότε σηκωθεισῶν τῶν ‖ σφαιρῶν καὶ
ἐπιγραφέντων αὐταῖς τῶν ὀνομάτων, ἐγ μὲν τοῦ ἑτέρου
κλη|ρωτηρίου τὰ τῶν Ῥωμαίων ὀνόματα, ἐγ δὲ τοῦ ἑτέρου
τὰ τῶν Ἑλλήνων κληρο[ύ]|σθω, ἕως ἂν {αν} ἐφ᾽ ἑκατέρου
γένους ἀνὰ εἴκοσι πέντε ἐκπληρωθῶσιν, ὧν ἀνὰ ἕ|να ἐξ
ἑκατέρου γένους ὁ διώκων, ἂν βούληται, ἀπολεγέτω, τρὶς
δὲ ἐξ ἁπάντων | [ὁ] φεύγων, ἐφ᾽ ὧι οὔτε [Ῥ]ωμαίους
πάντας οὔτε Ἕλληνας πάντας ἀπολέξει·

V

αὐτοκράτωρ Καῖσαρ Σεβαστὸς ἀρχιερεὺς μέγιστος |
δημαρχικῆς ἐξουσίας ιθ᾽ λέγει· | δόγμα συνκλήτου τὸ ἐπὶ
75 Γαΐου Καλουισίου καὶ Λευκίου ‖ Πασσιήνου ὑπάτων
κυρωθέν ἐμοῦ παρόντος καὶ συν|επιγραφομένου, ἀνῆκον δὲ
εἰς τὴν τῶν τοῦ δήμου τοῦ | Ῥωμαίων συμμάχων ἀσφάλειαν,
ἵνα πᾶσιν ᾖ γνωστὸν | ὧν κηδόμεθα, πέμπειν εἰς τὰς
ἐπαρχήας διέγνων καὶ τῶι | ἐμῶι προγράμματι ὑποτάσσειν,
80 ἐξ οὗ δῆλον ἔσται πᾶσιν ‖ τοῖς τὰς ἐπαρχήας κατοικοῦσιν
ὅσην φροντίδα ποιούμε|θα ἐγώ τε καὶ ἡ σύνκλητος τοῦ
μηδένα τῶν ἡμῖν ὑποτασ‹σ›ο|μένων παρὰ τὸ προσῆκόν
τι πάσχειν ἢ εἰσπρατ‹τ›εσθαι |

δόγμα συνκλήτου· |

85 ὑπὲρ ὧν Γάϊος Καλουίσιος Σαβεῖνος Λεύκιος Πασσιή‖νος
Ῥοῦφος ὕπατοι λόγους ἐποιήσαντο περὶ ὧν | αὐτοκράτωρ

let them enrol men who have half this qualification, and not less, to act as jurymen in capital cases of Greeks. If a Greek defendant, one day before the prosecutor begins to speak, being given the right to choose whether he wishes all his jurymen to be Romans or that half of them be Greeks, chooses that half of them be Greeks, then the lots shall be made equal and the names shall be written on them, and they shall be drawn, from one urn the Roman names and from the other urn the Greek names, until from each kind a total of twenty-five is completed, of which the prosecutor may if he wishes reject up to one of each kind, the defendant up to three altogether, provided that the three are not all Roman or all Greeks.

V

A proclamation of the Emperor Augustus, Chief Priest, Holder of the Tribunician Power for the thirteenth time:

A decree of the senate made in the consulship of Gaius Calvisianus and Lucius Passienus in my presence and with my assistance, concerning the preservation of the allies of the Roman people: in order that it may be known to all for whom we care, I have decided to send this decree to the provinces, and to put my own preamble above it, so that it may be clear to all those who live in the provinces how much care I and the senate take that no one of our subjects shall suffer harm or loss unjustly.

DECREE OF THE SENATE

On the subject on which the consuls Gaius Calvisianus and Sabinus Lucius Passienus Rufus held a meeting,

Καῖσαρ Σεβαστός ἡγεμὼν ἡμέτερος | ἐξ ξυμβουλίου
γνώμης ὃ ἐκ τῆς συγκλήτου κληρωτὸν ἔσχεν, | ἀνενεχθῆναι
δι' ἡμῶν {ι} πρὸς τὴν βουλὴν ἠθέλησεν, ἀνηκόντων | ἐς
τὴν τῶν συμμάχων τοῦ δήμου τοῦ Ῥωμαίων ἀσφάλειαν,
90 ἔδο‖ξε τῆι βουλῆι· τῶν προγόνων τῶν ἡμετέρων δίκας
χρημάτων | {ξε τη} ἀπαιτήσεως νομοθετησάντων, ὅπως
ῥᾷον οἱ σύμμαχοι ὑ|πὲρ ὧν ἂν ἀδικηθῶσιν ἐπεξελθεῖν καὶ
κομίσασθαι χρήματα ἀφαι|ρεθέντες δύνωνται, ὄντος δὲ τοῦ
γένους τῶν τοιούτων δικασ|τηρίων ἔστιν ὅτε βαρυτάτου καὶ
95 ἀηδεστάτου αὐτοῖς δι' οὓς ἐγρά‖φη ὁ νόμος, τῶν ἐπαρχηῶν
μακρὰν ἀπεχουσῶν ἕλκεσθαι μάρτυ|ρας πένητας ἀνθρώπους
καί τινας ἀσθ‹ε›νῖς διὰ νόσον ἢ διὰ γῆρας, ἀρέσ|κει τῆι
βουλῆι, ἐάν τινες τῶν συμμάχων μετὰ τό γενέσθαι τοῦτο τὸ |
δόγμα τῆς συγκλήτου χρήματα δημοσίαι ἢ ἰδίαι πραχθέντες
ἀπαι|τεῖν βουληθῶσιν, χωρὶς τοῦ κεφαλῆς εὐθύνειν τὸν
100 εἰληφότα, καὶ ὑπὲρ ‖ τούτων καταστάντες ἐνφανίσωσι τῶν
ἀρχόντων τινί, ὧι ἐφεῖται συν[ά]|γειν τὴν σύν[κλ]ητον,
τούτους τὸν ἄρχοντα ὡς τάχιστα πρὸς τὴν βουλὴν | προσα-
γαγεῖν καὶ συνήγορον, ὃ‹ς› ὑπὲρ αὐτῶν ἐρεῖ ἐπὶ τῆς {η}
συγκλήτου, ὃν ἂ[ν] | αὐτοὶ αἰτήσωσιν, διδόναι· ἄκων δὲ μὴ
συνηγορείτω ὧι ἐκ τῶν νόμων παρ|αίτησις ταύτης τῆς
105 λειτουργίας δέδοται.   ὧν ἂν ἐν τῇ συγκλήτωι αἰ‖τίας
ἐπιφέρωσιν ὅπως ἀκουσθῶσιν ὁ ἄρχων, ὃς ἂν αὐτοῖς πρόσοδον
εἰς τὴν | σύγκλητον δῶι, αὐθημερὸν παρούσης τῆς βουλῆς,
ὥστε μὴ ἐλάττους διακο|σίων εἶναι, κληρούσθω{ι} ἐκ
πάντων τῶν ὑπατικῶν τῶν ἢ ἐπ' αὐτῆς τῆς Ῥώμης | [ἢ]
ἐντὸς εἴκοσι μειλίων ἀπ{τ}ὸ τῆς πόλεως ὄντων τέσσαρας·

about which the Emperor Caesar Augustus, our leader, in accordance with the opinion of his council who have been selected by lot from the senate, wished that we should consult the senate, since these matters affect the safety of the allies of the Roman people, the senate decreed: whereas our ancestors established courts for extortion, so that it might be easier for the allies to avenge their wrongs by prosecuting and recovering the money of which they had been robbed, whereas, however, the nature of such trials is sometimes very onerous and unpleasant for those for whose sake the law was made, since the provinces are far distant for dragging as witnesses men who are poor or sometimes weak from illness or old age, the senate decides that if any of the allies, after the passing of this decree of the senate, wish to seek the restoration of money which has been exacted from them, either from communities or from individuals, without involving the capital trial of the man who extorted it, and if they appear before one of the magistrates who have the right to summon the senate, and lay information about it, the magistrate shall bring them as quickly as possible before the senate, and appoint for them as advocate, the man of their choice, to speak for them in the senate; no man shall be their advocate against his will, if he has the legal right to be excused such service. For those who bring their charges into the senate, so that they may be heard, the magistrate who gives them an entry into the senate shall on the same day, in the presence of the senate and provided that not less than two hundred members are present, select by lot four men from all the ex-consuls who are present either in Rome itself or within twenty miles of the city; simi-

ὁμοίως ἐκ τῶν στρατη‖[γ]ικῶν πάντων τῶν ἐπ' αὐτῆς τῆς
110 Ῥώμης ἢ ἐντὸς εἴκοσι μειλίων ἀπὸ τῆς πόλε‖[ω]ς ὄντων
τρὶς· ὁμοίως ἐκ τῶν ἄλλων συνκλητικῶν ἢ οἷς ἐπὶ τῆς
συνκλήτου γνώ|μην ἀποφαίνεσθαι ἔξεστιν πάντων, οἳ ἂν
τότε ἢ ἐπὶ Ῥώμης ἢ ἔνγειον εἴκοσι | μειλίων τῆς πόλεως
ὦσιν, δύο· κληρούσθω δὲ μηδένα, ὃς ἂν ἐβ<δ>ομήκοντα ἢ |
πλείω ἔτη γεγονὼς ἦι ἢ ἐπ' ἀρχῆς ἢ ἐπ' ἐξουσίας τεταγμένος
ἢ ἐπιστάτης κριτη|ρίου ἢ ἐπιμελητὴς σειτομετρίας ἢ ὃν ἂν
115 νόσος κωλύηι ταύτην τὴν λειτουργίαν ‖ λειτουργεῖν ἀντικρὺς
τῆς συνκλήτου ἐξομοσάμενος καὶ δοὺς ὑπὲρ τούτου |
τρεῖς ὀμνύντας τῆς βουλῆς ἄνδρας, ἢ ὃς ἂν συνγενείαι ἢ
οἰκηότητι προσή|κηι αὐτῶι ὥστε νόμωι Ἰουλίωι τῶι
δικαστικῶι μαρτυρεῖν ἐπὶ δημοσίου δικαστη|ρίου ἄκων μὴ
ἀναγκάζεσθαι, ἢ ὃν ἂν ὁ εὐθυνόμενος ὀμόσηι ἐπὶ τῆς
συνκλήτου | ἐχθρὸν ἑαυτῶι εἶναι, μὴ πλείονας δὲ ἢ τρεῖς
120 ἐξομνύσθω. οἳ ἂν ἐννέα τοῦ‖τον τὸν τρόπον λάχωσιν, ἐκ
τούτων ἄρχων, ὃς ἂν τὸν κλῆρον ποιήσηται, φροντι|ζέτω,
ὅπως ἐντὸς δυεῖν ἡμερῶν οἱ τὰ χρήματα μεταπορευόμενοι
καὶ ἀφ' οὗ ἂν | μεταπορεύωνται ἀνὰ μέρος ἀπολέγωνται.

οἳ δὲ αἱρεθέντες κριταὶ περὶ τούτων μόνον ἀκούε|τωσαν
καὶ διαγεινωσκέτωσαν περὶ ὧν ἄν τις εὐθύνηται δημοσίαι
ἢ ἰδίαι νε|νοσφισμένος, καὶ ὅσον ἂν κεφάλαιον χρήματος οἱ
εὐθύνοντες ἀποδε<ι>ξωσιν ἀπενηνέχθαι ἑαυτῶν ἰδίαι ἢ
δημοσίαι, τοσοῦτον ἀποδιδόναι κελευέτω|σαν, ἐφ' ὧι ἐντὸς
τριάκοντα ἡμερῶν οἱ κριταὶ κρινοῦσιν.

larly three men from all the ex-praetors who are in Rome itself or within twenty miles of the city; similarly two men from all the other senators or those who have the right to vote in the senate, who are in Rome or within twenty miles of the city. He shall not select anyone who is seventy years old or more, or who is invested with *imperium* or *potestas*, or who is president of a law court or overseer of corn-measures, or any whom illness prevents from performing this service (for this he shall make sworn disclaimer in the presence of the senate and shall produce three senators to swear to the truth), or anyone who is related or associated with the defendant in such a way as to be exempted by the *lex Julia iudiciaria* from giving evidence against his will in a public court, or anyone whom the defendant swears, in the presence of the senate, to be an enemy of his, with the limit that the defendant may not reject more than three men. When the nine men have been thus selected by lot, the magistrate who selected them shall ensure that within two days the plaintiffs and the defendant shall state their cases in turn.

Those who have been chosen as judges in this matter shall only hear and judge of those things which a man is charged with having appropriated either from individuals or communities, and shall order him to restore so much money as the plaintiffs shall show to have been taken from them, either from individuals or communities; the judges shall give their verdict within thirty days.

NOTES TO PART ONE

Chapter I: THE GROWTH OF THE EMPIRE

¹ The notion that what did happen had to happen is one which has particularly bedevilled the study of Roman history.

² It is likely that the first time this was done was for the provinces of Africa and Macedonia; for the original organisation of Sicily and Spain we have no exact information.

³ The usual mark of the *foedus iniquum* is the phrase (with its verb in the imperative) *maiestatem populi Romani comiter conservanto*. For this section I am indebted to Sherwin-White, *The Roman Citizenship*, Chap. VI.

⁴ Cic. II *Verr*. IV. 32 (Segesta); Plut. *Pomp*. 42 (Mitylene). Theophanes wrote a favourable history of Pompey's campaigns. Another way of acquiring *libertas* will be found in note 10 below.

⁵ The Asiatic cities may not have thought so in 88.

⁶ The idea of thus restricting *libertas* goes back to the settlement of Macedonia in 167, when the republics were declared free but had to pay tribute.

⁷ Cic. II *Verr*. V. 53.

⁸ *Ib*. II. 160. A few of these states had more genuine freedom; Marseilles had extensive territory and a long history of alliance; Rhodes was an island, and had been a great power.

⁹ The weakness of the *foederati* was exposed by Pompey when he was in Sicily. The people of Messana pleaded that they had a treaty with Rome, and his reply was 'Will you stop reading laws to us when we have swords at our belts?' (Plut. *Pomp*. 10).

¹⁰ It was also true that what Rome had given, if it was not guaranteed by a treaty, Rome could take away; but when they did so, Cicero, at least, thought it disgraceful (*de Off*. III. 87: non igitur utilis illa L. Philippi sententia, quas civitates L. Sulla pecunia accepta ex senatus consulto liberavisset, ut eae rursus vectigales essent neque iis pecuniam quam pro libertate

dederant redderemus. ei senatus est assensus. turpe imperio). This patron-client relationship has been illuminated by Badian in *Foreign Clientelae* 264–70 B.C.

[11] So Pompey in Asia Minor; see Chap. II.

[12] That is why in modern France the towns of Provence take their names from the towns of Roman times (*Nemausus*, Nîmes; *Arelate*, Arles), while in the rest of the country it is the names of the tribes which survive (*Lutetia Parisiorum*, Paris; *Durocortorum Remorum*, Rheims).

[13] Pompey's Bithynian charter laid it down that members of the local senate must be over thirty (Pliny *Ep*. X. 79), and to judge from the controversial *lex Julia municipalis* members of certain ungentlemanly professions were sometimes excluded. Any such regulations are likely to be, or to become, conservative. This is the normal dilemma of an imperial power, and the British empire has not escaped the charge: if you act through the local government you are in fact supporting it, if you try to change it you are interfering with local autonomy.

Chapter II: DEFENCE

[1] Much the same thing is said by Herodotus of the other enlightened empire of the ancient world, the Persian (Hdt. VI. 42).

[2] Evidence for Provence in the first century B.C. will be found in Cicero's speech for Fonteius, who had been governor of Transalpine Gaul from 76 to 73.

[3] During the Gallic war Caesar made sure by holding hostages, thus ensuring the loyalty of the tribes without interfering in local affairs. The Carthaginians had done the same in Spain, and so had Sertorius.

One other method of keeping the peace should be mentioned — the settlement of Roman citizens, either in new towns or in old towns which then received a new status, that of *coloniae*. They could ensure the loyalty, or at least the acquiescence, of the surrounding districts, and this method had been extensively used in the pacification of Italy. The planting of colonies overseas had to wait for the conjunction of military planning with the supply of sufficient Romans ready to emigrate. The schemes of Gracchus and Saturninus had as their primary aim the finding of homes for Romans, and were judged by their contemporaries in the light of the politics of the forum. With Caesar and Augustus, who had legions to demobilise, the garrison motive is again uppermost, and colonies played an important part in keeping the peace; their foundations in Lusitania are described by Sutherland, *The Romans in Spain*, pp. 122 and 148. Narbo Martius (founded 118 B.C.) was described by Cicero (Font. 13) as a watch-tower and bulwark of the Roman people.

⁴ Major uprisings, such as the slave revolts in Sicily, were another matter. The Sicilian cities, since they were not normally in danger, were quite unable to supply the troops needed in such emergencies.

⁵ Roman cavalry, whether *equo publico* or *equo privato*, were drawn from the upper classes, with a high property qualification. In view of their small numbers they could not be expected to provide the permanent overseas contingents which the Romans came to need. With the advent of the foreign wars, the Romans had to rely on allied cavalry,.

⁶ So on the outbreak of the civil war, the senate attempted to secure the loyalty of the king of Numidia by granting him this title. Since the Romans described all the provincials, including those who paid tribute, as *socii*, this word alone, being near the meaning of our word 'subjects', was not sufficiently honourable for those who were in any sense free allies. Hence the addition of the word *amicus*.

Even with this addition, however, the Romans regarded the *socii et amici* as clients, not as completely free agents. The trouble with Ariovistus was that he did not understand that friendship with Rome implied subservience. He did not owe his position to the Romans, regarded himself as an equal, and did not see why he should do what Caesar told him. The first client king to make this mistake had been Demetrius of Pharos in 220.

⁷ This is the dynamic of the expanding empire. To defend your own country you have to annex your neighbour's; to defend him you have to make a further annexation beyond; and so on. We sometimes blame the Republic for proceeding piecemeal, but what else do we expect? There were good moral

and strategic reasons for thinking that a more rapid advance
was undesirable, including, until the time of Marius, an acute
shortage of military manpower. Even so, with the conquests
of the triumvirs the empire was beginning to reach what might
be regarded as permanently satisfactory limits.

[8] Galatia, 25 B.C.; Cappadocia and Commagene, A.D. 17;
Mauretania, 42; Thrace, 46.

[9] Until the Social war these allies were mostly Italian; later
Spain and Gaul were the chief recruiting grounds. For the local
troops see Caesar, *B.G.* V. I (in Illyricum) *civitatibus milites
imperat.*

[10] For a full discussion see R. E. Smith, *Service in the Post-
Marian Army*, Chaps. I and II.

[11] Cic. *in Pis.* 44, *provincia maxime triumphalis.*

[12] They were kept up to strength both by fresh levies brought
from Italy, usually when a new governor came out, and by
recruitment from Roman citizens living in the province. On
discharge many soldiers settled in the country which had
become their home. Many of the things which we associate
with the empire had their roots in pre-imperial times.

[13] This is discussed by Smith (*op. cit.* Chap. II), who finds
that before the dictatorship of Sulla a governor who commanded
more than one legion had proconsular *imperium*, the rest pro-
praetorian; and that after Sulla all governors were proconsuls,
but only in a two-legion province was the governor himself a
consularis.

[14] Professor Last used to say that the Republic had 'not
standing armies, but chronic armies', and this is true of the
armies which fought the major wars.

[15] Legally, this was done by him in virtue of his *imperium*, but
senatorial sanction was considered necessary.

[16] Especially when he had been appointed in the first place
by a law of the people and not by decree of the senate (see
Chap. V).

[17] Rhodes was deliberately impoverished when in 168 the
Romans made Delos a free port (i.e. free from harbour dues);
this was a punishment for Rhodes for not assisting Rome in the
war against Perseus. The decline of Egypt did not need Roman
assistance.

[18] Even to Asia, their armies could march from Apollonia to the Hellespont; Lucullus in 85 collected a fleet, but only to guard the narrow crossing — he waited for Sulla at Abydos. In 171 the errant consul Longinus even marched to Epirus by way of Aquileia, but this was through very difficult country, and was not normally considered practicable. The Romans built the *via Egnatia* about 130, as soon as the annexation of Asia made it necessary, but of course the route had always existed.

[19] See Tenney Frank, *Roman Imperialism*, pp. 284 and 295.

[20] The father of this Antonius had campaigned against the pirates in 102, and in 100 the Romans had passed a law banning pirates from the ports of the empire. It remains true, however, that very little effective action was taken.

[21] Pompey did indeed campaign to the north-east, towards the Caspian, but the danger from here was the short-lived creation of Mithridates' Pontic empire. Goods from China, which are supposed to have reached the Euxine in Colchis, went on to the west by sea; so did the mineral wealth of Pontus (see Rostovsteff in *CAH* IX. p. 211).

[22] This road is described by Herodotus (V. 52). Calder (*C.R.* 1925) has conclusively shown that Herodotus was mistaken in thinking that it went by the northern route through Ankara and across the Halys (How and Wells' note can be abandoned). Croesus crossed the Halys to attack Cyrus, and Xerxes' army, which assembled near the upper Halys, used the northern route, but the Royal Road took the direct path through Iconium to the Cilician Gates — about 730 miles from Sardis to the Euphrates. This communication was as important to the Persians holding Lydia as to the Romans holding Syria.

[23] See Dunbabin, *The Greeks and their Eastern Neighbours*; in the eastern half of their empire the Romans followed where the Greeks had been before them.

[24] A narrative of Servilius' campaign is given by Magie, *Roman Rule in Asia Minor*, pp. 287 ff., who assumes that he advanced northwards from the sea. It seems more likely that he turned the Taurus range from the west, and was preparing to attack the pirates from the rear, where they had thought

themselves unassailable. He would also be contributing to the defence of Phrygia, now part of the province of Asia. That his son inherited the name Isauricus suggests that it was a distinguished campaign.

[25] Eleven regions, each with its city centre.

[26] One short part of the route is outside the province proper, when it passes through Cappadocia by Cybistra to the northern end of the Cilician Gates. Cicero follows this, but he is only nominally outside the province, the king of Cappadocia being dependent on him. It is clear that he could have marched east without leaving the province: reinforcements for Syria do not need to pass through Cappadocia. For the history of Cilicia I am indebted to Syme, in *Anatolian Studies Presented to W. H. Buckler*, pp. 299 ff.

[27] With an establishment of two legions. However, once the province was organised, and the defence of Syria effective, then, provided that the kings co-operate, this would be an unnecessarily large number of legions. The Romans seem to have thought so, and allowed their strength to diminish, until in 48 Pompey combined them into one.

[28] Syme calls this province a monstrosity. It gave rise to the theologians' dispute over St. Paul's epistle to the Galatians. Those who hold the 'North Galatian Theory' point out that the only true Galatians were the tribes of the interior, the Trocmi, Tectosages and Tollistobogii, and believe that St. Paul must have been writing to them. Others maintain that, since Pamphylia was at that time a part of the Roman province of Galatia, St. Paul could have used the word Galatians for the Hellenised cities of the coastal area, and that the philosophical tone of the letter makes it much more likely that it was written to them. The local governments of the cities of Phrygia suffered frequent confusion; rejected from the new province of Asia in 129, they were incorporated in it in 116; after Pompey's conquests they became part of the large province of Cilicia; Antony handed them over to King Amyntas, and on his death they were part of the province of Galatia. Strabo, himself a native of Amisus in Pontus, complained (p. 169) that the Romans drew frontiers for their own administrative convenience.

G

Chapter III: ADMINISTRATION OF JUSTICE

¹ There was always a pronounced difference between the
eastern and western parts of the Roman empire. In the west,
the Romans conquered, by painfully slow stages, peoples who
were less advanced in civilisation than they were themselves.
They imposed their own language, and, in varying degrees,
their own institutions. In the east they found a civilisation
more developed in many ways than their own, and more complex. Here the Greeks had been before them, and what the
Romans found was a mixture of orientalism with the rationalism
of European Greece; both Aristotle and the emotional re-
ligions of Asia. The conquests of Alexander had both Hellenised parts of Asia and orientalised Hellenism itself. The
official documents of the Roman empire had to be translated
into Greek for the eastern half, so that Augustus' *Res Gestae*
had two authoritative versions. This difference persisted,
being particularly conspicuous in the different attitudes to the
deification of human beings. The basis for the eventual division into the eastern and the western empires had existed from
the first.

² Inheritance rouses strong feelings and is often important.
A difference between national laws on this subject was the
casus belli of the Hundred Years War. Sicilian practice, however, was similar to Roman (*II Verr.* I. 118).

³ By a *lex Cornelia*; since abuses are not remedied before
they occur, and since Cornelius, though a vigorous tribune,
was not an unreasonable one, we should assume that there had
been some scandals; and Cicero tells us (*II Verr.* I. 119) that
Verres, when *praetor urbanus* in 74, had frequently given judgements contrary to his own edict.

⁴ *Edictum perpetuum* is the edict which remains in force
throughout the year, as opposed to particular administrative
regulations; *edictum tralaticium* is that which is handed down
unchanged from one praetor to another. Most of the *edictum
perpetuum* is also *tralaticium*. Clauses of the edict are preserved
in the Digest in such forms as *qui . . . , in eos iudicium dabo*.

⁵ *Recuperatores* were a board of assessors, either three or five
in number, who delivered judgement in much the same way as

the *unus iudex*. Their origin was probably in cases between litigants of different nationalities, which could not be settled in accordance with the statute law of either party. Perhaps it was felt that the single *iudex* might be influenced excessively by the civil law of his own country. The use of *recuperatores* was not confined to international cases. We do not know the rules which decided whether the magistrate should appoint a *iudex* or a board of *recuperatores*, but it appears that the court of the *iudex* was more formal and less expeditious; if a quick judgement was required, and legal niceties were not likely to be involved, *recuperatores* were more efficient. Since they are connected especially with peregrine law, and not with the laws of Rome, they are frequently employed in the provinces: the edict of Verres provided for *recuperatores*, not a *iudex*, to hear taxation disputes in Sicily. For their use in the extortion court before Gracchus see p. 160. Compare Livy xxvi. 48.— a board of two advocates with a neutral chairman.

⁶ For this formula, or a travesty of it, see p. 111. The task of the *iudex* will include investigating the right of Servilius to the estate, and questions of law as well as fact may well arise. We hear, for instance, of famous judgements by a pupil of Scaevola, Aquilius Gallus, one of the best legal minds in Rome in Cicero's time. It will be noticed that in Roman law the words 'condemn' and 'acquit' are used in civil law judgements.

⁷ The *civitates liberae*, of course, used their own laws, and this was such an important part of their freedom that Livy describes the grant of *libertas* to the Oresti with the words *suae leges redditae* (p. 95). In other cities which have their own codes of law difficulties will arise if those codes conflict with the provisions of the governor's edict; it could happen that normal administration followed one principle, but that when a law-suit was taken to the governor's assize he followed another. Unless the edict left him free to enforce Syracusan law at Syracuse and Lilybaean law at Lilybaeum, there could be continual trouble. In any case some difficulty must be expected when a judge brought up under one legal system sits in a town which has a different one; the eventual compromise will depend on the enlightenment or obstinacy of the people concerned, and will differ widely in different times and places.

Cicero in Cilicia was dealing with Hellenised communities, which had had civilised legal codes before the Romans arrived; they were not 'free', but he arranged that at least the provincials should themselves serve as *iudices*, and claims that this gave them the feeling that they were free (p. 109). Even Verres assumed, when he was appointing a priest at Syracuse, that in a matter of that kind he had to observe the letter of the Syracusan law (p. 99). In general, however, Cicero's own pronouncement that he would take the *urban* praetor as his model showed, even at that time, that it was Roman law which was likely to prevail.

⁸ He was expected to choose advisers both from his own staff (see Chap. V) and from the *conventus civium Romanorum*; it was considered that a board composed of his staff alone would not be sufficiently independent. To condemn Sopater, Verres got rid of those of his *consilium* whom he could not bully; the fact that the rest of the Roman citizens could walk out while the Syracusans did not dare to do so is the clearest evidence of the difference in status (see note on p. 229, *praeter Siculos*).

⁹ It seems that since the *lex Porcia* of 199 (the tribunate of M. Porcius Laeca), citizens had the right of *provocatio* in Italy and the provinces; before that, it had applied only in Rome (see note on p. 234, *civis Romanus*). If a dispute occurred in which a Roman of sufficient influence was involved, it might be sent to Rome (*ad fam*. XIII. xxvi). But in *II Verr*. I. 85 Pericles the Ephesian had obstructed a quaestor, which was an insult to the Roman state, and he was summoned to Rome.

¹⁰ He would either give instructions to the *recuperatores* that 'if it appears that the Salaminians have borrowed the money at 48 per cent interest, then condemn them to pay such and such sum of money', or that 'if it appears . . . then, since the maximum permitted interest is 12 per cent, condemn them to pay . . .'. The board would not be deciding the rate of interest, which was the essence of the dispute.

It is also possible that even when a case would normally be settled by the formulary process, the governor could reserve it for his own *cognitio* (see A. H. Jones, *Studies in Roman Government and Law*, Chap. V).

¹¹ Further details of this loan will be found in the note on

p. 235, *de Bruto*. Cato's part in the transaction has been examined by Oost (*Classical Philology*, 1955), who points out that when the Salaminians approached their patron Brutus, they can hardly have failed also to ask their other patron Cato, especially as he was particularly interested in provincial affairs, and that Cato must have endorsed his son-in-law's extortionate contract; he also suggests that even if Cato would not extort money for himself during his stay in Cyprus, he may have allowed Brutus to do so: it is suspicious that he did not leave a copy of his accounts in the island. His influence in the east was increased by a well-publicised journey described in Plutarch (*Cat. Min.* 15); that of Brutus extended far beyond the city of Salamis, and included the making of large loans to the king of Galatia (see p. 126) who had been one of his father-in-law's clients.

Chapter IV: TAXATION AND FINANCE

[1] During the war with Spartacus, Sicily had supplied the Roman armies, without payment, with corn and leather (Cic. *II Verr.* II. 2). In the Sertorian war Pompey requisitioned supplies from Transalpine Gaul (Id. *Font.* 13): cavalry, pay and corn.

[2] From the figures in *II Verr.* III. 163 (p. 131) we can deduce that the total money value of the Sicilian corn tithe in one year of the seventies was about nine million sesterces. It was paid in corn, which is likely to have been used in the beginning for the Punic and Spanish wars, and later to have been sold at Rome.

[3] The state did acquire a modest revenue from the Macedonian republics in this year, which will not have been unconnected with the remission of taxation; but it is likely to have served rather as a diminution of burdens than as a positive surplus. These judgements of quantity are very difficult; it is not a question of whether taxation was paid, but of how much, and how far the money went. It is certain that over thirty years later Tiberius Gracchus could not finance his land reform out of existing revenues (even in 63 it is Pompey's *manubiae* which figure prominently in the land bill of Rullus: see Cic. *de leg. ag.* II. This lack of public funds and the dependence on war booty made the demobilisation of large armies so difficult).

There is also an element in the calculation which it is impossible to estimate — the cost to Italy of the absence of the men.

⁴ Buildings are listed by Scullard in *JRS* (1960), p. 70, note 44 (add the *via Postumia*). Mummius, who triumphed in 146, was again using some of his spoils when censor in 132.

⁵ *Imp. Pomp.* 6; we do however suspect that the real cause of Roman anxiety was the loss of the money being made by the equestrian business men, rather than that which was accruing to the state. A comparison with Chap. I will show that the revenue-producing provinces were those for whose annexation the impulse came from outside the senate.

⁶ According to Plutarch (*Pomp.* 45), Pompey advertised at his triumph that he had increased the imperial revenues from fifty million drachmae to eighty-five million, besides bringing into the treasury in booty the sum of twenty thousand talents. At the rate of 1 drachma = 1 denarius = 4 sesterces, this gives a figure of fifty million denarii, or two hundred million sesterces for the revenue of the empire before Pompey. For the taxes of the province of Asia at this time Magie (*Roman Rule in Asia Minor*, p. 1115) accepts an estimate of fifteen million denarii. For comparison, the tribute which Caesar later imposed on the Tres Galliae was forty million sesterces (also for comparison, Cicero claims — *II Verr.* I. 27 — that Verres would be shown to have illegally taken the sum of forty million sesterces in three years; this relationship between public and private finance is an important and sometimes neglected feature of the history of Rome).

It would be interesting to set beside these figures the sums required to pay the Roman armies; before Caesar doubled army pay, the legionary received 5 asses a day, with free clothing, but with deductions for food and arms; in Pompey's time this would amount to 114 denarii per (solar) year (so Watson in *Historia 1958*, disputing the traditional 120 *denarii* a year); if we accept Smith's estimate of fourteen legions in the standing armies at this time (*Service in the Post-Marian armies*, p. 29), and assume a normal strength of nearly five thousand men in a legion, the annual wages bill alone of these legions will come to nearly eight and a half million denarii, and this is not the sum total of military expenditure.

The total of Pompey's war booty is enormous (1 talent = 6,000 drachmae), and does not include the very large sums which he will have divided among his troops and kept for himself. Some remarks on Clodius' corn law will be found in note 31 below.

[7] To take only the senators mentioned in this book, we know of historical writings by Cato the censor, Piso Frugi, Rutilius Rufus, Sulla, besides Cicero, Caesar and Sallust.

[8] Hence crown lands commonly became *ager publicus populi Romani*; they were usually let out to tenants and the rents collected by *publicani* for the Roman treasury. Mines were usually administered in the same way. The territories of the cities of Carthage and Corinth were also *ager publicus*. For the Spanish mines see Sutherland, *The Romans in Spain*, p. 107.

[9] *ad Q.f.* I. i. 33. p. 150. The tribute of Spain was mostly paid in silver, which was mined in both provinces. At first this was coined locally for the purpose, and the consistency of the coins suggests Roman supervision. By the first century it is being paid in bullion (Sutherland, *op. cit.* p. 55).

[10] The bid was made in bushels, not in money. If Hiero sold the corn, his income would be fairly steady, since a poor harvest would mean high prices. The Romans could do the same, or use the corn to feed their armies.

[11] Our ignorance of what was happening in the thirties and twenties of this century makes it difficult to form a right judgement of Gaius Gracchus. We need, for instance, to know more about the trial — and acquittal — of Aquilius, and about Gracchus' quarrel with Calpurnius Piso Frugi (Cic. *Font.* 38). On the whole, the history books do less than justice to Gracchus; our ultimate sources are senators, naturally hostile to public corn, equestrian juries and reform by legislation, and silent about the abuses which he was attacking. If only Cicero could have prosecuted Aquilius.

[12] These *societates* went back at least to the second Punic war, when public contracting became big business, and when senators were excluded from trade; and most censors had had important building contracts to let out. Cato's experience in 184, when he accepted the most competitive tenders (Livy XXXIX. 44), shows that there were already strong vested interests. But the tax collecting in Asia was more lucrative than anything yet

known. A story of corrupt wartime contracting with senatorial connivance will be found in Livy, XXV. 3–4.

[13] See Jones, *JRS* (1956), p. 22. It appears that they also engaged in that other great moneymaking activity, the slave trade.

[14] This case has been examined by Badian in *Athenaeum* (1956), pp. 104 ff. He finds that the administration of Asia had become notorious; that the governors, who were only praetorian, were having difficulty in standing up to the powerful business interests; the *lex Aquilia* was not much help, especially as it had been framed before the days of the *censoria locatio*. Q. Mucius Scaevola (the Pontifex) was a distinguished lawyer, was consul in 95, and was sent out in the following year as *consular* governor of Asia; his edict was carefully framed, and was intended to provide the province with a permanent charter. He took with him as his *legatus* Rutilius Rufus, a very senior *consularis* who had been a distinguished soldier. Since Scaevola himself came home after nine months, leaving Rufus in charge of the province, we may guess that the rules which Scaevola framed Rufus executed. This, more perhaps than his enmity with Marius, may explain why it was Rufus who was prosecuted in the extortion court. His condemnation was the one great blot on the record of the equestrian juries — they had to find a way of discrediting the new deal in Asia. However, our ultimate source for all this is probably Rufus' own memoirs, so there may have been more in it than we know.

[15] By lending the cities the money with which to pay (see above). It is often assumed that Sulla diminished their opportunities by abolishing the *censoria locatio*; this is very doubtful (see note on p. 241, *consulibus*, and p. 264, *Sulla*), but even if true, the taxes still had to be collected by somebody, and the cities themselves could hardly do other than employ the *publicani* who were experts; their bargains might well be no better than the censors'.

[16] Their whispering campaign at Rome encouraged the disloyalty of his troops, and helped to persuade the senate to take away his provinces one by one behind his back; eventually, his supersession by Pompey became a military necessity.

[17] Cicero, attacking Gabinius in the *de Provv. Coss.* 10,

accused him of not allowing a *publicanus* in the same city as himself; what he said about this when he defended Gabinius in court we do not know. In his speech for Fonteius, since they supported his client, they are *homines honestissimi* (13).

[18] Some were instituted (*instituerunt*) by the censors of 179, whose building programme was exceptionally expensive (Livy XL. 61); but Livy does not say whether these were in Italy or in the provinces, so that we do not know who really paid for the original *basilica Aemilia*.

[19] *II Verr*. II. 171; the rate of tax at Syracuse was 5 per cent.

[20] See Chap. I, p. 99.

[21] Cic. *ad Att*. II. xvi. 1 (see also *ad Q.F.I*. i. 33). Even this one remaining tax could be avoided by informal manumission.

[22] These include *vasarium*, payment for the upkeep of the governor's household; *cibarium*, for the maintenance of his officials; *frumentum in cellam*, the right to buy corn at a fixed price; there might also be *aurum coronarium*, a special gift of gold from the provincials to a successful general (the *lex Julia* forbade this unless the general also received a triumph). The word *salarium* does not occur in Republican literature: naturally, since a special allowance for salt must always be, practically as well as etymologically, a salary.

[23] Cic. *Pis*. 86; *II Verr*. I. 36; *ad Att*. VII. i. 6 (below). Though the sums may be exceptional, the Verrines passage is worth quoting, to show where the money went: accepi, inquit, viciens ducenta triginta quinque milia quadringentos decem et septem nummos. dedi stipendio, frumento, legatis, pro quaestore, cohorti praetoriae HS mille sescenta triginta quinque milia quadringentos decem et septem nummos. reliqui Arimini HS sescenta milia (2,235,417 – 1,635,417 = 600,000).

[24] Tac. *A*. II. 33. auctu imperii etiam privatas opes adolevisse.

[25] The clearest expression of the various degrees of honesty is to be found in *II Verr*. III. 195. p. 134; especially noteworthy is the phrase: *honestus atque concessus*.

[26] It also instructed the governor, at the end of his tour of duty, to publish his accounts in the province. This is a step

in the right direction, though it may not ensure more than a surface respectability.

[27] The story of Scaptius will be found on p. 38.

[28] During the Sertorian war Pompey's army wintered in Gaul, and injustices connected with this were part of the subsequent accusations brought against the governor, Fonteius (Cic. *Font.* 16).

[29] They had of course obeyed Mithridates' order for a massacre of Romans and Italians, 80,000 of whom were killed; and they had paid no taxes for several years. But they could well feel that the Romans had begun by letting them down, and in any case being invaded does not help the economy, and they were quite unable to find the sum of twenty thousand talents to finance Sulla's return to Italy. In addition, they had not only to have the troops billeted on them through the winter but also to pay them, and that at exceptionally high rates. Sulla's troops were being cheated of the booty they might have gained from an invasion of Pontus, and their loyalty was going to be very important to their commander in the following year. For all this Asia had to pay.

The five years' taxes are probably for the years 88 to 84, which owing to the war had not been paid. It is possible, however, though less likely, that it was an advance payment for the years 85 to 81; but that Miletus built ships for Murena (propraetor 84–1) *ex pecunia vectigali* (*II Verr.* I. 89) does not settle the matter — inevitably the payment would come to be spread over the next few years.

[30] Lucullus' measures are described by Appian (*Mith.* 83). He scaled down the most oppressive debts, established a limit of 12 per cent on interest rates, and settled the indemnity by exacting 25 per cent of crops and a tax of 25 per cent on the value of houses and slaves.

[31] The whole business of the corn laws needs examining with a mid-twentieth-century eye. The books are still full of Victorian righteousness. Gracchus has grudgingly been allowed to be respectable, since Last calculated (*CAH* IX. p. 59) that his corn need not have cost the state anything, but Clodius remains a villain. Cary, for instance (*CAH* IX. p. 524): 'It mattered nothing to Clodius that this gratuity absorbed more

than one half of the new revenues accruing from Pompey's conquests, and that it completed the pauperisation of the Roman proletariat.' We may surely credit Clodius with knowing before he began that the money was available, and as for pauperisation, a modern unemployed man who was offered two loaves a day for himself and his family would not think he was being pampered. Best of all, find work for them, of course, and we should notice that both Gracchus' and Clodius' corn laws followed determined efforts to put the urban unemployed back on the land — the agrarian laws of Tiberius Gracchus and Caesar respectively. When that has been tried, it is a proper care of the government that those who cannot be moved shall be able to live. The nation which had conquered the Mediterranean world could not be expected to allow its citizens at home to starve to death. Caesar's retrenchment has sometimes been taken as a condemnation of Clodius, but what he attacked was not free corn but administrative laxity. Nor did the emperors find a better solution to this intractable problem: a century and a half later, Tacitus describes the Roman populace as 'vulgus cui una ex re publica annonae cura' (*H.* IV. 38). If it is a question of *how much* help the government ought to have given, we must admit that we do not know enough of the economics of the life of the poor at Rome, but it seems probable that, in the absence of factories, there was not a living wage for all.

Chapter V: THE EXECUTIVE

¹ So long as the proconsul remained in his province and the consul at Rome, conflict was unlikely; it is possible that the consul while at home could send orders to the proconsul, but we know of no instance, and Henderson in *JRS* (1957) argues that the consul's *imperium* was in no way superior to the proconsul's. Conflict between proconsuls was not likely to arise so long as their provinces were geographically separate; but when Pompey fought the pirates he had to be able to disembark, and was given, by the *lex Gabinia*, an imperium up to a distance of fifty miles from the coast in all the maritime provinces. Since it was equal to that of the provincial governors, conflict could arise—and did arise in Crete. Remember-

ing that, Messius, when he was proposing a similar command ten years later, wrote in his bill (which was not passed) that the commander should have an *imperium maius*.

[2] Verres had three, but that was because Arrius (pr. 72), who was to have succeeded him, was kept in Italy by the war against Spartacus. One reason for not taking a province after the praetorship is suggested in the note on p. 221, *oportet*.

[3] On the conservative assumption that four ex-praetors returned from their provinces each year, at an age, on the average, of forty-four, and that senators are retiring from active life at about sixty. By the time a man is a *consularis* he can have governed two provinces, and some of them had.

[4] For all that he was pleased with his success as an administrator, Cicero's letters home are full of requests to his friends to see that he was not kept abroad for another year. In writing to Quintus in Asia, he had assumed that he would feel the same.

[5] Some remarks about senatorial morality in this field will be found on p. 84. The close link between city and provincial office was loosened by Pompey in 52, when he enacted that there should be a five-year gap between the two. This, by putting the monetary reward further off, would at least make the money-lenders hesitate.

[6] *II Verr.* iv. 45.

[7] He would have claimed that this was his right; the unofficial salaries of Roman provincial administrators are discussed in Chap. IV.

[8] The technical phrase was *ornare provincias*. This was the process for the praetorian provinces, and, until the tribunate of Gaius Gracchus, for the consular also. Gracchus seems to have considered either that the consuls were unduly influencing the selection of their own provinces — the use of provinces for profit was one of the things which aroused his anger — or else that his opponents were using their majority in the senate to the disadvantage of his progressive friends; when Fulvius Flaccus (cos. 125) had been on the point of forcing the issue of the allies, they abruptly sent him (while still consul) to Transalpine Gaul; and even if it was necessary for the consuls to draw lots to decide which of them should have which of the chosen provinces, it was open to the senate to choose the best

when both consuls were supporters of the regime. He therefore enacted, by the *lex Sempronia de provinciis consularibus*, that the consular provinces should be chosen before the election of the consuls who were eventually to hold them. To ensure that it should be done in time, he expressly exempted this choice from the tribunician veto, since otherwise such a veto would automatically prevent the elections from being held. Again, our judgement of Gracchus is made more difficult by our lack of evidence. How bad were the abuses which he was trying to stop? Were they bad enough to warrant this loss of flexibility? The more we consider his legislation, the more we feel this lack.

A further difference between consuls and praetors is described in Chap. II, note 13. It was a difference in military rank, and was only important to the governor himself; in his dealings with his provincials a propraetor had as much power as a proconsul.

That provinces should be selected by the senate was an essential part of the system. They knew the facts, as the people in the streets could not. There were occasions, however, when they were overridden by the assemblies in these appointments, and of course when a law had been passed they could not but obey. The first occasion was probably the appointment of Marius to the African command in 108, and this was imitated by the abortive *lex Sulpicia* of 88. Sulla tried to prevent a repetition, but the *lex Gabinia* of 67, in this respect disastrous, re-established the precedent that commanders could be appointed by the people. Clodius carried this a step further, since by one of his *leges Clodiae* he altered the allocation of ordinary provinces, where no great military emergency existed, and was therefore interfering in administration, not planning the strategy of a war. The effects of some of these appointments on the growth of the empire were very great, but they do not properly belong to the subject of provincial administration. It may be convenient to list them here, and then dismiss them:

108	Marius	Africa	?
88	Marius	Mithridates	lex Sulpicia
67	Pompey	the Pirates	lex Gabinia
66	Pompey	Mithridates	lex Manilia

59	Caesar	Cisalpine Gaul and Illyricum	lex Vatinia
58	Piso	Macedonia	
	Gabinius	Syria	lex Clodia
55	Caesar	Gauls and Illyricum	lex Pompeia Licinia
	Pompey	Spain	
	Crassus	Syria	lex Trebonia

9 Since they had no independent *imperium*, there was a limit to the decisions which they could take. They needed to be able to refer to their superior. When therefore the *lex Gabinia* gave Pompey his command against the pirates, a command which included the whole length of the Mediterranean, it was seen that ordinary *legati* were inadequate, especially in winter. A deputy would have small authority in Pamphylia if the source of his power was at New Carthage. For this purpose, therefore, Pompey was given fifteen *legati* who themselves had *imperium*, so that they could take decisions and give orders with more confidence on the spot. Their *imperium* was praetorian only, and they were under his orders. Later, when the compact of Lucca enabled him to stay in Italy while governing Spain, the same problem arose, and was solved in the same way. The Spanish provinces were administered by deputies, who were given praetorian *imperium*; a precedent which was to prove useful to Augustus.

10 In the *Divinatio*, Cicero is concerned to show that Caecilius would be an unsuitable prosecutor of Verres because he had been his quaestor; he may therefore be exaggerating the closeness of the tie (*Div. in Caec.* 61). Pompey and Caesar had sometimes chosen their own quaestors — Antonius had not followed Caesar by chance (*ad Att.* VI. vi. 4). Caesar as quaestor in Spain had held assizes (Suet. *Div. Jul.* 7); the young Crassus in Gaul had commanded troops (Caes. *B.G.* V. 24). In Sicily, where the Romans had inherited the east end of the island from the Greeks and the west end from the Carthaginians, they maintained two quaestors, one at Lilybaeum and the other at Syracuse.

11 In his army, the general's bodyguard was known as the *cohors praetoria*.

12 *II Verr.* II. 27.

[13] Though some of the staff were also liable to prosecution, as the *lex Acilia* shows. Rutilius had been Scaevola's legatus (see Chap. IV, note 14).

[14] Readers of E. M. Forster's *A Passage to India* will realise that relations between rulers and ruled may be socially as well as officially difficult. Though the Romans never had to face a difference in colour.

[15] It did not, for instance, occur to them that in the event of an earthquake the imperial government might help.

[16] But these letters from Rome were usually asking favours on behalf of Romans, which were not likely to do the provincials much good. A whole book of Cicero's letters (*ad fam.* XIII) is devoted to letters of recommendation.

[17] The phrase *res repetere* was an ancient one. By fetial law, before declaring war the Romans had to send representatives to their enemy who should demand restitution (*ad res repetendas*). Only when the enemy had refused was it permissible for the Romans to declare war. This was still observed in declaring the foreign wars of the second century though by then the demand is made by senatorial *legati*, not by the *fetiales*. The same phrase was now used of the court which ordered restitution when a Roman had abused his official position for his private gain. We mostly hear of provincial governors being tried in this court, but it could apply to any magistrate, or his legatus, and it was here that senators could be prosecuted for accepting bribes.

[18] The dates when the other *quaestiones perpetuae* were established are uncertain, but Sulla left seven such courts.

[19] *II Verr.* IV. 17, *communis arx sociorum.* See also *Div. in Caec.* 18.

[20] Messana (*II Verr.* IV. 15); Cicero spared no pains to denigrate this embassy.

[21] Fonteius was prosecuted in 69, the year after the introduction of the tripartite juries (see note 23); his acquittal must have come as a disappointment to those who hoped for better things.

It has been suggested (by Badian, *Foreign Clientelae 264–70*) that Pompey was interested in the condemnation of Verres; if that is so, Cicero was not taking such a chance after all. And having been quaestor in Sicily, he was trying to become a *patronus* on his own account. Verres apart, his career was based on his services to the nobility in the courts, and he would naturally much rather defend than prosecute. Whether contemporary or not, the author of the *Commentariolum Petitionis* had a shrewd understanding of his motives (see especially *Com. Pet.* 20).

The doctrine enunciated in Cic. *Off.* II. 49–51 is instructive: a man could make a reputation for eloquence by undertaking a prosecution in his youth, but only once, *semel igitur aut non saepe certe*; it is disadvantageous to be labelled as a prosecutor. As a result, a governor was likely to be defended by experienced barristers and prosecuted by a young man displaying his eloquence.

22 A deception by which, when a man had to be prosecuted, the prosecution was undertaken by an accomplice, who would do it so badly that the court had to acquit. This had been the intention of Caecilius, if he had succeeded in the *divinatio*.

23 It may be convenient to summarise here the changes which were made from time to time:

Before 149   the *recuperatores* appointed in 171 were senators.

149   (by the *lex Calpurnia*) senators.

123   (by a law of Gracchus) the non-senatorial well-to-do; those whom we later call equestrians.

106–101   It is possible that between the *lex Servilia* of Caepio and the *lex Servilia* of Glaucia the juries were composed either of senators or of a mixture of senators and equestrians.

104   Gracchan *iudices* again.

89   (by the *lex Plotia*) juries drawn from all classes.

80   (by a law of Sulla) senators only (but now more than half of the senators are men who were recently equestrians; I have discussed the ensuing corruption in *Greece and Rome*, 1962).

70   (by a law of the praetor Aurelius Cotta) equal proportions of senators, equestrians and *tribuni aerarii*. These last were in effect the next most wealthy class in Rome after the senators and *ordo equester*; it turned out that their sympathies were likely to lie with the

equestrians, so that it is sometimes said that two thirds of the juries were equestrians; they were not very successful as umpires in this matter.

59   (by a law of the praetor Fufius Calenus) the votes of the three sections were counted separately.

55   (by a law of Pompey) the poorest members of each section were excluded.

45   Caesar removed the *tribuni aerarii* from the juries.

[24] Several acquittals by equestrian juries are mentioned by Cicero in his speech for Fonteius (23–27); Cicero approves of them, but we have no means of checking the merits of the cases.

[25] The maltreatment of Gavius was as shocking as any crime in the catalogue of Verres, and makes a stirring finale to the book which deals with jurisdiction. But it can be seen from Cicero's language that it is only marginally relevant to the case the court had to decide.

[26] If the text of Vel. Pat. II. 8, is right, C. Cato (cos. 114) was condemned for extortion in Macedonia when the subsequent *litis aestimatio* came to only 4,000 sesterces; set beside Cicero's claim that Verres' extortions amounted to forty millions this does not seem very much (but see the *apparatus criticus* of *O.C.T.* on *II Verr.* IV. 22, where the same case is mentioned; even here, however, the figure accepted by the editor is only 8,000). This was in the days of equestrian juries, *tum cum severa iudicia fiebant*.

[27] There was no such review at Rome either, but there the magistrate had to take account of a vigorous public opinion, while a really serious case, if not dealt with by a *quaestio perpetua*, would come before the people.

Chapter VI: AUGUSTAN EPILOGUE

[1] This is not to say that he had no difficulties; but it is broadly true.

[2] Syme (*Roman Revolution*, p. 502) states that no *nobilis* commanded an army in the emperor's provinces in the first decade of the reign of Augustus.

[3] It is unfortunate that the one military enterprise of Augustus which was clearly beyond the powers of the Republic did

not succeed. It was a fine conception, strategically, none the less.

⁴ Interest in geography was growing at the time; Strabo was born within a year of Augustus. A great map of the whole known world was publicly displayed in Rome by Augustus' general Agrippa.

⁵ Tac. *A.* I. 11.

⁶ So, in fact, could the governor of an imperial province.

⁷ Technically this was trial by the consul, with the senate as his *consilium.* But the extortion court was still the *normal* procedure in the early principate.

⁸ Augustus himself sent a copy of the decree to the governor of Cyrene.

⁹ For the germ of *appellatio* under the Republic see Chap. V, p. 66. The *lex Julia de vi publica* made it illegal to obstruct a citizen from exercising his right of *provocatio,* and is therefore particularly valuable to those who lived a long way from Rome; unfortunately we have no date for it, and the usual ambiguity of the name *lex Julia* prevents us from being certain whether it was passed by Julius or Augustus. On this subject I am indebted to A. H. Jones, *Studies in Roman Government and Law,* Chap. IV.

¹⁰ By *commendatio* and *nominatio;* the emperor was entitled to issue two lists of candidates he approved of; those 'commended' were considered elected forthwith; those 'nominated' still had to be elected, but had at least gained the emperor's approval. Caesar had done much the same thing (Suet. *Div. Jul.* 41). Anyone who aspires to govern Rome through the established order must have some control over elections. Pompey had tried to govern by influence alone, but without success. Tiberius abolished election by the people altogether.

¹¹ It had been proposed for Pompey in 57. The precedents of the civil war were best forgotten.

¹² See especially *ad Q.f.* I. i. 16. p. 148.

¹³ The story that Julius Caesar intended to move the capital of the empire to Troy or Alexandria is not to be taken seriously.

¹⁴ *Aen.* VIII. 675–713:

> hinc Augustus agens Italos in proelia Caesar . . .
> hinc ope barbarica variisque Antonius armis . . .

The intensity of feeling in Horace's Ode (III. 37) is evidence of the success of Octavian's propaganda.

[15] By the granting of Latin rights to towns outside Italy, which gradually produced a local aristocracy of Roman citizens; by the granting of citizenship on discharge to provincials who have served their term in the *auxilia* (*ipsis liberisque posterisque*; a number of these *diplomata* have been found in Britain, and can be seen in the museums); and by grants to individuals for the equivalent of the modern 'political and public services'. The advantages of Roman citizenship were sufficient to make it a coveted distinction. For the admission of provincials to the senate the most notable text is the speech of Claudius (Bruns, *Fontes Iuris Romani*. p. 195, reported by Tacitus in *A*. XI. 24).

The idea that Roman citizenship could be given to individuals for services to Rome was not an invention of the empire. In fact Livy (XXVI. 21) records an instance as early as the second Punic war; it then seems to have been forgotten, until in 101 Marius enfranchised two cohorts of Umbrians at the battle of Vercellae. In 89 Pompey's father, Cn. Pompeius Strabo, enfranchised a cohort of Spanish auxiliary cavalry in the field at Asculum in Picenum *virtutis causa*. In the first century wars the honour was given to a number of non-Italians abroad, and was not always confined to bravery on the field of battle; the Balbus family of Cadiz, and, exceptionally and scandalously, Theophanes of Mytilene (see p. 9), who became Cn. Pompeius Theophanes. In *Foreign Clientelae* App. B. Badian lists over forty such grants under the Republic, excluding those who owed it to Caesar.

In theory, such grants could only be made by the *populus Romanus* itself; Strabo recorded (Dessau *I.L.S.* 8888) that he was acting *ex lege Julia* (the law of 90 which helped to end the social war: it may be doubted, though, whether it was meant to cover grants to non-Italians); and Pompey's enfranchisements during the Sertorian war were legalised by the *lex Gellia Cornelia* of 72; in both these cases the grants had to be made *de consilii sententia* (*I.L.S.* 8888 and Cic. *Balb.* 19) — it was a matter for careful consideration. But Marius' action at Vercellae was never legalised (Plut. *Mar.* 28), and it seems that such grants by Roman generals began to be accepted without further ceremony.

Caesar was more prodigal. Besides completing the unification of the Italian peninsular by the enfranchisement of the Transpadanes (according to Antony he planned to do the same for Sicily), he gave citizenship more freely to individuals, and his overseas colonies will in fact have given it to many more. In this, as in other things, Augustus was more conservative.

16 The development of the *ordo equester* is described by Stevenson in *CAH* X. pp. 186–8. He probably underestimates the work of the freedmen of Augustus. The emperor's varied work could not have been done nor his huge estates managed without skilled assistance, and the equestrians did not yet supply it. From the last chapter of Suetonius' Life (*Div. Aug.* 101) it is clear that the bulk of his money was being handled by freedmen and even slaves. By the time of Claudius the work had become so important as to generate titles, and then Rome realised what had been happening; eventually the equestrians came to think these apparently servile posts worth holding, but it is not until the time of Hadrian that they take over, and gradually most of the freedmen disappear from the limelight.

17 So St Paul, *Acts* XXV. 12.

18 Augustus himself organised a census in Gaul in 27 (Dio. LIII. 22); Germanicus in A.D. 14 was *agendo Galliarum censui intentus* (Tac. *A.* I. 31). Before long the phrase *ad census accipiendos* begins to appear in the inscriptions of governors.

19 Though in the *Res Gestae* Augustus boasts of the money he has spent on the public good, the machinery of his financial control is hidden from view. The most plausible assumption is that the accounts (not the cash) of each province were kept in the *aerarium*, which was nominally under the control of the senate; since important provinces were administered by the emperor, and since the emperor (unlike other proconsuls) was himself in Rome, he can hardly have avoided regarding a large part of the *aerarium* as his concern. The grouping together of these offices and their eventual separation from the rest of the treasury was only a matter of time, but it does not seem to have happened until the reign of Claudius; then, the *aerarium* does

only senate's business, the *fiscus* does the emperor's. (When Augustus speaks of *mea pecunia* he means his own personal wealth, which was derived from estates, inheritances and spoils of war.)   Jones (*JRS* (1950), p. 22) would put the division of the treasury later, and holds that throughout the Julio-Claudian period *fiscus* is the same as Augustus' *mea pecunia*.

[20] So in Britain in 61 the procurator Classicianus advised the government to supersede Suetonius Paulinus (Tac. *A*. XIV. 38).

[21] Tac. *A*. II. 47.

[22] See, for instance, Ehrenberg and Jones, 224 (=*ILS*. 9007).

[23] *Decline and Fall of the Roman Empire*, Chap. III.

[24] Book X of Pliny's letters contains his correspondence with the emperor while Pliny was in Bithynia.   His lack of initiative may well have irritated Trajan, but it ensured that his interference in local affairs was kept to a minimum.

[25] Tac. *H*. I. 4 (of the year 69): evulgato imperii arcano posse principes alibi quam Romae fieri.

[26] 'It is a fact never to be lost sight of that *dignitas* at Rome implies less what the possessor owes to others than what he claims as due to himself' (Wirzubski, *JRS* (1954), p. 10).   The financial aspect of this sense of ownership is discussed in Chap. IV.   In Tac. *A*. XV. 21 Thrasea Paetus is referring back to the ideas of the Republic.

[27] Though for the circuses the state only paid a basic sum; the extravagances came out of the pockets of the magistrates. In this spending the careful Augustus outdid all his predecessors;   three thousand five hundred wild animals were only part of the story (*Mon. Anc.* 22. 3).   On p. 189 it is argued that we ought not to complain unduly about the bread;   circuses on this scale are harder to justify.

[28] In 43 Octavian found enough money in it to pay his soldiers a lump sum equivalent to ten years' pay (Appian *B.C.* III. 94).

[29] *Odes* II. xv. 13.   In *JRS* (1950), p. 26, Jones is writing of Augustus, but it had always been true: 'The state was so poor that a rich man's private resources were comparable with it.'

[30] Dio XXXIX. 37; Tac. *A*. II. 33.

[31] But Roman sentiment always allowed more to a triumphator than to a governor.   Some of Mummius' loot was housed

in the temple of Luna on the Aventine, as the Sicilian 'trophies' of Marcellus had been in his temple of Virtus and Honos outside the Porta Capena. Velleius Paterculus has the story that when Mummius appointed contractors to convey his antiques to Rome he stipulated that if any were lost on the way they should be replaced. This passion for collecting did not end with the Republic; even Mummius could not be compared with Nero or Constantine.

[32] Tacitus' phrase is meant to be inclusive: *dilectum ac tributa et iniuncta imperii munera* (*Agr.* 13).

[33] This was a difference between the Roman empire and the Athenian; the Athenians were born interferers.

[34] Despatch to Cyrene (p. 168).

[35] It is true that early Republican coins carried the helmeted head of Roma, and this type was not unimpressive. But these issues do not compare in interest with the coinage of the empire, while the personal types of the late Republic were aimed at the glorification of individuals and will not have endeared Rome to her allies.

Almost all the coins used in the empire were issued by mints under the emperor's control, and carried his head on the obverse; many have been found in India and Ceylon. His was the most widely known face in the world: '*Whose is this image and superscription? They say unto him, Caesar's.*'

Besides using the obverse to make themselves personally known, the emperors used the reverse to celebrate their achievements and announce their intentions. Augustus had first to secure his position in the Roman state, so that most of his announcements were addressed primarily to Romans — some, like the *corona civica* series, with the legend *ob civis servatos*, solely to Romans. But the great mint at Lugdunum produced a large number of coins with the device of the provincial temple to Rome and Augustus, and on some coins of Tiberius we find *civitatibus Asiae restitutis*. It was not, however, until the time of Hadrian that we find an important part of the imperial coinage directed to the provincial public.

Economically, of course, it was beneficial that all the money of the west, from the smallest silver coin upwards, was on one standard; bronze, for local use, was different: the Spanish coins of Republican date shown by Sutherland (*The Romans in Spain*, Plates II–IV) are interesting as showing the spread of peaceful conditions and the absence of a centralised policy. The number of mints coining in bronze increases in Baetica and the coastal strip in the first century B.C., and there is a mixture of types: some have a crude Roma, some have the Spanish charging lancer. In the east, where there was already a multiplicity of coinages, the denarius circulated, but here the Romans also struck on the standard of the Attic drachma (1 dr. = 1 d.). Here too the continued existence of local bronze was tolerated: Laodicea and Cibyra were striking coins under the early empire, and may well have been doing so when Cicero was their governor.

However, it is difficult to estimate how big a part civilian economics played in Roman thinking; the army was a big user of coins, and army pay was doubtless a primary consideration: issuing coins was within the rights of a general. But the general was also a civilian governor, and it is certain that at least the governments of Augustus, Tiberius and Claudius were not ignorant in financial matters.

The most accessible photographs of coins in sufficient quantities are likely to be the plates in Mattingly, *Roman Coins*, Sutherland, *Coinage in Roman Imperial Policy 31 B.C. to A.D. 68*, and Grant, *Roman History from Coins*. Grant, Chaps. III and IV are relevant to the subject of coins in the provinces.

³⁶ It is not easy to be sure of the feelings of the people. According to Tacitus (*A*. XIV. 31) the inhabitants of Colchester regarded the temple of Claudius with loathing, *quasi arx aeternae dominationis*; but this is the language of malcontents at a time of revolution. In A.D. 15 the people of Tarraco asked to be allowed to build a temple to Augustus (*A*. I. 78); but they were Roman citizens, since it was a colony, and he had treated them with special favour when he was in Spain; we need not assume that this is typical of the feelings of Spaniards.

³⁷ Because the feeling on which it was based was spontaneous. In a letter to the Alexandrians, the emperor Claudius tried tactfully to moderate the over-enthusiastic honours which they wanted to pay him; it was published in Alexandria by the Prefect, with the preamble: 'So that you all may marvel

at the greatness of Caesar our God' (Nos. 1 and 2 in Charlesworth, *Documents Illustrating the Reigns of Claudius and Nero*). A full, but rather optimistic, account of the means by which the Roman emperors won the loyalty of the provinces, east and west, will be found in Sherwin-White, *Roman Citizenship*, Chap. XII.

[38] The Roman attitude to druidism is instructive. The evidence has been collected by Last in *JRS* (1949), who finds that the hostility of the government was caused by the druidic practice of human sacrifice. The early empire began by forbidding Gauls who were Roman citizens to profess this *dira immanitas* and proceeded to root it out of the empire altogether. It is at times when western civilisation is in danger that the legacy of Rome is most appreciated, and the writings of Professor Last before and after the second world war are a tribute to the slow but abiding effect of Latin culture in Europe.

We will end these notes on the imperial regeneration with the elder Pliny's post mortem on Druidism (*N.H.* XXX. 13); nec satis aestimari potest quantum debeatur Romanis qui sustulere monstra in quibus hominem occidere religiosissimum erat, mandi vero etiam saluberrimum.

[39] At the risk of spoiling this picture of the imperial harmony, it should be pointed out that where the Romans of the empire are conquering free peoples there is abundant evidence of hostility; it was late in the reign of Augustus that an Illyrian rebel complained 'You send us not shepherds or sheepdogs, but wolves'; and it was not in the time of the Republic that the damning epigram was coined, *ubi solitudinem faciunt, pacem appellant.*

NOTES TO PART TWO

Chapter 1: THE GROWTH OF THE EMPIRE
Livy, XXXIII. 32–34.

32. Isthmiorum: after the defeat of Philip of Macedon in
197, the Romans had made peace with him on condition that
he withdrew all his troops from Greek cities by the time of the
next Isthmian Games, which were due to be held in the summer
of 196. These were one of the four great national festivals of
Greece, and were held at Corinth every two years.

quo ... visuntur: where people go to see. ...

artium: musical competitions formed a part of most Greek
festivals.

virium et pernicitatis: Pindar's surviving Isthmian odes
celebrate two victories in the chariot race and five in the
pancration.

usus: accusative plural. At this time Corinth is the
wealthiest city of mainland Greece, and since King Philip II of
Macedon had made it the centre of the Hellenic League in 338
it can claim to be the most important.

exspectatione: Macedonian troops have left Greece, a commission of ten senators has arrived and was known to be
advising Flamininus.

liberos, immunes: both these words are important; it was
possible to be *liberi* without being *immunes*. **suis legibus:** this
is an essential part of *libertas*.

33. ludis dimissis: the end of the first day of the games.

adire: depends on *cupientium*.

lemniscos: ribbons attached to the *coronae*; crowns decor-
ated in this way were given to victors in the public games.

trium ferme et triginta: and he had been consul two years
earlier (198). The *lex Villia annalis* had not yet been passed,
and he had distinguished himself in the Hannibalic war. The

sources of his support have been discussed by Scullard, *Roman Politics 220–150. Chap. VI*.

fructus: this word, which is derived from *fruor*, is sometimes used of enjoyment of the mind.

esse aliquam: the motives of the Romans have been called in question in modern times, and of course they did not send an army abroad unless they thought it was in their own interests; and it was in their interest to weaken Philip. But to deny the philhellenic generosity of Flamininus and his supporters is unnecessarily churlish. He certainly made a favourable impression on the Greeks, apart from their delight at this proclamation, as can be read in Plutarch (*Flam*. V, VI, etc.)

ius fas lex: morality, religion and law; *ius* is what is binding by its own nature, a wider conception than *lex*. (Hence its use in the phrase *ius gentium*.)

atque Asiae: the Greek cities of Asia Minor were always trying to claim the privileges of being Greeks, but even the Spartans in the fourth century had abandoned them to Persia.

34. **legationes:** the grand declaration has not settled everything; the Romans, having declared that the Greeks were free from all foreigners, now have to settle the future status of the liberated cities and tribes. First, Antiochus, king of Syria, had to be warned off, and that from Asiatic Greeks as well as from an invasion of Greece itself; next, self-government was guaranteed to the tribes north of Thermopylae; then the claims of the Aetolian and Achaean leagues had to be settled. To describe the details would take us deep into the tortuous history of second-century Greece; even without them it will be clear that the lot of the liberator was not an easy one. The Romans will be in some measure responsible for their arrangements, and may have to keep the peace which they have made.

suae leges redditae: this is the essence of *libertas*.

excepta: with the exception of these two towns.

Eumeni: King of Pergamum; he and his father had been staunch supporters and willing protégés of the Romans, whose Asiatic policy was based on their alliance. They are now being rewarded by the senatorial commission, but Flamininus had more idealistic views, and to the credit of the government at home he prevails in the end.

Caesar, *de Bello Gallico*, VII. 32–33.

32. 2. **hieme confecta**: the winter of 53–52; Caesar had surprised the Gauls by the speed with which he began his campaign against the great revolt of Vercingetorix. The capture of Avaricum had eased his supply position, but until then it must have been very difficult. Caesar's commentaries are full of references to *commeatus* and *res frumentaria*, and if his efficiency in this department has been neglected it is not his fault.

Aeduorum: they lived between the Seine and the upper Loire, not far from the boundary of Caesar's original province of Gallia Transalpina. They were *socii et amici* of Rome, and it was at their appeal that Caesar had attacked the Helvetii. He relied on their loyalty to keep the peace in central Gaul. His policy of indirect control is described by Sherwin-White in the bimillenary number of *Greece and Rome* (March 1957). Caesar's account of the beginning of the revolt of the Aedui has been challenged by Stevens in *Latomus* (1953).

3. **magistratus**: the title of the chief magistrate, who had the power of life and death, was *Vergobret* (*B.G.* I. 16). That the office was annual suggests a higher degree of civilisation than that of most of the northern tribes whom the Romans absorbed.

5. **clientelas**: the word is frequently used to describe the real sources of power in the Roman state.

33. 2. **deminuisse**: the Aedui were allies, not a conquered tribe, and Caesar avoids giving offence, but in virtue of his *auctoritas* (**32.** 6 above) he summons them to meet him.

Decetiam: on the Loire; in this instance the place-name has survived into the modern *Decetia* (see, by way of contrast, note 12 p. 175).

3. **civitas**: local centres within the tribe of the Aedui.

vetarent: careful provision against the domination of one family.

per sacerdotes: royal power and religious authority are seldom far apart.

intermissis: when the present holders relinquish their office.

Cicero, *II in Verrem*. II. 122–127.

122. Halaesini: the town of Halaesa, near the north coast of Sicily, had been a native Sicilian, not a Greek or Carthaginian foundation. In Timoleon's partition of the island in the fourth century it was in the Greek east, but not far from the frontier, Himera being Carthaginian. In the first Punic war she joined the Roman side early (hence *meritis* and *beneficiis*), and was repaid by the grant of freedom. By the time of the elder Pliny (*N.H.* III. 8) the Halaesi were *stipendiarii*, but what caused this fall from grace we do not know.

L. Licinio: L. Licinius Crassus, the orator (not the father of the triumvir) and Q. Mucius Scaevola (the Pontifex) were consuls in 95.

petiverunt: as a free city, they had no *need* of Roman approval.

C. Claudius: he happened to be praetor at the time; he was *patronus* of Messana (II *Verr*. IV. 6). According to Pliny (*N.H.* VIII. 7), he had another title to fame — he was the first man to make elephants fight in the arena.

Marcellis: ever since M. Claudius Marcellus captured Syracuse in the second Punic war and ended the revolt in the island the family had been acknowledged patrons of the Sicilians (see p. 67, and note on p. 272, quattuor).

dedit: a law which is imposed on a *civitas* which has not passed it for itself is for it a *lex data*; at Rome a law which the Roman people has passed is a *lex rogata*.

aetate: thirty was the minimum age for the quaestorship at Rome, after which a man passed into the senate.

quaestu: some trades were considered so inferior that those who practised them might be disqualified; it is evident from *ad fam*. VI. xviii. 1 that auctioneers might be so excluded.

censu: property qualification; at Rome there seems to have been no official *census senatorius* until the time of Augustus, but in fact a senator needed to be rich. Regulations such as these could hardly fail to be conservative in effect. Romans naturally took with them their ideas of what was fitting.

auctoritate: Roman magistrates had no power to interfere in the affairs of a free city, but their opinions could be expected to carry some weight.

senum: boys of sixteen or seventeen; the distributive numeral implies that there were several of them.

socii et amici: a very honourable appellation (see p. 176, note 6). It is possible that Cicero is exaggerating the status of the Halaesini.

123. **Agrigentini:** Agrigentum had been of great strategic importance in the first Punic war, being at one time the Carthaginians' port of entry into central and eastern Sicily. Its dealings with Scipio (Africanus the elder) date from 206, when he was in Sicily collecting an army for the invasion of Africa.

T. Manlius: if this man is the Mamilius of Livy, XXVII. 36, and the colony belongs to the year 207, it would explain the need for Scipio's interference; we should guess that Manlius (or Mamilius) had failed to find a satisfactory compromise between the old citizens and the new.

deduxit: this verb is regularly used of the founding of colonies.

dilectum atque discrimen: all criteria of selection.

permiscuit: he did not observe the qualifications of age, rank or profession. That *ordo* appears to be the equivalent of *census* above tells us something of the importance attaching to wealth.

124. **demortuus:** this compound is used when a man's death creates a vacancy.

praetore: this word is frequently used of a provincial governor, regardless of his exact status; it was in fact not until the time of Sulla that it was the established practice for a magistrate not to go out to a province until after his term of office in the city.

commercium: who should not even have been concerned in the transaction.

tantulum: so little.

125. **Heracleae:** this is Heraclea Minoa; it was a Greek colony, but being at the mouth of the Halycus, which was Timoleon's frontier, it was ruled by the Carthaginians, and in the Punic war was one of their ports of entry into the island. It became part of the Roman province, and in 131, after it had suffered severely in the slave war, its population was increased

by new Sicilian colonists settled there by the Roman commission. The same problem of the two communities therefore arose.

In both these cases Verres was doubtless breaking the law in not observing the balance between the two, but since they had been living together in the same cities for many years (a hundred and fifty at Agrigentum, sixty at Heraclea), we may doubt whether the distinction between old and new citizen was any longer important — or desirable — except to the defeated candidates. Possibly it was high time it was abolished.

126. **curationes:** at Rome this word came to be used officially of the public boards established by Augustus to manage such things as the water supply of the city and the sacred buildings.

Iovis: since the time of Timoleon this priesthood had been an annual office of great importance; the holder gave his name to the year — as, for instance, did the priestess of Hera at Argos.

127. **revocatur:** this verb was used for the last stage of a process; so, when an argument ends in a fight, *res ad manus revocatur*; similarly, *res redit ad triarios*. The combination of election and lot was well known at Athens; it ensured that only suitable men were elected, and then left the final choice to the gods. It had the effect of diminishing the temptation to bribe the electors.

pro suffragio: in the voting.

cuium: *cuius* declined as an adjective was used in early Latin, rarely as late as this.

fas: this is much more emphatic than *licet*, carrying the notion of divine sanction.

Extracts from the *Lex Antonia de Termessibus*.

The site of Termessus was a very strong one, on a hill commanding the defile which leads from Pisidia into Lycia and Lycaonia. In the year 91 it was still outside the bounds of the Roman empire, since there was then no territorial province of Cilicia and Roman Asia did not extend so far east. For 'the consulship of Marcius and Julius' we must therefore suppose some treaty between Rome and Termessus; the Romans may have been preparing for trouble with the Cilicians and Isaurians, or with Mithridates. In the event Termessus did resist Mithridates, and its territory suffered severe damage. Sulla compelled Mithridates to retreat, and later constituted the province of Cilicia, the territory of which surrounded, and probably included, Termessus; he did nothing else to help the reconstruction of Asia Minor. Lucullus did make some attempt to do justice to the allies of Rome, and we may see his hand in this law. He was proconsul of Cilicia both in 72, which was taken as a cardinal date for establishing ownership, and in 68 the other possible date of the passing of this law.

The text of these extracts is taken from Wordsworth, *Fragments and Specimens of Early Latin*; it is also to be found in Bruns, *Fontes Iuris Romani*, and there is a translation in Hardy, *Six Roman Laws*. In accordance with the usual practice, it was engraved on tablets of bronze, and posted on the wall for all to see. One of the tablets was found in the ruins of the temple of Saturn (which was the *aerarium*) at Rome. The letters in italics are supposed to have been on the tablet, those in brackets complete what the engraver abbreviated.

mai(oribus): We presume that there was also a Lesser Termessus, but nothing is known of it.

Corne . . . : Cornelius; the law was inscribed on four or five sheets of bronze, of which we have only one, and the heading extended along the top of them all. There is room probably for all the tribunes, and it is likely that they all put their names to it. From a fragment of another law the names of nine of them can be recovered. Their tribunate is dated to 68 by Broughton (*Magistrates of the Roman Republic*, p. 144), but there is no direct evidence.

de s(enatus) s(ententia): a common formula; it may be that in Sulla's constitution tribunes could propose laws provided they had senatorial approval; if that is so, then this law and these tribunes could belong to the year 72.

rogaverunt: this is what the proposer of the law does. His proposal is a *rogatio*, and if the people pass it it is then a *lex rogata*. From the point of view of the Termessians, who have not passed it, it is a *lex data*.

scivit: in a law passed by consul or praetor the formula is *populus iussit*; but tribunes were originally officers of the plebs, and their resolutions *plebiscita*.

in . . .: this would be the place of meeting; for the *comitia tributa*, which is not in theory a military body, it is frequently the forum.

a.d.: the date.

principium: they recorded the name of the tribe which voted first (it was selected by lot), which is sometimes called the *tribus praerogativa*, and of the first voter.

L. Gellio: this is the year 72.

socieique: the words are usually reversed, *socii et amici*; see Chap. II, note 6. Archaic spelling survived in legal texts.

sunto: the imperative is used in laws, the subjunctive in *senatus consulta*. This, and similar matters, are lucidly discussed by Daube, *Forms of Roman legislation*.

quod advorsus: provided it is not contrary to this law.

Thermensorum: the engraver was not sure of the spelling or declension of this foreign noun.

praeter loca agros: section 2 of the law has made provision for land and buildings; this section deals with moveable property.

preimum: when the law was passed, the second Mithridatic war had begun.

usei fructeive: this combination of *utor* and *fruor* gave rise to the noun *ususfructus*, our usufruct, the right to occupy.

quod eius: such part of the property; **ipsei:** the owners.

uutei: a mistake of the engraver; *utei* in the previous line is for *ut*.

hiemandi: the obnoxious billeting of troops; this practice is discussed in Chap. IV.

quo: although this sentence does not contain a comparative.

nisei senatus: since the Romans are giving *libertas* they can lay down limits to it; see Sherwin-White, *Roman Citizenship*, p. 154. So Appian (*Iber.* 44., writing of the second century) says that it was the Roman practice to make such grants 'for as long as it seems good to the senate and people'.

lege Porcia: (this is Cato the censor) a law passed during his praetorship in 198; an early predecessor of Caesar's famous law.

maritumeisque: Termessus was nowhere near the sea, and the use of this word here suggests that we have a formula, and that there were other recipients of this *libertas*.

deixserint: future perfect (*pace* Hardy, who translates 'may have been laid down'); for the past this law uses the perfect indicative.

fructus: *quos fructus transportabunt, eorum. . . .*

Chapter II: DEFENCE

Cicero, *ad familiares.* III. iii.   (*All the letters in this chapter were written on the way to, or in, Cilicia in the years* 51–50 B.C.)

AP. PULCRO: Appius Claudius Pulcher (COS. 54) was governor of Cilicia 53–51; Cicero has been appointed to succeed him, and, before leaving Rome, had written him a goodwill letter. Now he is worried about the military situation. Appius was a brother of Clodius and Clodia, and nearly related to the Metelli; a man of importance in the counsels of the oligarchy, he was censor in 50 and was made proconsul in the war against Caesar. Of his self-importance Cicero ironically coins the word *Appietas* (*ad fam.* III. vii. 5). The character of his administration can be judged from the extracts in Chaps. III and IV.

1. **Brundisium:** Cicero is on his way to Cilicia; he had reached Minturnae in southern Latium by May 5, and was still at Brundisium on June 5. He eventually reached Laodicea on July 31.

Vergilianus: at least one of Appius' *legati* has returned home ahead of the governor. This type of *agnomen* shows that its owner has been adopted: this man was born a Vergilius and has been adopted by a Fabius; he takes the *nomen* of his new family (and *cognomen*, if there is one), since he now legally belongs to it; but he retains the adjectival form of his original *nomen*. So Augustus was born C. Octavius, and became, on adoption, C. Julius Caesar Octavianus.

censebant: imperfect, because the decree was not finally put to the vote.

H

meis et Bibuli: Bibulus had not gone to a province after his consulship, and he was therefore, like Cicero, pressed into service to fill the gap made by Pompey's law of 52 (see p. 192, note 5); he went to Syria, and stayed there a year, being back in Italy for the beginning of the civil war. The defeat of Carrhae is still recent, and some people in Rome are afraid of a Parthian invasion. If it comes, the danger must be met by the armies of Syria and Cilicia. It was common practice for a new governor to take reinforcements of Italian legionaries with him. But at this moment Caesar has nine or ten legions in Gaul, and there are seven in Pompey's Spanish provinces, so that there is naturally opposition to further recruitments and military expense. In 50 the senate eventually decided that Pompey and Caesar must each release a legion for service in the east.

Sulpicius: as consul he refuses to put the motion, and by his opposition he prevented such a decree being passed. This is Sulpicius Rufus, Cicero's friend, who had been a consular candidate as far back as 63, and has now achieved an honour he must have despaired of.

litteris iis: this is Cicero's letter to Appius mentioned above, which we know as *ad fam.* III. ii.

cura ac diligentia: with *complectare*; I hope you will take great pains not to omit any of the services with which a governor can assist his successor.

benevolentiori: that I could not be succeeding a more kindly man.

2. **exemplum**: a copy; the letter will have been sent, like the two letters printed below, to the magistrates and the senate.

dimissos: the governor naturally had control of routine enlistment and demobilisation of individuals within the province. If there are not many Roman citizens resident there, then unless the home government sends reinforcements the strength of the legions will decline. This was happening in Cilicia.

cogitasse: this *had* been your intention.

pro eo quanti te facio: for the high opinion I have of you.

Pomptinum: he was the military man among Cicero's legati, having celebrated a triumph over the Allobroges, though under circumstances of great bitterness. Praetor in 63, he never became consul.

exspectabam: I am waiting for; Roman letter-writers frequently used this 'epistolary' imperfect, because by the time the letter is read the action will be in the past. It will be found frequently in this book, and no further comment will be made on it.

Cicero, *ad familiares*, XV. ii.

COS. PR. TR. PL.: Cicero addresses his letter to those magistrates who have the right to summon the senate. The language of this letter is naturally more polished than in some of his more private letters.

1. **S.V.V.B.E.E.Q.V.**: *si vos valetis bene est, ego quoque valeo*.

neque maturius: in view of the fact that he left Rome in the first week in May this is a surprising statement. To judge from the letter to Appius referred to above, the senate had thought that there was no time to be lost.

quam facultate et copia: doubtless a covert reference to their failure to vote him reinforcements.

iter mihi faciendum: Cicero's journey can be followed on the map on p. 16. He follows the same route as Xenophon, the Persian royal road. In a narrow sense Cappadocia is outside his province, but the governor of Cilicia at this time has also the task of protecting and controlling the king, and Cicero felt himself free to enter the kingdom.

eos: a repetition of the accusative *Parthos*; this hardly seems necessary, and *eo* has been conjectured.

2. **Cybistra**: the map on p. 16 should be carefully studied. The nearest part of the province to the enemy is the Pedias, and if the enemy comes through northern Syria Cicero will have to meet them at the Syrian or Amanian Gates. He does eventually go there, passing the scene of Alexander's victory at Issus. But instead of fighting their way through Syria, they could pull out of it (*ex Syria egredi*) to the north, and march up the Euphrates to Melitene, or even, as Cicero seems to fear, advance north-westwards through Commagene (it will be

obvious from the map that this is very unlikely). From eastern Cappadocia it would be possible for them to make their way to Lycaonia, and in that case they would have to pass close to Cybistra, but their most likely course would be to the upper Halys and along it to Galatia, which had been Xerxes' route. As a means of protecting Cappadocia, the Cybistra position is not very adventurous, but Cicero dares not move far from the pass into the Pedias. The fact is that it was not really possible for one army to defend the frontier both north and south of the Taurus range, as Vespasian recognised when he made Cappadocia a consular province; and it was a sensible change when the Pedias was attached to the province of Syria, whose army was well placed to defend it. We should not, however, be led by Cicero's dilemma into harsh criticism of the government's defence policy. Against ordinary incursions by local princes the native forces of Cappadocia were adequate, and the sheer distance (even as the crow flies, Melitene to Cybistra is two hundred and sixty miles) was a protection to the Roman provinces. Apart from the frontier province of Syria, which was well garrisoned, Roman Asia Minor would only be endangered by a concerted and purposeful Parthian invasion, and of that there was no likelihood. The next hundred years demonstrated the truth of this judgement, since apart from the quite exceptional invasion of 40 B.C. nearly all the fighting was east of the Euphrates.

quocumque animo: Artavasdes had assisted Crassus in the expedition which ended at Carrhae in 53, but since then had made a marriage alliance with the Parthian royal family. His subsequent career was equally ambiguous, until he was captured by Antony in 34, and led in a triumph through the streets of Alexandria.

non procul: in fact the march to the Armenian frontier could hardly take less than a fortnight.

Deiotarum: king of Galatia; another preoccupation of the governor of this large province, but also a supplier of troops to assist the depleted legions.

4. auctoritas: This was a decree in favour of the king: see 7 below, where *consultum* and *auctoritas* appear to be identical.

intercessisset: because the necessity for protecting Ariobarzanes, from internal as well as external enemies, was a distraction from the Parthian war.

Eusebem: a title very near in meaning to the Roman *agnomen* 'Pius'. 'The Philo-Roman' might not be a popular title in his own kingdom, but it appears on his coins, and had been borne by his grandfather. The importance of Cappadocia to the peace of Asia Minor, the poverty of the king and the instability of the monarchy made this a matter of great concern to the governor of Cilicia.

5. **in consilio:** the governor chooses them, almost certainly including one at least of his *legati*; it made the interview more formal, with the king in the position of a defendant.

commendationis auctoritas: the effectiveness of your instructions.

interitus paterni: we assume from this passage that his father Ariobarzanes II Philopator was murdered; his grandfather, Ariobarzanes I Philorhomaeus, had a chequered career, being four times placed on the throne by the Romans.

6. **Ariarathe:** he eventually succeeded his brother, and took the titles *Eusebes et Philadelphus*.

idem faceret: *sc.* fleret.

compluris: accusative plural.

sollicitatum esse: had been approached and urged to consent.

Those who have access to Joliffe's lurid indictment, *Phases of Corruption in Roman Administration* will find (p. 66) a reconstruction of this conspiracy unfavourable to Ariarathes. Jolliffe also suggests that Ariobarzanes' debt to Pompey was money promised for advancing his interest in the senate, and that Pompey chose Cicero as governor of Cilicia because he knew that he would not embezzle the money.

7. **cohortatus sum:** Cicero always fancied himself as the power behind the throne.

contentionem: they must be frightened rather than actually maltreated.

ex auctoritate: see note on *auctoritas* in 3 above.

8. **nullo postulante:** of your own accord.

Cicero, *ad familiares*, XV. iv. 7–11.

Cicero writes a long letter to Cato, in the hope that he will use his influence to persuade the senate to vote Cicero a triumph. He surveys his strategy during the Parthian scare of the summer of 51 (described in the preceding official despatch), and then gives this account of his December campaign against the hill tribes of the Amanus range.

7. **Antiocheam:** this is the Antioch on the Orontes, the chief town of Syria; if the cavalry were detached from this force, they will have crossed into Cilicia by the Syrian Gates.

cohorte praetoria: the headquarter cohort, which is normally attendant on the commander. In his first year in Gaul, to stimulate their loyalty, Caesar said publicly that he would treat the tenth legion as his *cohors praetoria* (*B.G.* I. 40). It is this official designation which is parodied when the governor's civilian followers are called his *cohors*. Although they are supposed to be his bodyguard, these troops have not gone westwards to meet Cicero, but remained no doubt where Appius had stationed them; Epiphaneia is well placed for blocking the road from either of the two passes of the Amanus.

occidione occisum: were massacred.

aversas: that they had turned their backs on Cappadocia. Cicero at last realises that they are not going to use the difficult northern route.

recessisse: this was the work of Cassius, now proquaestor, before the arrival of Bibulus.

Bibulum: at last.

cur abesset: Cicero is right of course; but the Galatians will have marched some seven hundred miles by the time they get back to Ancyra.

8. **utrique provinciae:** Cilicia and Syria; Cicero now turns from the great crisis to a necessary piece of border warfare.

expedito: in battle order, without heavy equipment; this has nothing to do with the use of light armed troops, the Latin for which is *levis armatura*.

cohortibus: these are legionary cohorts; since at least the time of Marius, the cohort has been the usual tactical unit of manoeuvre of the legion in battle; in the *auxilia* it is also their highest administrative unit.

aliis: dative, governed by *praeesset*; Cicero has all his *legati* with him. Quintus had served with Caesar in Gaul, but

Pomptinus was the most distinguished soldier present (see note on p. 212, *Pomptinum*).

interclusi: since their escape was cut off. We know nothing about these hill villages. In a letter to Atticus (V. xx), Cicero adds that he was saluted as *imperator* by his troops. Perhaps he omits it here because he is afraid that Cato will not approve.

9. **Aras Alexandri**: doubtless the name dates from Alexander's march in 333; we are not far from the battlefield of Issus.

10. **Pindenissum**: it is a pity that we cannot put the scene of Cicero's Christmas victory on the map, but he does not even tell the direction of his march.

ne regibus quidem: there were client kings within the confines of the province: Tarcondimotus, for instance.

fugitivos: usually of runaway slaves; here, probably, of deserters from the army; if they are actually going to join the enemy they are *perfugae* or *transfugae*.

quo facilius: the justification of many Roman expeditions beyond the frontiers, Pompey in the Caucasus, Caesar in Germany and Britain.

vallo et fossa: the same digging process makes both the rampart and the ditch. *fossa* is a continuous ditch surrounding the town to prevent a sortie or a break-out; *vallum* is the rampart associated with it; *agger* is a mound formed by bringing up piles of brushwood, stones or earth, at the point where the attack is to be made, as a platform for artillery or battering rams; *vinei* are mantlets, probably made of brushwood, to protect soldiers attacking the walls; *turres* are small towers from which covering fire can be given, constructed on the *agger*, or, if necessary, on wheels so that they can be pushed up to the walls; *tormenta* is the general word for pieces of artillery.

labore meo: most generals would give credit to the troops.
sumptuve: more will be heard of this consideration for the provincials in Chaps. III and IV.

Quintum fratrem: Marcus had to leave the army, and go first to Tarsus and then back to Laodicea for the assizes. His timetable is set out in the note on p. 220, *Laodiceae*.

11. **nunc velim**: now we come to the purpose of the letter.
admonendum: remind.

praedicatione: open expression of approval.

Chapter III : ADMINISTRATION OF JUSTICE

Cicero, *ad Atticum*, VI. i. 15. (*All the letters in this chapter were written from Cilicia in the years* 51–50 B.C.)

Bibuli: for his appointment to the province of Syria see note on p. 212, *meis et Bibuli*.

exceptionem: this is the part of the edict concerned with the enforcing of contracts. Bibulus is pledged to enforce a contract unless it is in some way defective. Since, according to Atticus, it implicitly condemned one of the parties, it is probable that it excepted contracts in the making of which one of them had acted in bad faith — like the *exceptio doli*, which became part of the Roman praetor's edict (i.e. the praetor would uphold contracts provided they were not made *dolo malo*). It is a sorry commentary on the conduct of Roman businessmen that such an *exceptio* could be considered to be a slur on them.

ordinem nostrum: Atticus was an equestrian; though much richer than many senators, and mixing socially with them, he kept out of politics. Apart from the noble families, the ordinary senators were of no higher class than the equestrians, only that the equestrians had chosen a business instead of a political career. There was, however, some feeling that this was an ignoble choice. It was the non-political Atticus who survived the dangers of the civil wars and married his daughter to the revolutionary leader Agrippa; if Tiberius had died about the year A.D. 20 Atticus would have been the great-grandfather of an emperor.

ἰσοδυναμοῦσαν: having the same effect; this *exceptio* did not specifically refer to the intentions of the parties at the moment of signing the contract.

Q. Muci: for Scaevola's model edict see p. 186, note 14; the eastern districts of Cicero's Cilicia had been part of Scaevola's Asia.

P. f.: Publi fili; it was necessary to be careful in distinguishing the Scaevolas. This is the Pontifex; the Augur was Quinti filius.

EO STARI: to stand by it.

libertatem: in *civitates* which the Romans had declared to be *liberae* the governor had no right to interfere in the local courts; in others it was sensible of him to interfere as little as possible, so that they might feel that they also were free. In Greek cities this was still important.

διαίρεσιν: division; Cicero divided his edict into two sections.

provinciale: things which concern the official administration of the province; the second section deals with matters of private concern only, but which are likely to end up in the courts and for which therefore a statement of policy will be helpful. As with many such classifications, the facts are somewhat recalcitrant; usury, for instance, affects private individuals as well as states or tax collectors.

rationibus: accounts; that Greek cities could mismanage their finances is clear from the letters which the younger Pliny wrote from Bithynia. The object of his mission (A.D. 110 or 111) was to set them straight.

usura: we learn from *Att.* V. xxi. p. 124, that Cicero's edict did not recognise interest rates in excess of 12 per cent.

ἄγραφον: unwritten; we have had two sections of detailed clauses on subjects in which Cilician practice might be different from Roman (laws of inheritance, for instance, may differ greatly). For the rest, Cicero avoids overloading his edict, by stating that he will follow the practice of the urban praetor at Rome. It is to be hoped that the Roman edict was made accessible in the province. It was in ways like this that Roman legal ideas spread throughout the empire, and not only in the previously untutored west.

peregrinis: non-Roman; in this case Greek.

nugatoribus: worthless men. For Roman opinions of Greeks see *ad Q.f.* I. i. 16. p. 148.

αὐτονομίαν: freedom; this is the right to use their own laws, in their own courts (see p. 95, *suae leges redditae*).

Cicero, *ad Atticum*, V. xxi. 9.

Februariis: this is the year 50, and Cicero has been in his province since the previous July.

dedi: *dare* is regularly used of sending a letter.

forum agere: to hold the assizes. *Cibyraticum*, *Apamense*, *etc.* are adjectives agreeing with *forum*.

Laodiceae: evidently this town was now considered to be the capital of cis-Tauric Cilicia, as Tarsus was of the Pedias. It seems quite extraordinary that the Lycaonians should have had to travel some three hundred miles for their justice, especially as the governor had to pass through their territory three times in six months. We are reminded that Sopater, who lived at Halicyae in western Sicily, had to go to Syracuse (*II Verr.* II. 68. p. 116). The rule that a man might not be summoned to appear outside his *forum* loses some of its value if his *forum* can be held as far away as this; though the Cypriots were protected (*Att.* V. xxi. 6. p. 140, a regulation doubtless made by Cato). This inherent improbability has led Tyrell and Purser to believe that only the first three assizes were to be held at Laodicea, and that Cicero will then go to Pamphylia and the others. But this is against the clear meaning of the sentence, and it is highly dangerous, when translating Latin, to force the words to mean what we should like them to mean. In any case, the matter is settled by *Att.* VI. i. 24, where Cicero says that he will be at Laodicea until the Ides of May. As far as we can tell, he never visited Pamphylia. In the previous summer he heard suits as he went eastwards, at Apamea, Synnada, Philomelium and Iconium; but that was a more impromptu affair, since there had not been time since his arrival in the province to organise full-scale assizes; at that time Cicero wrote of his *iurisdictio*, but did not use the phrase *forum agere* (*Att.* V. xx. 1).

Cicero's letters give us a fairly accurate account of his movements during his year of office, and it may help to understand the activities of a provincial governor if we recapitulate them here. (It must be remembered that the Julian calendar was not then in force.)

51	May 5	Left Rome.
	July 31	Arrived at Laodicea; the year begins.
	Aug.	Travelled eastwards, stopping at Colossi, Apamea, Synnada, Philomelium and Iconium.
	Aug. 24	Camp near Iconium.
	Aug. 28	Reviewed troops, then marched eastwards.

	Sept. 20	At Cybistra, in Cappadocia.
	Oct. 3	Arrived at Tarsus.
	Oct. 7	Left Tarsus for Mount Amanus.
	Oct. 11	Battle.
		Camp at Issus; Pindenissa campaign.
	Dec. 17	Capture of Pindenissa.
	Dec. 26	Still at Pindenissa; then back to Tarsus.
50	Jan. 5	Left Tarsus for 'Asia'; Quintus Cicero left in charge of 'Cilicia' and the army.
	Feb. 11	Arrived at Laodicea. Assizes in February, March and perhaps April, covering the whole cis-Tauric province.
	May 15	Left Laodicea for Tarsus.
	June 5	Arrived at Tarsus.
	June 21	*in castris*.
	July 17	Still at Tarsus; then to Laodicea.
	July 30	Left Laodicea; the year ends.
	Nov. 24	Arrived at Brundisium.

κέρας: I will look for a horn for Phemius. In *Att.* VI. i. 13 we learn that he did send it. κέρας is a musical instrument, and Phemius, since he has the name of the minstrel who sang to Odysseus in the palace of Alcinoos, is probably a musical slave or freedman of Atticus. We must suppose that Pamphylian horns were famous, and that Cicero will make enquiries of the Pamphylians who come to Laodicea to the assizes.

redeuntibus: Cicero expects to leave by the way he arrived, travelling the long land route for the fourth time. Appius had left by sea from Tarsus, but Cicero had not enjoyed even his crossing of the Aegean in the previous summer. In fact he did not leave Tarsus until after the middle of the month. From there to Laodicea is about five hundred miles by the main road.

oportet: The normal practice about leaving a province appears to have been as follows: if the senate decided that a province should have a new consular (or praetorian) governor, the available *consulares* (or *praetorii*) drew lots to decide which of them should go to it; the selected man travelled at his leisure, usually in early summer, and the moment he set foot in the province he was the governor. His predecessor had thirty days in which to hand over and leave. Caesar apparently left Spain in 60 in a hurry, without waiting for his successor to arrive, for fear that he might be too late for the consular elections (Suet. *Div. Jul. 18*. It is possible that his successor was deliberately dallying, so that Caesar would be unable to be elected that year; in any case, it was not easy for a man to govern a praetorian province for two years and be elected consul *suo anno*, and many of the most distinguished nobles do not govern a province until after their consulship).

If the senate did not send a successor, then they might instruct the present governor to remain for another year (this is what Cicero was afraid of, and what they had done in Quintus' case; see note on p. 262, *ad Q. f.* I. i.; but they might also authorise him to delegate the province to one of his officers and himself to return to Rome; it is clear from *ad Att.* VI. vi. 3 that this is what they eventually did for Cicero. If the senate did none of these things, it is not clear what ought to happen; probably the governor himself would decide whether to stay or not. When Caesar was in Gaul it was assumed, both in 56 and in 50, that if nothing was done at Rome he would remain.

However, when Cicero wrote this letter, he did not yet know what was going to be decided in his case (he did not know ten days later, when he wrote his next letter to Atticus. VI. i, see § 14). It is a sad commentary on his sense of values that he preferred to leave a consular province to a not very satisfactory quaestor rather than to remain himself. Of course he knew that important things were likely to be happening at Rome very soon.

praefici: if someone was to be left in charge, it would naturally be one of the *legati*; in the end, after some hesitation, he left his new quaestor, a heavy responsibility for a young man of thirty.

Pomptinum: he would also have been suitable (see note on p. 212, *Pomptinum*), but seems to have been in an even greater hurry than Cicero.

Postumia: probably sister of Postumius, who was a friend of Cicero. We do not know why Pomptinus was anxious to see the brother.

Cicero, *II in Verrem*. II. 30–42, 62, 68–75.

30. **hos quaestus**: Cicero has been describing Verres' methods

of extortion by proxy, by which he causes lawsuits to be decided in favour of his friends.

cohorte: it was not illegal for a governor to form his *consilium* from his *cohors*, but, since it could obviously not be really independent of him, it was generally considered to be wrong.

dant: this is the praetor at Rome, the governor in a province.

intercedere: this is true of the provinces, the tribunes' veto being valid only within the first milestone from the city of Rome.

31. **in ea verba:** this is the formula; the same phrase is used of an oath of allegiance: *in verba imperatoris iurare.*

Balbus: a member of the present jury. He had also been a member of the jury which in 74 condemned Oppianicus for murder, and when discussing that case Cicero (*Clu.* 107) speaks highly of his legal knowledge and integrity. Now he is imagining that Balbus is the *unus iudex* in a private suit, and the point is that not even he could avoid giving a verdict which would result in injustice.

SI PARET: this is a parody of a formula, but is typical, according to Cicero, of Verres' administration of the law. Cicero uses the names of jurymen (Servilius and Catulus were also on the panel) to invent a sample of Verrine justice. In this imaginary case, Catulus is claiming land which is in the possession of Servilius. A true formula would read, 'If it appears that the land belongs to Catulus, and if it is not restored to Catulus, condemn Servilius to pay to Catulus the value of the land; if it does not, acquit.' Then justice would be done; the land, or its value, would go to the rightful owner. By altering the names, the praetor, who frames the formula and sends the case to the *iudex*, can compel the *iudex* to award the land or its value to the plaintiff (Catulus) when in fact it belongs to the defendant (Servilius).

EX IURE QUIRITIUM: full freehold possession, of which only Roman citizens were capable. *populus Romanus Quiritium* is the formal title of the Roman people in their civil and religious, as well as political and military capacity. It is used, for instance, according to the patriotic Roman myth, in the solemn vow by which Decius Mus offered his life to the gods if they would give the Roman people the victory over the Latins (Livy, VIII. 9. 340 B.C.).

NEQUE RESTITUETUR: this is the *exceptio*; if the defendant is guilty he can avoid condemnation by restoring the property.

SI NON ACCIPIT: more legal absurdity. Verres is supposed to be addressing a debtor, who is offering to repay a sum smaller than his real debt. '*If he does not accept what you say you owe, bring a charge against him; if he sues you (for the remainder of the debt), put him in prison.*' With Verres' assistance, the debtor will avoid some at least of the repayment.

iudicabant: this word is supplied by the editor of the *OCT*; it, or a word like it, is clearly necessary. The *lex Rupilia* (see below) ordained Sicilian jurors for Sicilian disputes, Roman for Roman; Verres has reversed this.

32. **domi:** in the city to which both parties belong.

Rupili: after the end of the slave war in 131 the island was reorganised by P. Rupilius (cos. 132), who was assisted by the customary commission of ten senators. He gave his name to the *lex provinciae* of Sicily.

vocant: at Rome these provincial charters were instituted by decrees of the senate, and were not technically laws; the provincials would regard them as *leges datae*.

privatus: it is against the natural meaning of the Latin to assume that these cases must be between an individual and a *civitas* other than his own. But if we do not, a difficulty arises in the case of Heraclius (38, below). Each party has the right to reject a senate proposed by the other, and if this happens the praetor appoints one himself.

civis Romanus: this is an important regulation, since provincials were likely to complain that Roman citizens received preferential treatment; that there were in fact such complaints is shown by the decree of Augustus in Cyrene (p. 166).

conventu: this official phrase seems to imply legal recognition of a social fact. In most of the larger cities of Sicily there would be likely to be such a *conventus*.

decumanos: tithe collectors; see Chap. IV.

Hieronicam: originally the law of Hiero's kingdom of Syracuse (see map on p. 30). The Romans applied it throughout the island. Its inspiration was Greek, and it combined detailed accuracy with equity in a way new to the Romans. The king was Hiero II, who died in 215 after a reign of over fifty years.

33. **praeconem:** these are all members of Verres' *cohors*.

COGNITURUM: Verres is not saying that he will rehear the original case, which he has no right to do, but that he will hear a criminal case against the *iudex* who will be punished for having given a wrong verdict. *IUDICASSET* and *COGNOS-SET* are for original future perfects.

34. **negotiatoribus:** traders who are not registered as members of the *conventus*, perhaps because they were not permanently resident; but it is not clear why they should be expected to serve on the juries. They were *propositi*, not *selecti* — perhaps volunteers in places where the resident *conventus* was small. But there may be a distinction here which we do not understand.

copia: this abundance of jurymen was supplied by the staff; the staff, not of Scaevola, but of Verres. For Scaevola's reputation as a governor see p. 186, note 14.

sicubi videtis: in whatever place you find this edict, I will show you that that senate has given a verdict contrary to its real feelings.

datus: appointed to hear a case.

sortitio: juries were appointed by lot from those qualified to serve.

Hieronica: courts which heard controversial suits which arose out of the *lex Hieronica* were undermined by Verres.

uno nomine: by this one declaration.

35. **Hieronis:** no connection is claimed with the old Syracusan royal family; *domi nobilis* is a favourite phrase of Cicero to describe the local gentry outside Rome — he was one himself. The Heraclii were certainly very wealthy, to judge from the value of this inheritance.

triciens: the usual abbreviation for *triciens centena milia*, HS standing for the genitive *nummum sestertium* (which was always written for *nummorum sestertiorum*). *HS* itself is *IIS nummus*, (*S, semis*), the 'two-and-a-half coin', since it was a quarter of a denarius and the denarius was originally equivalent to ten asses. Late in the second century (in *Num. Chron. 1934* Mattingly argues for 122 B.C.), when the denarius was made equivalent to sixteen asses and the sesterce therefore to four, the name remained unaltered. When written in figures, *triciens* is usually $\boxed{\text{XXX}}$; the distributive numeral *tricena* would stand for *tricena milia sestertium*, which in figures is usually $\overline{\text{XXX}}$ (it is not uncommon, however, for these lines to be omitted: *e.g.* in II. 93. p. 156, *HS D* is obviously not just 500 sesterces; see also II. 69. p. 117). *Triginta sestertii* is thirty.

stragulae vestis: soft furnishings, not clothes.

36. **adfines:** especially used of relatives by marriage; through their wives Verres had become one of the family.

refertam: if this text is correct *rem* must be the property; *domum refertam* has been suggested, and may well be the correct reading.

neminem: the provincial who had no friends at Rome was at the mercy of the governor. The Marcelli who were consuls in 51, 50, 49, were not yet old enough to be important, and the previous generation of the family was less distinguished. In any case, they could be invoked on both sides in a dispute between Sicilians. However, when Heraclius went to Rome he did not do so badly after all (see 62 below, *commendati*).

deberet: there was a clause in the will which stated that in order to inherit he must put up the statues.

palaestritae: the officials in charge of the *palaestra*.

commissam: if the gift to Heraclius failed, the money would go to them.

37. **auctor est:** *auctoritas* is the unofficial (or semi-official) exercise of power.

dica: a law suit; Syracuse was a Greek city, and Cicero, who knew the island, uses the Greek word.

nossent: the sort of people who knew Verres.

sortiturum: the beginning of the Syracusan assizes, since the first act in a case is to select the jury by casting lots. So far there is no irregularity.

diebus xxx: thirty days must elapse between summons and hearing. This was the normal interval at Rome, though it could be longer, and Cicero had been granted a hundred and ten to collect the evidence against Verres.

alteram: the second assizes. Heraclius expected Verres to hold the first assizes as planned, and then the court would not be sitting at Syracuse again for perhaps six months; by that time there might be a change of governor. Verres foiled him by putting off the assizes altogether until the first day on which his case could be heard.

Q. Arrium: the praetor of 72; he was to have succeeded Verres, but was kept in Italy by the slave war. He would normally have taken over in the spring of 71.

38. aequo iure: the point at issue is who are the judges to be. Heraclius is claiming that the *palaestritae* are the *populus Syracusanus*, in which case this is *populus a privato* (see 32 above); the difficulty is that in that case Verres should appoint a neutral senate, and the narrative shows that this was never considered. If in 32 *populus a privato* does refer to a *different* civitas, then it is not relevant to this case, and we do not know what jury Heraclius was asking for. The *palaestritae* ask for judges who are individual Sicilians from anywhere in the assize area, chosen by Verres, a request which we are told was contrary to the *lex Rupilia*. Their legal grounds are not clear, and it may be that Cicero deliberately suppressed them because they had some validity. Verres and his confederates were not usually without ingenuity.

convenirent: an assize district might contain a number of cities.

39. urbana: Verres had been *praetor urbanus* in 74. The first book of this indictment (*II Verr.* I) is an attack on his administration in that year.

Chelidone: Verres' relations with her during his praetorship are the subject of occasional hints. By the time he composed the second Philippic Cicero could do much better than this.

non neminem: it is also true that some men when away from Rome and in responsible positions turned out much better than might have been expected.

consules: in the Sicilian slave war of 104–1 Roman consuls had operated in the island; the last of them, the younger Aquilius, was prosecuted for maladministration but acquitted.

quinque: a number frequently employed for *recuperatores*, who often heard cases in the provinces which at Rome would go before a *unus iudex*. Cicero calls these men *iudices*, but he may be speaking loosely. We do not know whether the difference between the five appointed here and the three in 42 below implies any difference of procedure. *Recuperatores* may be three or five in number.

40. **imperatoris**: Rupilius.

41. **de amicorum sententia**: a very clever sentence; it prevents us from asking the otherwise obvious question, why did Heraclius run away? *Itaque* does the same. It turned out to be an unwise decision, as well as not a very brave one; even Cicero does not say that his life was in danger. The same words are used of Sthenius (II. 91. p. 156).

instituto suo: his usual custom.

horam decimam: very late in the day; at Rome a senator would be home to dinner by then.

42. **tris**: see on *quinque* in 39 above.

62. **Epicrates**: Cicero has just described the case of Epicrates of Bidis, whose property also Verres handed over to the local authority, by a similar trick.

Romam: influence at Rome was the provincial's best hope.

barba: not going to the barber was a mark of mourning.

Metellus: Verres' successor in Sicily; he was praetor in 71, and eventually consul in 68.

commendati: they had found friends in Rome to recommend them to the care of the new governor. We have examples of such recommendations in *ad fam*. XII. xxi. p. 143, and XIII. ix. p. 143.

68. **capitalium**: we now come to the administration of criminal law; the governor hears the case himself and pronounces judgement, assisted by a consilium of qualified advisers, chosen by himself.

Halicyensis: Halicyae was a city of western Sicily, not far from Lilybaeum. It was a *civitas libera* (III. 13. p. 128), but Sopater was tried on a capital charge at Syracuse by the Roman governor, both by Verres and his predecessor, and Cicero does not claim that that was illegal. In Chap. I it is argued that the free cities were not really free, and this case supports the argument.

Sacerdotem: Verres' predecessor as governor of Sicily.

detulerunt: to put a man's name on the list was the technical term for instituting a prosecution. From this verb was derived the ill-omened noun *delator*.

Syracusis: it seems a long way for him to be summoned, especially as we learn from V. 140, that Verres did at least once hold an assize at Lilybaeum. Livy (XXXI. 29) knew of assizes held at Syracuse, Messana and Lilybaeum. Compare Cicero's assizes at Laodicea (p. 220, *Laodiceae*).

69. **splendidus:** see note on p. 233, *splendidissimo*.

priore: in the first hearing; after the short speeches of the *actio prima*, Cicero had produced some of his witnesses.

HS LXXX: this must be eighty thousand, i.e. *octogena* (see note on p. 225, *triciens*); eighty sesterces would be a paltry sum.

70. **quid . . . faciendum:** two of the MSS omit these words; a copyist could have added them, remembering what he had copied in the previous chapter, and *videret* is more sinister without them. In general, however, it was a dictum of Professor Clark that in copying a manuscript 'it is easier to omit than to invent'.

conventu: this is the local *conventus civium Romanorum*, from whom the governor chose his *consilium*. These men need not *all* have been on Sacerdos' *consilium*.

71. **solebant:** it seems that, like the modern bench of magistrates, some turn up more often than others. This was a good attendance (*frequentes*).

operam dare: that he should go and get on with a private suit for which he was the *iudex*.

adesse: to give support by being present in court.

cohorte: it was considered wrong for the governor to have only members of his staff on his *consilium*.

72. **Graeculo:** the diminutive is contemptuous; Verres is talking as one Roman to another.

me quoque: Minucius was prepared to walk out on his client.

73. **in se:** against Verres.

negotiaretur: 'since he was not prepared, even for business purposes, to abandon his rights, and thought it wrong to advance his interests in the province by sacrificing his liberty.'

praeter Siculos: they were more at the governor's mercy.

This incident shows, more clearly than any theoretical discussion, the difference in status between Roman citizens and provincials: the Romans could boycott proceedings of the governor. Verres was naturally in a dilemma.

74. **conventus:** the court was crowded; this is not the *conventus civium Romanorum*.

75. **unus et alter:** one or two.

indicta: no speech was made for the defence.

scribae: Verres' *consilium* now consisted of three members of his staff.

Cicero, *II in Verrem*, III. 25–28.

25. **edictum:** this is a matter of administrative law. Verres is giving the tax collectors privileges not open to private citizens. Normally, when a man claims that another owes him money and will not pay it in full, he must first go to law to establish his claim. Only then can action be taken to compel payment. Verres is laying down the principle that when the tax-collector makes his demand, the tax-payer must first pay whatever is demanded, and only when this has been done will the court consider the validity of the claim. It is possible of course to say that in the end the result will be the same, but by this method the collector, instead of being a *petitor* who has to establish his right to make the demand, becomes the man in possession, and the tax-payer has the more difficult task of compelling him to make restitution. According to Cicero, it was a device to exact more, but the object may have been to ensure punctuality of payment; if the farmers were putting off paying until the last possible moment, and fighting every case in the courts, this would be an effective counter-measure; but naturally we have no evidence on this point.

edidisset: the tax-collectors published an official list.

dato: this form of the imperative is often used after a clause which contains a future perfect; a 'delayed imperative'. This is a dialogue between Verres and a farmer.

26. **professionem:** a public and official declaration; here it is the formula for taxation, like the instructions on which the modern Notice of Assessment is prepared. The clerk reads the central part of the document, which states the tax-payer's

liability to pay; on the same document (*codex*) is the statement of his procedure if he thinks he has been unjustly assessed.

negat: Cicero is imagining Verres' reaction; the speech was never delivered in court. It was his practice to publish afterwards speeches which he wanted to be on record, whether they had actually been delivered or not. We know that he circulated a copy of his *consulares oratiunculae*, the speeches of his consulship.

octuplum: if the tax-collector lost the case, he had to make restitution of eight times the disputed sum (i.e. eight times the difference between his demand and the true figure). It seems a large enough penalty; the difficulty was to enforce it.

27. **vectigalibus:** any payment to the state; it may include tithes, customs dues, rents of public lands; in Italy at this time there were still public lands, mainly in Campania, customs dues and the manumission tax.

pignerator: if a man is owed money and is not paid, he takes the case to court (as a *petitor*), and, if the court agrees, an order is made that the money shall be paid. The man who owes it then has a statutory time in which to pay up (in the Twelve Tables it was thirty days); if by then he has not paid, further action can be taken. If it is an individual to whom the money is owed, that individual has to take the debtor before a magistrate (this is *manus iniectio*) who uses his power of *coercitio* to compel payment. But if the money is due to a public company — and this includes the tax-collectors — they have a quicker way of getting it: without having to go to the magistrate again, they can take possession of part of the man's property (*pignoris capio*), and if he still does not pay they can sell it. It is this process which is indicated by the word *pignerator*. This puts the company in a better position than an ordinary plaintiff for actually extracting the money, but they must still go to law in the first place to establish their right to it. When the case *first* comes before the court the company is *petitor*, not *possessor*. It is therefore different from Verres' procedure, under which they could demand the money before they had proved their right. We remember that the emperor Claudius, a bureaucrat but not a tyrant, gave his procurators the power to act as judges in their own cases (Tac. *A.* XII. 60).

honestissimo: Roman literature, from Plautus to Vergil, is full of the doctrine that there is something especially moral about living on a farm. The early Romans had been a farming people, and this is part of the backward-looking notion which puts the golden age in the distant past.

integra: that the case should go to court first, before anything has been done.

digito: the *publicanus* had gained the right to collect the taxes by bidding at the auction; this tells us something about the conduct of Roman auctions.

singulis: the small farmer, with only one plough. In III. 120 Cicero has figures read out to show that during Verres' three years of office the number of farmers in four Sicilian states fell from 773 to 318. We can probably trust the figures, since the *lex Hieronica* demanded exact documentation; whether Cicero is right that the cause was extortionate collection of the tithe we cannot check, but it looks black for Verres.

Larem: according to Warde Fowler (*Religious Experience of the Roman People*, p. 77), the Lar was essentially the god of a farming household, worshipped by all members of the *familia*.

Syracusas: see note on p. 229, *Syracusis*.

28. **exspecto:** the speaker must be a Sicilian in the audience at the imaginary trial.

reicere: Verres is giving orders that the case shall proceed; the first thing is to select the judges, by a process in which the parties have the right to reject a certain number of those whom the lot selects.

decurias scribamus: the word *decuria* is used of the whole list of men liable to serve on a jury. (At Rome after the year 70 the three orders were enrolled in three separate decuriae; see p. 194, note 23.) The plaintiff and his counsel are suggesting that they begin by writing down the names of the men who are available. Verres then shows that the whole proceeding is a farce by limiting them to members of his staff. This story is very effective in exposing the trickery of Verres, until we remember that it is wholly imaginary — even Cicero does not say that it ever actually happened.

iniquos: this might well be true.

Cicero, *II in Verrem*, V. 160–163.

160. **Consanus:** presumably from either Cossa in Etruria or Compsa in Samnium.

illo numero: Cicero has said that Verres sent so many Romans to penal servitude in the Syracusan quarries that the quarries became a *domicilium civium Romanorum*; not a very likely story.

Messanae: in the third century bands of ex-mercenaries of the Syracusan tyrant Agathocles settled in Messana and called themselves *Mamertines* (children of Mars); in Cicero's day the town is called *Messana*, its people *Mamertini*. They were a *civitas foederata*, but collaborated with Verres; he did not call upon them to provide the one warship which they were obliged by their treaty to supply when required, and they were the only city which on his departure sent an embassy to Rome in his honour.

praetorio: the governor's headquarters.

161. **meruisse:** Gavius will have served in a legion, and that fact is a guarantee of citizenship; Raecius was probably his *tribunus militum*, and as such would have been already an equestrian; but he might have been a centurion, who had subsequently become an equestrian.

splendidissimo: this word is especially used of Roman equestrians, or of provincials who, being *domi nobiles*, were of equivalent dignity. The corresponding word used for senators, made popular by Cicero, was *amplissimus*.

fugitivorum: the followers of Spartacus; the slave revolt in Italy was started by escaping gladiators in 73 and was not finally crushed until 71. In 73 they had been masters of most of southern Italy, and in 72, when they marched southwards again, they may have been intending to cross into Sicily. It is possible that Verres should be given some credit for preventing this, but Appian (*B.C.* I. 118) says nothing of how they failed in this, and of course Cicero would not. Verres was right to be on the alert, and this visit to Messana may have been connected with this; a full account of what happened in western Sicily during the war in Italy might throw a different light on the whole affair. It is most unlikely that a Roman citizen would

have been in league with the slaves, but for all we know Verres
may have denied that Gavius was a citizen.

162. **civis Romanus:** the keeping of law and order in the
provinces depended on the governor's *imperium*, and for non-
citizens there was no limit to the punishment he could inflict.
Citizens, however, had some protection. Against capital
sentences, and eventually also against corporal punishment and
even against fines above a certain amount, they could appeal
to the Roman people. Originally, this appeal, like the tribunes'
veto, was only valid in Rome, but in the second century, when
Romans began to settle abroad, it was gradually extended.
The details of the extension are obscure; Cicero, in a short
survey of the *provocatio* (*Rep.* II. 54) says that there were three
leges Porciae, the work of three different men. On the basis of
general probability and such evidence as there is, A. H.
Macdonald suggests (*JRS* (1944), p. 19) the following scheme:

199   (tribunate of P. Porcius Laeca): *provocatio* (against
      capital sentences) extended to citizens in Italy and
      the provinces.

198   (praetorship of M. Porcius Cato): *provocatio* allowed
      against scourging.

154   (consulship of L. Porcius Cato): *provocatio* allowed
      against execution on active service.

If this is correct, a combination of the first two *leges Porciae*
should have protected Gavius.

crux: a punishment normally reserved for slaves. Verres is
punishing Gavius for having been concerned in the revolt of
Spartacus, like the six thousand slaves whom Crassus crucified
along the Appian Way.

pestem: if the text is sound, this must refer to Verres.

163. **lex Porcia:** see note on *civis Romanus* above; Cicero
may be making a mistake in speaking of one *lex Porcia* and
more than one *lex Sempronia*. C. Gracchus passed a *lex
Sempronia*: *ne de capite civium Romanorum iniussu vestro
iudicaretur* (Cic. *Rab. Perd.* 12, where it is coupled with *Porcia
lex*). This had a specific purpose: after the death of Tiberius
Gracchus, the senate had ordered the consuls to hold a special
trial of his supporters, and they had disregarded the right of
appeal. C. Gracchus' law reaffirmed this right, and as a result

of it Popillius, one of the consuls, went into exile to avoid trial. (Gracchus' legislation on this subject is discussed by Ursula Ewins in *JRS* (1960), pp. 94 foll.).

tribunicia: this is not really relevant, since the tribunes' power of veto still extended no further than the first milestone from Rome. But its original purpose was to curb the power of magistrates. Nor is it likely that Sulla took from them the right to protect citizens, since according to Cicero's own phrase he left them the *potestas auxilii ferendi* (*Leg.* III. 9. Nor was Palicanus inactive in December 72, see p. 159). In the seventies the restoration of the full powers of the tribunes has been one of the chief subjects of popular agitation (*desiderata*), culminating in full reinstatement by Pompey early in the year of Verres' trial.

aliquando: at long last.

fascis: the bundle of rods carried by the governor's lictors; except when the magistrate is in Rome, each bundle is surmounted by an axe, a symbol of the power of life and death (a power which, over Roman citizens, they no longer have).

Cicero, *ad Atticum*, V. xxi. 10–12, VI. i. 3–7.

V. xxi. 10. **de Bruto**: this is a long story; the people of Salamis in Cyprus had wanted to borrow money in Rome, which was forbidden by a *lex Gabinia*. Brutus had an interest in the island, having been there in 58 to help his uncle, Cato, to organise it as part of the empire; his influence procured for the intending lenders an exemption from this law. So the money was lent. The creditors then realised that the law still took away their right to sue for the recovery of the money if that should prove necessary. A second *privilegium* restored this right. Cicero's predecessor, Appius Claudius, had been trying to force the Salaminians to pay up, but without success, and the arrears of interest are mounting. Brutus has asked Cicero to help, but has still not told him that he himself is the creditor. Perhaps there was still some reluctance on the part of senators to admit that they were making money in this way. Usury had once upon a time been forbidden to any Roman, but there was no special bar to senators, so that when commercial progress made moneylending essential there was no law to keep them out of it. They could not become merchants on their own, because of the *leges Claudiae*, but by lending money they could have some part, on a preference share basis, of the growing affluence of the business world. Still, it did not accord well with the *dignitas* of the Roman senator. (I have discussed some consequences of this in *Greece and Rome*, 1962.)

We can reconstruct, with some degree of probability, the history of this loan; the money had been borrowed in Feb. 56 (February was the month when provincial representatives were most likely to be in Rome); periodically thereafter, probably each February, the account was rendered, deducting what had been paid and adding in the interest, and a new agreement was made for the next year. This was done in Feb. 52, when the total indebtedness was 85 talents. During these four years the interest had been calculated at 48 per cent, the rate stated in the contract, the governors being Lentulus Spinther and Appius Claudius. After this no further payments were made, and in 51 no new contract was negotiated. The Salaminians were clearly defaulting, and Scaptius was given his military rank. By the beginning of January, when Cicero heard the case, twenty-two months had elapsed, by which time 85 talents would have become 199 at compound interest of 48 per cent, or 106 at 12 per cent. Cicero is only adjudicating the interest to be charged since the last contract in 52, but already this huge discrepancy has developed. Unfortunately we cannot calculate the amount of the original loan, since we do not know how much the Salaminians paid in the first few years. Nor are we told the purpose for which they borrowed the money.

ex Cypro: Cyprus was part of the province of Cilicia; Cicero did not visit the island himself, but did send a representative there to hear lawsuits (see p. 140, and notes on p. 253, *cives Romani* and *evocari*).

praefecturam: the rank of *praefectus cohortis*, so that he can have the use of official status and troops to enforce a private claim.

petenti: Pompey, who had large financial interests in the east, had asked for a similar rank to be given to Sextus Statius; Cicero had refused. Torquatus similarly for M. Laenius.

turmas: squadrons of cavalry; these are allied contingents, but part of the Roman army.

vexabat: Scaptius still had the troops.

11. **praestarem:** keep my promise.

Tarsum: the chief town of Cilicia Pedias; Appius had been holding an assize there when Cicero reached Laodicea. The Salaminians could not be compelled to attend there, but are eager to settle their debt on the terms of Cicero's edict.

a me: at my expense.

praetori: the word is frequently used of a provincial governor, whatever his rank.

nomine: account.

vectigali praetorio: the requisitions which the governor could make in the province.

translaticio: the part of the edict which Cicero had taken over from his predecessor.

centesimas: since the Romans reckoned their interest monthly, this is equivalent to 12 per cent in our idiom; *quaternas* is 48 per cent.

anniversario: with compound interest on a yearly basis: at the end of the year, not at the end of each month, if the interest has not been paid, it is added to the principal for the calculation of future interest.

Lentulo Philippoque: 56 B.C.

12. **versuram:** this word should mean the borrowing of money in order to pay off a debt; we are no nearer to knowing what they wanted money for in the first place.

lex Gabinia: dating from the tribunate of Gabinius in 67. The legislation of that year is well described by Last in *CAH* IX, pp. 341–5.

quaternis: doubtless the fact that it was illegal enabled them to push up the rate of interest.

fraudi: this is the usual word for a crime in legal language.

non ut alio: some such phrase is clearly necessary; the creditors can now sue for the return of their money, but are not exempt from the normal provisions of the law, among which, in Cilicia, is the limit on the rates of interest. Obviously Appius had taken the opposite view.

Graecis: Greek was the language of business in the eastern

Mediterranean, and the word *Greek* is used loosely; this is not a statement about their nationality.

in fano: the debt would then be discharged, whether Scaptius accepted the money or not.

contentus erat: since Scaptius was *not* content, this reading cannot be right. The rest of the sentence seems genuine, and it may be that we should read *contentus non erat.* **bono nomine:** either 'to which he had a good claim' or 'which he had a good chance of receiving'.

VI. i. 3. **ilico:** quickly; Atticus might think he was being blamed for having taken Brutus' side.

libellum: we begin to get some idea of the ramifications of *gratia.*

Ariobarzane: king of Cappadocia; his grandfather had been restored to the throne by Pompey.

mecum: see p. 104.

procuratoribus: Pompey's agents; compare *procurabant* below. Under the empire, *procurator* is the title of the equestrian civil servant. We see again how near Pompey was to being the first emperor. He was one of the richest men of the time; the family fortunes, based on land in Picenum, were very great, and his profits from triumphs in three continents exceeded anything Rome had yet seen. His financial stake in Asia Minor dated from his Mithridatic command. **sescentis:** hundreds'.

putatur: this is the local rumour in Cilicia, understandable if the Parthian danger is being exaggerated. Few at Rome expected it, and Pompey had other preoccupations.

XXXIII: we do not know the rate of interest, but thirty-three talents a month indicates a huge loan; no wonder that repayment on this scale was crippling the king's finances.

tributis: for *tributum* and *vectigal* see note on p. 239, *vectigalium.*

sorte: the principal; there seems to be little chance that Pompey will recover his money. However, the investment was not wasted — Ariobarzanes fought for Pompey in the civil war. Pompey is enlarging his *clientela* rather than augmenting his income.

solida: hard cash.

solvit: *sc*. Ariobarzanes.

Appi instituto: Cicero's predecessor had done his best for the king — or for Pompey.

4. **Deiotarus:** king of Galatia. Brutus does not neglect any means of persuasion.

non habere: had no resources.

tutela: the governor of Cilicia was expected to look after the king.

Glabrione: he was a grandson of Q. Mucius Scaevola, and when he was in debt his grandfather would not let the money-lenders be paid in full.

fenus et impendium: interest and expenses; if these were exorbitant Scaevola might have refused to pay them. The word *fenus* can mean capital lent on interest, but it is less likely that Scaevola could have cancelled that — or that Cicero would want to disappoint Brutus to that extent. In Brutus' Cypriot loan it was the interest, not the principal, which he reduced.

M. Scaptio: not the Scaptius of the Cypriot affair. Brutus' request seems to us quite scandalous, and Cicero's excuse, that these men were operating in Cappadocia, not Cilicia, is weak. Cappadocia was under his care, and in any case, if he gives a commission he cannot escape the responsibility for it.

sic agere ut: made a bargain that.

Chapte. IV: TAXATION AND FINANCE
Cicero, *II in Verrem*, III. 11–15, 18–20, 147–148, 163, 188–197.

12. **tripertita:** of the following extracts, the first three deal with the tithe, the fourth (163) with *frumentum emptum*, the last (188–197) with *frumentum aestimatum*.

vectigalium: the normal usage of these words appears to be as follows: *vectigal* is the most general word for public revenue; it includes the payment of taxes in kind, and is therefore used for tithes; *stipendium* is payment in money. The whole field of taxation is included in the contemptuous description of Hannibal in Livy XXI. 41, *vectigalis stipendiariusque populi Romani*. *Stipendium* had other meanings — military pay and military service — and in this sense of fixed taxation it was often replaced by *tributum*, and we find *tributum* (for which the adjective is *stipendiarius*) as the opposite of *vectigal*; an instance of this is Cicero's description of Ariobarzanes' revenue (p. 126). In Caes. *B.C.* III. 32, 'head-taxes' are *tributa* both because they were payable in money and because they did not vary with the value of the head (see note on p. 250, ἐπικεφάλια). *Vectigalium* is here an adjective.

plerisque: in Africa there were large estates of *ager publicus populi Romani*, including the former municipal territory of the city of Carthage.   There were also a number of free cities in Africa. Cicero here speaks of the remainder of the province.

13. **perpaucae**: if *is ager* means the tenancy of the land, then the Roman people are still the owners, and *redditus* means presumably that they did not evict the sitting tenants; if *is ager* is the right to collect the taxes, then the ownership has been entirely restored to the cities.

foederatae: Messana (this is the *civitas Mamertina*, see note on p. 233, *Messanae*) had made a treaty with Rome at the beginning of the first Punic war, Tauromenium (Taormina), which was then in the kingdom of Hiero, not until the second. In V. 133, Cicero mentions a third *civitas foederata*, Netum in Southern Sicily; presumably he forgot it at this moment.   The names of the other cities are Centuripa, Halaesa, Segesta, Halicyae, Panhormus (or Panormus, this is Palermo).

14. **certo tempore**: it was important to wait until it was possible to estimate the quality of the harvest.

in Sicilia: in fact the auctions were held at Syracuse, a separate auction for the tithe of each *civitas*.

15. **iis**: the Sicilians.

convellere: so in 19 Cicero says to Verres '*totam legem Hieronicam sustulisti*'; in fact, what Verres' irregularities seem to have amounted to (and Cicero will not have left anything out) are as follows:

(i) He rigged the auctions so that the taxes should be collected by his friends — particularly Apronius.

(ii) If the farmer disputed the amount due, he had first to pay what the collector asked, and then go to law to recover the excess; if he was successful at law, the collector had to pay eightfold restitution.

(iii) By two other edicts he compelled the farmers to pay punctually.

(iv) He allowed the tax-collector to summons a farmer to appear at a distant court. This and the edicts mentioned in (iii) were inventions of his last year.

(v) He ordered the farmers to make declarations of the acres they had sown. This is represented by Cicero as the invention of an additional form, so that the farmers could be punished for not filling it in correctly; it probably looked like that to the farmers — farmers in all ages resent filling in forms — but that can hardly be the whole truth.

(vi) By his control of the courts, mainly by threats that he would use his own staff as *recuperatores* in order to obtain a conviction, and would then inflict corporal or capital punishment, he assisted Apronius in collecting much more than the law allowed. This is the main body of the accusation, as far as the tithe is concerned, and it is supported by numerous instances; in some cases physical violence was actually used. The difference between the bid at the auction, which was the amount actually sent to Rome, and the total collected, was scandalously large — sometimes more than 100 per cent — and the bulk of the excess went to Verres. It is the fact that he himself profited by it which makes it a proper case for the court *de rebus repetundis*.

The subject of this chapter is Roman taxation, not the exactions of Verres; those interested in criminology will find a choice selection in sections 53–57, 61–63, 67–69.

18. **consulibus:** they were consuls in 75. When there were no censors, public contracts were handled by the consuls; the fact that after Sulla there were no censors until the year 70 should not therefore be used as evidence that he abolished the auction of the Asiatic taxes; these consuls could perfectly well have let out that contract. Both in 80 and in 75 the consuls let out contracts for the repair of temples in Rome (*II Verr.* I. 130).

minutarum: vegetables.

quaestores: there were two in Sicily, but the corn tithes at least were all auctioned at Syracuse; in Verres' administration Cicero does not give the impression that the quaestors had much to do with it all. In 75 he was himself quaestor at Lilybaeum.

Romae: it is not clear why these contracts should be dealt with at Rome, while the much more valuable corn tithe was not disturbed.

adderent: the consuls have passed the law and the auction is being held at Rome.

neque tamen: the amendments suggested were not unreasonable in themselves.

Sthenius: for his history see p. 153. **hospes:** the jury have already heard what that friendship was worth to Sthenius.

causam: this seems to have developed almost into a lawsuit; the consuls, aided by a *consilium* of experts, hearing both sides and pronouncing their decision, in which they reject the request of the *publicani*.

19. **amplificatione:** although it would have brought in a greater revenue.

atque adeo: or rather.

exitio: elsewhere Cicero admits that under Verres the tithe revenue was increased, but says that his exactions, by impoverishing the farmers, would reduce the future yield.

20. **segetibus:** in the cornfield. Verres' edict demanding a return of crops sown suggests that there were in fact possibilities of evasion here (see note on *convellere* above).

Siculum: a Sicilian Greek; Roman opinions of Greeks are discussed on p. 263.

147. **Leontini:** see map on p. 30.

magno: a few words, such as *magnus, maximus, plurimus*, are used in the ablative for buying (and selling), in the genitive for valuing; some, like *plus, minus*, in the genitive for both; exact sums of money always in the ablative.

reliquas: has not left the farmers the means of paying future tithes.

non ... ita est: by paying a higher price the *publicanus* does not buy the right to collect a larger amount from the farmer.

148. **pro portione:** proportionately to their harvest.

tritici: of wheat; the contractor (in this case Apronius) guaranteed to deliver to the government 216,000 modii of wheat. The phraseology is the same as for sesterces: see note on p. 225, *triciens*.

doceo: Cicero goes on to say that a company headed by a Roman equestrian, Q. Minucius, had been prepared to offer 30,000 *modii* more for the Leontine tithe than Apronius had paid; Verres' defence being that Minucius' offer was made too late.

Alba: it occurred to Cicero to use the name of Aemilius Alba as a typical biased judge because he has just been describing how Alba had been saying in the market that Verres had saved himself by bribing the jury.

163. **empto:** in the mid-seventies there was a shortage of corn in Rome, and in 73 a law was made authorising a distribution. The Sicilian tithe was not now sufficient for all the needs of the state, so it was decided to buy further corn from the Sicilian farmers with public money. The price was fixed by the senate, and evidently the farmers could not refuse.

Terentia et Cassia: the consuls of 73 were C. Cassius Longinus and M. Terentius Varro Lucullus; it seems to have been the senate's decision rather than theirs. Verres went to Sicily in 73, and was the first governor to administer this law. Licinius Macer, tribune in 73, describes it in contemptuous terms as an attempt to buy the loyalty of the people with five *modii* of corn, 'which is no better than prison rations' (Sall. *Or. Macr.* 19). But the senators should rather be given some credit because when they saw the need they did themselves what they had abused Gracchus and Saturninus for doing.

The history of the corn laws between Gracchus and Clodius is very uncertain, and almost every stage involves controversies which can not be argued here. In general the truth seems to be that the public sale of corn at a fixed price was begun by Gracchus in 123, abolished by a tribune Octavius in 119, restored by Saturninus in 103, abolished by Sulla, restored again by the senate in 73 (laws on the subject by the younger

Drusus in 91 and Lepidus in 78 were immediately repealed).
As to price, Gracchus made it 6⅓ asses per *modius*, Saturninus
the same (this involves a textual emendation, but an easy one);
the price in 73 we do not know. The amount a man could buy
from this source was limited in 73 to five *modii* a month,
enough to make about two 1¾ lb. loaves of bread a day. As to
the number of recipients, Clodius certainly limited it to the
poor, and, though this has been disputed, it is likely that there
was always some limit. To the numbers in 73 we have a clue
in this section: the extra corn brought in by the *frumentum
emptum* would provide five *modii* per month for about 73,000
people. However in III. 72 we find a much lower figure: there
Cicero calls the amount paid by Agyra (198,000 *modii*) *plebis
Romanae prope menstrua cibaria*; this can hardly mean anything but 'nearly the monthly ration of the Roman people',
and implies about 40,000 recipients. We must allow for an
orator's rhetoric, and should probably prefer the higher figure.
Ten years after Clodius, Caesar found 320,000 recipients, and
reduced the number to 150,000.

Whatever the details, from the time of Gracchus there were
men in Rome who believed that it was the duty of the government not to let the people starve. As would happen in any
state, this got mixed up in party politics, until what had once
been heresy became orthodox. On p. 189 it is argued that
Clodius' free corn (which was continued by Augustus) was no
more undesirable than modern forms of national assistance.
At the growing end, which directly concerns the provinces, the
more assured and steady market at Rome should benefit the
farmers of Sicily, provided that the official price was reasonable
(which it was), and the collection fair (which for the first year or
two it unfortunately was not).

unum decumanum: the editor of O.C.T. suggests *unum
decumarum alterarum, alterum quod praeterea* . . . , which is
much clearer, and could easily have been corrupted. The
simplest thing was to use the existing machinery of collection.
It seems that this large order put up the market price, so that
they had to pay more for the additional quantity.

aequaliter: the same word is used of Sulla's exactions in
Asia (*ad Q.f.* I. i. 33. p. 150); this makes Tenney Frank's

emendation *aequabiliter* less probable in spite of *II Verr*. V. 52, *aequabiliter emi*. In either case it cannot mean that each *civitas* paid the same amount, but that the load was distributed fairly, not equally. Elsewhere (*Flacc*. 32) Cicero says that Sulla's *descriptio* was made *pro portione*.

decernebatur: unless it was authorised by a *lex*, which rarely happened, money was only paid out of the treasury on the strength of a *senatus consultum*.

nonagiens: nine millions. This tells us the expected size of the Sicilian corn harvest: the senate expected to pay 9,000,000 when buying a tenth of the crop at 3 sesterces per *modius*. This puts the tithe at 3,000,000 *modii*, and the whole harvest at 30,000,000, equivalent to 7,125,000 bushels, or nearly two hundred thousand tons.

erogatum: this compound is used of money paid out of the treasury.

188. decumano: this is the normal tithe; the 'second tithe' is included under *empto*.

in cellam: besides his *vasarium* (see Chap. IV, note 22), the governor was entitled to buy corn from the provincials for himself and his staff. This is called *aestimatum*, because the senate, instead of giving him the corn, gave him what they thought it was worth. The 'estimating' which the governor did for himself in the province was irregular; it was, however, very frequently done, and, as it was more important to the farmer, Cicero often speaks as if this unofficial estimation was the origin of the name. There was a limit on the amount which could be bought in this way.

In principle it was a reasonable arrangement. We note the price: whereas for *frumentum emptum*, when the money went direct to the farmers, the senate's price was three sesterces, at most three and a half, for *frumentum aestimatum*, which was part of the governor's allowance, it was four. (It would be naïve to suppose that the governor would buy for the state at wholesale, and for himself at retail prices.) But the cause of the trouble was that it was possible for him to convert part of this allowance into money and to make a profit on it. Some

Roman nobles were expert at turning an expense account into a salary.

adiecto: he was allowed to buy so much wheat and so much barley; he added both quantities together and put the total down as wheat.

denariis ternis: twelve sesterces; the usual method of making a profit was to pay the farmer less and pocket the difference; Verres is after bigger game.

abstulisse: Cicero is now describing a normal honest transaction; the money was first paid over to the farmer — to get his receipt on the books — and then the farmer provided money instead of corn. If the two prices were reasonable, no one need be the poorer by it; but it all depended on the prices. Since this was regularly done by innocent men, Cicero cannot be meaning that the farmer, instead of selling corn at the market price, gave money and received nothing.

189. **H.S. ternis:** this was the senate's price for the 'second tithe'. We do not have Verres' letter to Hortensius, but even the assured Roman market will not prevent some fluctuations in price.

190. **qui tamen:** unlike Verres.

in ultima: Agricola found the same thing happening in Britain: Tac. *Agr.* 19: *devortia itinerum et longinquitas regionum indicebantur.* The empire did not put a stop to all abuses.

ita multi ut: although many have done it.

191. **utrisne tandem:** two interrogative words, and *tandem* for even greater emphasis; **credo** is ironical.

ne portarent: to avoid having to transport it.

Philomelio: at the far end of Phrygia, beyond Synnada (see map on p. 16). At this time it was part of the province of Asia. Its distance from Ephesus was about three hundred and fifty miles. Ephesus was the headquarters of the governor of Asia, and he could demand that this corn be delivered to him there at the price fixed by the senate. It would obviously pay the Phrygian farmer to give him the money, or even to buy corn in Ephesus for delivery to the governor, rather than to cart his own all that way.

inter annonam: the difference in the prices. *annona* is the yearly produce (*annus*), then the corn supply, the price of corn.

192. **Phintia**: these three towns are the nearest seaports to Henna, one on each coastline (see map on p. 30). They would be reasonable delivery points.

eodem die: the distances are rather over fifty miles.

193. **eligas**: are you going to select?

194. **controversia**: if these facts are not in dispute, the case is as good as over; there is nothing more to wait for.

coactae conciliatae: this is the language of the *lex Acilia*, p. 161.

an vero: these words introduce the ironical question which closes the argument: 'Or are you really going to pretend that . . . ?'

195. **prompsisset**: this verb is used for bringing something out of the store cupboard: *deprome quadrimum Sabina*. So IV. 32, *promi*, p. 153.

Frugi: first on the roll of honour of upright governors; he was tribune in 149 when he passed the *lex Calpurnia de rebus repetundis*, the law which established the *quaestio perpetua*. He was consul in 133, censor in 120. He wrote a history of Rome, *Annales*, taking the view that the morality of the Romans was on the decline, and that the censorship of 154 was a milestone on the downward path (Pliny *N.H.* XVII. 244).

rettulisses: this is a counsel of perfection; but in similar circumstances twenty years later Cicero did the same, to the exasperation of his staff (*ad Att.* VII. i. 6 below). Perhaps such standards were not as rare as we are tempted to believe.

ambitiosi: to give the farmer the benefit of the senate's overestimation might be due to generosity; it might also be an attempt to gain support in the province, to increase one's *clientela*, to buy *gratia* with someone else's money.

honestus atque concessus: an admirable expression of average opinion; a morality which is not confined to Romans. *honestus* means that there was no disgrace in doing this.

ne emisses: if you had done what most people do, you would not have bought at all.

196. **optime**: the farmer's reply; what follows is a conversation between him and Verres. The *denarius* is worth four sesterces.

sperabam: I was expecting.

Attendite: to the whole audience; it is a story worth hearing; **vos**: the jury themselves have to judge Verres' part in it.

197. **cistam . . . fisco**: both words originally meant a basket. *fiscus* is already being used of public funds, especially on provincial account; since the emperors' accounts were mainly provincial, the word comes, in the time of Claudius, to be used of the emperor's treasury (see p. 198, note 19). Verres is transferring the *denarii* from the state money-chest to his own.

octonos: this is two *denarii*; since Verres also kept the original money he was getting three, and could buy such corn as he needed in the open market at about two sesterces. The farmer, instead of making a profitable sale, is being robbed.

The complete transaction has been as follows: the senate *estimated* wheat at 4 s. and barley at 2 s., and paid Verres for so many *modii* of each. Verres in theory gave the money to certain Sicilian farmers, and was then entitled to receive that amount of corn from them. He chose to take money instead; and he *estimated* the value of the corn at 12 s. per *modius*, for both wheat and barley (in fact he took a short cut here, see 197 above). Such corn as he needed he could buy in the open market for 2 or 3 s. Verres has therefore made a profit of about 10 s. for each *modius* of his allowance, of which 2 have come from the generosity of the senate's *aestimatio*, and 8 from the rapacity of his own. There is also an additional profit if the quantity allowed by the senate was greater than his actual needs.

Livy, XXXII, 27. 2.

eadem aestate: the year is 198.

elephanti: these will be African elephants, of whom there are two distinct species. That elephants could be used in war was first made known to the Mediterranean world when Alexander the Great encountered them in India. As a surprise weapon, or if wrong tactics were employed against them (as by Regulus in Africa), they could be very effective, and they were much used in Hellenistic warfare; but against an enemy who knew how to deal with them they could be a disastrous failure, and unless they were going to win battles, the difficulties of fodder and transport made them an encumbrance. After Thapsus their use was confined to processions and the arena. The problems posed by their use are well described by Glover in *Greece and Rome*, 1948.

tritici: it is from occasional references like this that we find out how the Romans fed their armies (see also note 1, p. 183). For *modium* as a genitive plural see note on p. 225, *triciens*.

Masinissa: king of Numidia from the second Punic war to 148; he was a friend of Africanus the elder, and remained loyal to Rome throughout his long reign. As the perfect client king, and a man of great age and wisdom, he figures in Cicero's *Somnium Scipionis*.

in Graecia: under Flamininus; the second Macedonian war.

Sicilia Sardiniaque: the provinces which would normally provide a surplus of revenue over expenditure.

commeatus: literally a going-to-and-fro; hence used of supplying an army and of the supplies themselves.

M. Marcellus: a son of the M. Claudius Marcellus who suppressed the revolt of Syracuse in the second Punic war. We do not know whether this province came to Marcellus by lot or, as sometimes happened, by special arrangement.

Cato: *pr.* 198, *cos.* 195, *censor* 184.

habitus: thought to be too harsh; in the introduction to his *de Re Rustica* he says that the early Romans considered the usurer to be worse than the thief. For his interest in the welfare of the provinces see Smith in *Greece and Rome*, May 1940.

sumptus: this abuse appears early in the history of the empire; see p. 100, *lege Porcia*.

Cicero, *ad Atticum*, V. xvi. (Except where otherwise stated, the letters in this chapter were written from Cilicia in the years 51–50 B.C.)

1. **publicanorum:** one of the unofficial services which they performed was to allow their agents to carry letters, and Cicero does not want to miss an opportunity.

mandati: Atticus had urged him to write regularly.

2. **plane eversam:** yet Cicero was anxious not to be associated with the prosecution of Appius. Of course the provincials have probably been exaggerating their distress.

Laodiceae: see map on p. 16. Cicero is moving along the old Royal Road.

ἐπικεφάλια: poll taxes; such is our ignorance of the finances of Cilicia that we do not know what these were. It was not the normal Roman practice to levy a poll-tax, except in Egypt. The exactions of Metellus Pius Scipio in Asia in 48, as described by Caesar (a hostile witness), included *tributa* levied *in capita singula servorum ac liberorum* (*B.C.* III. 32). But Caesar says that these demands were exceptional, inventions of Scipio (*excogitabantur*), and ruinous to the province. If Appius had been doing the same — and from *ad fam.* III. viii. 5 below it seems that he had — there would naturally be vociferous complaints. Such taxes would not be what we should normally call poll-taxes, since the number of heads is only being used as means of calculating the tax-payer's wealth, but they might be colloquially known as 'head-taxes'.

ὠνάς: everybody's tax arrears have been sold; if a man failed to pay his tax to a state official, the debt could be sold to a private company, which would be expected to make a profit in return for their services in collecting it. This is only done with taxes not already being collected by *publicani*, and the reference here may be to local taxation within the cities. In any case it implies a wholesale inability to pay.

monstra: inhuman behaviour.

3. levantur: Cicero was obviously sincere about this; the self-made man from Arpinum was far less avaricious and more scrupulous than many Roman nobles.

quemquam: we hear nothing of Cicero's *comites*.

foenum: fodder for horses and wood for fuel were normally requisitioned by the governor without payment. The *lex Julia* of 59 laid down strictly what could be requisitioned, and Cicero is not even availing himself of his legal rights.

4. Appius: it was a curious province, with poor communications between the Pedias and the Asiatic dioceses. But the thirty days of the *lex Cornelia* were meant for handing over, not for continuing to exercise a governor's authority.

Bibulus: though it is already the first week in August, and Syria needs its governor. The Roman nobles travelled in leisurely fashion. We do not know why it was imagined that

Bibulus should want his year of office to last into the autumn of the next year.

tridui: *sc. iter.* Cicero joined his army at Iconium.

ad familiares, III. viii. 1–5.

1. **ad urbem:** in the neighbourhood of Rome. A proconsul's *imperium* lapsed the moment he entered the city itself, and if Appius wanted a triumph he would have to remain outside the *pomoerium* until it was held. Cicero himself, on his return from Cilicia, had exaggerated hopes and did not enter the city for several years. It was possible to live very comfortably in the neighbourhood of the Campus Martius, as Pompey was now doing, being proconsul of Spain.

levissimo: a word often used by Romans of Asiatic 'Greeks' (see *ad Q.f.* I. i. 16. p. 149).

2. **superiore . . . aequo:** both on the judge's tribunal and off.

legatos: these are the laudatory delegations sent to Rome in honour of a retiring governor.

tuo nomine: on your account.

solvendo: solvent.

3. **delectari:** on the contrary, the Roman noble set great store by such tributes to his *dignitas*; more important still, Appius had reason to fear a prosecution for extortion, and Cicero is removing testimony which he will badly need.

sua sponte: by his own character.

locum: the senate did not always hear their carefully prepared orations.

eorum: the people of Midaeum.

bene merito: since you had deserved well of them.

laudaturum: I should think well of anyone who should do it at his own expense. **legitimo:** if he keep within the expense laid down by law (this will be either the *lex Cornelia* or the *lex Julia*). **infinito:** if he exceed the limit.

4. **edictum:** more information on Cicero's edict will be found in notes on pp. 218-9.

Samum: the *publicani* would naturally scrutinise a new governor's edict with great care, and someone must have sent them a copy in advance. They had to make their representations before he reached the province and began his jurisdiction. Cicero found the *publicani* waiting for him at Samos and the Salaminians at Ephesus.

totidem verbis: word for word.

caput: the section.

tralaticium: Appius had evidently been allowing, or encouraging, the cities to do things which were forbidden in his own edict.

privatae rei: Appius' excuse was that these were private affairs, while the law only limited public delegations; but it is obvious that they were being paid for publicly. *publicum orbis terrae consilium* is a fine description of the senate.

neque . . . exclusi: it was indeed difficult for the provincials of cis-Tauric Cilicia to reach Cicero when he was at Tarsus or in the Amanus mountains, but if Appius thought that they ought to have used that as an excuse to proceed with their delegations, it was indeed *irridendum*.

dioecesium: administrative districts; our word *diocese*. Being a Greek word, it is particularly used in the Greek-speaking east. Presumably they coincided with the assize areas (*ad Att.* V. xxi. 9. p. 110).

5. **venditionem:** that further unnecessary expenditure should not be added to their existing difficulties. For the poll-taxes, and the sale of tax arrears, see the previous letter.

tributum: properly used of the payment of a fixed sum by the *civitas* to Rome, as was done in Spain, but it is most unlikely that the normal direct taxation of Cilicia was paid in this way (see note on p. 239, *vectigalium*).

quam tu non ignoras: it seems clear that Appius was guilty of extortion.

capitum: see note on ἐπικεφάλια in the previous letter.
ostiorum: a tax on doors, as in England there was once a window tax. If Scipio's activities in Asia in 48 (Caes. *B.C.* III. 32) had any precedents, it was possible for a governor to raise money in ways not sanctioned in Rome.

magistratus suos: they had had the task of collecting these taxes which have now been sold to private companies; and if they were to head the deputations to Rome they would want them to be done in style.

ad Atticum, V. xxi. 6–8.

aestivis confectis: when the campaign was over; *aestiva* is properly a summer campaign, but this one had gone on until Christmas. The word is also used of a summer camp, as opposed to *hiberna*.

hibernis et Ciliciae: the army was naturally stationed at the eastern end of the province, in the Pedias. Since Cicero is going west of the Taurus he appoints a deputy.

Volusium: it was usual to delegate jurisdiction to a *legatus*, or sometimes to a *quaestor*; this man was neither, and we do not know what position he held. He may have been a suitable person, but it follows that Cicero did not think the task very important. **certum:** reliable; *abstinentia* is a very important virtue in a provincial administrator, and Cicero claims it for himself in *ad. Att.* V. xvi. 3. p. 136; not without reason.

cives Romani: presumably the native Cypriots could be left to manage their affairs without Roman assizes. **pauci:** the island, having been brought into the empire by Cato in 58–56, did not offer much attraction to Roman business men; Cato's administration may have been scrupulously accurate (though there were those who did not believe it), but a great deal of money was taken out of the island (Plut. *Cat. Min.* 39, see also note 11 on p. 182).

evocari: Cypriots could not be compelled to come to the assizes at Tarsus, doubtless a regulation made by Cato. The Salaminians had come there, but they came voluntarily, as they wanted to persuade Cicero to settle their affair (Chap. III, p. 39).

7. Asiam: the Phrygian dioceses of Cilicia had once been part of the province of Asia; Cicero sometimes seems to be using this name for the whole of the cis-Tauric part of his province.

admiratione: for the justice of his administration, or because a proconsul was being so energetic as to cross the Taurus range in winter.

dioecesium: see note on p. 252, *dioecesium*.

hospitem: had had no one billeted there.

quaestu: perhaps the most scandalous of all the recognised means of extortion, and very profitable to those governors who employed it. **quotannis**: this suggests that it went further back than the two winters of Appius' term of office. The amounts they were prepared to pay show how unpleasant it was to have to billet the troops — who might be legions of Roman citizens or cohorts of allies.

Cyprii: the whole island; this is just the amount which the single city of Salamis was quite unable to repay to Brutus; it is equivalent to nearly five million sesterces.

ὑπερβολικῶς loquor: exaggerate.

statuas: statuary to commemorate public benefactors was as common then as in the nineteenth century (so *ad Att*. VI. i. 17, *turma inauratarum equestrium*).

fana: we hear of divine honours being paid in the east to individual Romans, to Flamininus in Greece, for instance; and there was a festival in honour of Scaevola, the *Mucia*, in Asia. But we may doubt whether Cicero was in danger of being honoured on quite this scale.

τέθριππα: chariots; to set up a statue of a man in a chariot was itself almost a divine honour.

8. **Graeci**: see note on p. 237, Graecis. *et Graeci et cives Romani* includes everybody.

compresserant: the danger of famine leads to hoarding, which in turn makes the famine worse. This letter was written in the middle of February.

ad Atticum, VI. i. 16.

16. **habeo in deliciis**: I treat them as pets (compare Catullus II, *passer deliciae meae puellae*). **laudo, orno**: when Cicero later spoke of playing on the vanity of Octavian he used these words (*ad fam*. XI. xx. 1, *laudandum adulescentem, ornandum, tollendum*); in that case he was less successful.

Τὸ παραδοξότατον: most surprisingly.

pactionibus: this is the usual word for the compacts made by the *publicani* with the *civitates*. The *societates* who collected the taxes were in the habit of lending the money themselves and then recovering it at high rates of interest. But we are very ignorant of the details.

Servilius: Servilius Vatia Isauricus; for his governorship of

Cilicia see Chap. II, p. 26. **etiam** implies that he was not normally a friend of the *publicani*; also that these rates of interest were exorbitant, and that the process had been going on for thirty years. Cicero's idea was ingenious and effective, though not strictly legal. We must make allowances for a temporary proconsul confronted with a system which has become recognised from habit. Gabinius' treatment of the *publicani* in Syria had been more direct — and disastrous to himself; his condemnation was still a recent memory.

gratissima: the *promagistri* were pleased to be flattered; we may doubt whether the investors in Rome were so pleased at receiving only 12 per cent.

se quisque maxime: each one thinks himself my favourite.

ad familiares, II. xvii. 1–5.

SALLUSTIO: nothing is known of him apart from this letter.

stator: an official messenger.

a.d. XVI: in February Cicero had written to Atticus (V. xxi. 9. p. 110) that he intended to spend July in travelling from Tarsus to Laodicea, in order to leave his province on the 30th; but the military danger compelled him to move with his army towards the frontier with Syria (see the timetable of his movements in note on p. 220, *Laodiceae*).

neque quemquam: for the situation which is created when no successor is sent see note on p. 221, *oportet*; Cicero is proposing to leave a deputy to look after the province for a whole year.

Parthico: the military situation of Cilicia is described in Chap. II.

puerorum: Quintus Cicero's sons had accompanied their father to the province. Since Marcus will reach the coast at Ephesus, Rhodes is out of his way.

quam primum: unlike his leisurely outward journey, which took almost three months.

successor tuus: the quaestor will usually arrive and leave with the governor; but the system was sometimes very lax.

2. **rationibus referendis**: the *lex Julia* laid it down that an outgoing governor should publish his accounts in two cities in

his province. But Bibulus had, as Caesar's colleague, opposed the whole of the Julian legislation of 59, and was taking this opportunity of showing that he did not consider that the law was valid.

incommodum: since the armies of both provinces had been involved in the border fighting, their finances were in some measure interlocked. Hence Sallustius' anxiety that Cicero may be inconvenienced, and his request to see a copy of Cicero's accounts.

servandam: though it is hardly likely that a quaestor would actually be prosecuted for obeying the orders of his superior. Sallustius was in a difficult position.

3. **Apamea**: this is not the Phrygian Apamea, but in Syria, in Bibulus' province. Evidently Sallustius had been criticising his commander-in-chief in his letter to Cicero, and may have helped to provide material for the *sermones malevolorum*. Cicero's reply is in the nature of a reproof. Bibulus had cause to be displeased with his proquaestor.

Parthi: Cicero has no doubt that the Parthians did not on this occasion cross the Euphrates, and that no one but Sallustius thought they had.

4. **verum**: reasonable.

Apameae: the Phrygian Apamea, which is on Cicero's route to Laodicea. The accounts had to be published in two cities, and we know that the other was Laodicea; it is possible that we should read *Apameae et Laodiceae*. We might have expected Tarsus instead of Apamea, but the accounts were not ready before Cicero left the Pedias.

praeda: spoils of war were an important part of a governor's budget. The two urban quaestors were in charge of the treasury at Rome. It is strange that the Romans left the care of the treasury to such junior officials, who cannot have had much control over the office staff. The story of Cato's quaestorship (Plut. *Cat. Min.* 16–18) is instructive. But of course they had no share in framing financial policy.

praedes: Cicero is depositing the money with the *publicani*, who act as bankers for the state (so Jones, *JRS* (1956), p. 22). As little money as possible is actually sent to Rome.

drachmum: genitive plural, as with *sestertium*, *denarium*, *modium*; see note on p. 225, *triciens*. We do not know what this figure refers to.

praefectis: army officers handled the spoils of war, the provincial quaestor handled the rest of the public moneys.

5. **legionibus**: in the spring of this year the senate decided to send two more legions to reinforce the Syrian army against the threat from Parthia; they called on Pompey and Caesar to supply one each from their armies, and as Pompey sent one which he had lent to Caesar, both of them in fact came from Gaul. By the time they reached Rome it was clear that the Parthian danger had been overestimated and they were retained in Italy, and formed an unreliable element of Pompey's army in 49.

otium: peace; more often this word is used of peace within the state, *pax* of peace in relation to foreign enemies. The people in the province are no longer occupied with preparation for war.

Marium: Sallustius' successor.

ad Atticum, VII. i. 6.

6. **gloriosum**: it is indeed creditable to Cicero, but highly discreditable to the system which made it possible. We must add that he had paid for things in the province which he could legally have requisitioned. Exact sums of money are seldom mentioned in the literature, but when they are the picture is the same: gross overestimation of requirements. In practice, the unpaid nobility were paying themselves very substantial amounts.

annuum: enough to last him for another year, until the arrival of the next governor in the summer of 49. He will not have to keep up the same state as a proconsul, and will not have any *legati*. The more we consider the task facing Coelius, the more we are surprised that he should have been left in charge.

referre: a thousand sesterces is much too small a figure to be the cause of so much fuss; the true sum is probably a million, which could have been written $\overline{\text{CI}\mathfrak{I}}$ or $\lceil \text{X} \rceil$.

invenirer: as if I was being found out to be.

Phrygum et Cilicum: we are continually being reminded of the dual nature of the province.

honorifice: but the staff, it seems, would have preferred hard cash.

ad familiares, XIII. xxi. 44 B.C.

CORNIFICIO: governor of Africa; a great deal of land in Africa was owned by Roman senators.

legatione libera: see p. 53. The governors of the provinces had no say in these appointments.

dignitatem: this word is specially kept for senators.

sum solitus: during his year in Cilicia, some seven years ago.

lictores: a mark of a magistrate; the Roman senator expects to travel in style.

factitatum: that it had always been done.

ad familiares, XIII. ix.

CRASSIPEDI: P. Furius Crassipes, a wealthy young man, had been the second husband of Cicero's daughter, Tullia. They have by now separated, and just about this time she was married to her third husband, the highly unsatisfactory Dolabella. The *publicani* have appealed to Cicero to use his influence with his ex-son-in-law, although the two men seem to be on terms of formal politeness.

socios: throughout this letter this word means the members of the *societas* which had contracted to collect the taxes in Bithynia. They were Roman equestrians, and are losing no opportunity of bringing pressure to bear on the administration to advance their interests. That Cicero, who was more zealous than most men for the protection of the provincials, should write this sort of letter shows the strength of the forces at work. In the same year he wrote a similar letter (*ad fam*. XIII. 65) to the governor of Bithynia on behalf of another *promagister*. Cicero spent much of his life acquiring *gratia*, and the letters in Book XIII show one of the ways in which he used it.

quorum res agitur: the shareholders.

2. **ordini**: the use of this word for the *publicani* shows that they are being identified in people's minds with the equestrians. Cicero always prided himself on his friendship with the class to which he had belonged. According to Pliny (*N.H*. XXXIII. 34) the word *publicani* was beginning to be used at Rome for

the non-senatorial well-to-do when Cicero found for them the more honourable word *equites*.

tribuerim: do what I can for them.

constat: its directors were also directors of other companies.

Men.: for *Menenia tribu*; this is the man's formal description, and if Rupilius had had a cognomen it would have followed the name of his tribe. A cognomen was originally the mark of a patrician, but by this time it is becoming fashionable among plebeians also. Some families, however, are still without one, the Antonii, for instance, and the Octavii.

magister: the managing director, who lived at Rome; his overseas manager is *pro magistro*.

3. in operis: in the service of.

expertus: Cicero had had equestrian support in his political career.

ad familiares, V. xx. 1–2, 7–9. 49 B.C.

RUFO: Mescinius Rufus was Cicero's quaestor in Cilicia, and Cicero said some hard things about him in his letters (Coelius Caldus was Rufus' successor, and only arrived in the province just in time to be left in charge of it). Before leaving Tarsus, Cicero wrote (*ad Att*. VI. vii. 2) that he expected to meet Rufus at Laodicea so that he could then publish his accounts before leaving the province, as the *lex Julia* demanded. It is clear from this letter that Rufus did not meet Cicero, and the accounts had to be made up without him. Cicero himself had no head for figures, and the work was done by his clerk and a cousin of Rufus. The accounts having been published in Cilicia, Cicero had to hand in an identical copy to the treasury at Rome. The quaestor also had to send in his accounts at Rome, and Rufus, having found a mistake in Cicero's, is naturally uncertain what to do. Cicero's reply is friendly, but not very helpful.

1. eo: Cicero had expected to meet him at Laodicea.

noluisti: evidently Rufus had begun his letter with suitable politeness.

M. Tullius: when a slave is freed, he often marks his new status by taking the full three names of the Roman; for this he usually adopts his *praenomen* and *nomen* from his patron, retaining his own name as a *cognomen*. This man's *cognomen* is Laurea, which betrays the Greek origin which we should in any case have expected in a secretary. In Laurea's absence Cicero is helpless over the details.

referendis: *refero* is to hand in to the treasury, *confero* to make up by comparing the various documents.

scientem: consciously; especially used of doing wrong (so in the *lex Acilia*, p. 162, *sciens dolo malo*).

rem aut existimationem: your interest or your reputation.

ius vetus: before the *lex Julia*.

necessitudinis: for the bond which was supposed to exist between governor and quaestor see p. 192, note 10.

2. **totidem verbis:** word for word.

ad meum arbitrium: to make you toe the line; Cicero had not deliberately sent in his accounts early in order to prevent Rufus from questioning them.

scribam: I put my secretary at your disposal.

Mindium: a banker and a cousin of Rufus.

me absente: Cicero was never interested in financial matters.

servo: Tullius was really a freedman, but in view of the social gulf which lay between them a noble could use the word *servus* of an ex-slave.

ut eundem: as if I had received it from your cousin; *frater* is sometimes used for *frater patruelis*, a cousin on the father's side.

honestum et utile: these words are often used together; *utile* corresponds with *rem* in 1 above, *honestum* with *existimationem*.

maxime: where I thought I most certainly ought to publish them; but the adverb is grammatically strange, and the conjecture *maximae* is tempting.

pro relatis: as good as handed in to the treasury, since the treasury copy had to be identical.

7. **beneficiis:** the retiring governor submitted a list of soldiers who had served the state well; a kind of honours list (military division), which was sent in as a supplement to the accounts. The quaestor, who also submitted his accounts, could do the same.

tribunos militaris: officers of the legions, as *praefecti* are of the *auxilia*. **contubernales:** the young men of senatorial family who accompanied a commander-in-chief in order to gain experience of the army. For this purpose they counted as commissioned officers.

ambitioni: by putting a man's name on this list you would gain his support for the future; there was no reticence in the careerism of the senator.

nihil uterer: in his early years Cicero had been a master in the art of winning support, as the *petitio consulatus* (if indeed it is genuine) clearly shows.

centurionibus: the rules for recommending non-commissioned officers and lesser fry were not so stringent.

in integro: you have a clear field.

8. **Myrina:** on the coast of Asia Minor, north of Phocaea; Rufus must have known that Cicero had to publish his accounts before leaving the province, and if he went off to Myrina and left the work to others he was hardly in a position to complain if a mistake was made.

pro ea spe: Cicero thought that when he returned to Rome he would be wealthy, and it sounds as if he had let Rufus understand that he would himself reimburse him if things went wrong. As it turned out, Cicero lost the whole of his provincial profit, and was not in a position to part with a hundred thousand sesterces.

sic accepisse: I do not regard your letter as a demand for repayment of debt. **haec tempora:** the civil war was beginning and creditors were becoming anxious about their money.

9. **apud publicanos:** they acted as international bankers.

eam omnem pecuniam: 2,200,000 sesterces seems a good profit for a man who had been scrupulously honest, and whose military successes had not been outstanding. No wonder the great commanders were wealthy men. Pompey's agents were already at work in the east, which was to be his source of power in the struggle with Caesar.

HS centum: a hundred thousand, of course; Cicero abbreviates figures where there is no doubt.

cibariis: the allowance which the governor received for the subsistence of his staff. This passage makes it clear that the staff also expected to do well out of the state.

tulisses: if you had entered this money as paid to me; *i.e.* if you had lent it to me yourself.

quae est: such is your kindness.

aestimationem: to take my land in payment, at a valuation. It was common for senators to have the bulk of their fortunes invested in land (they were excluded from many forms of business); they had little which could readily be converted into cash, and for their living expenses they frequently ran into debt. They were therefore vulnerable if the value of land fell, which was now happening as a result of the civil war. Caesar's remedy, which became law at the end of the year, was that a creditor could be compelled to accept land at its pre-war value as repayment of a debt. This passage, though Cicero does not mean Rufus to take him seriously, shows that such a solution was already being talked about in January 49.

This way of living and its apparent insolvency was blamed by Cicero in his consulship, when he complained that the size of their debts had driven men to support Catiline (*Cat.* II. 18). It explains the recurrent rumours of *novae tabulae* which accompany all revolutionary designs (Lepidus in 78, Catiline in 63; it was even said of Caesar in 49), and the influence of such different men as Crassus and Atticus, who provided the ready money.

numeratum: hard cash.

ut ego te: as I have no doubt you do.

conscindi: you need not destroy; a friendly gesture, allowing Rufus to use Cicero's letter in his own defence. The MSS. read *non scindi*, which would mean just the opposite. This is against the tone of the letter (Cicero does not seem to be bothered for his own sake), and can hardly be right.

Chapter V : THE EXECUTIVE

Cicero, *ad Quintum fratrem*, I. i. 15–16, 32–36; ii. 10–11.

When Quintus Cicero had been governor of Asia for two years, and then (60 B.C.) had his term extended for a third year, Marcus wrote him two long letters of condolence and encouragement. In fact he took the opportunity of writing a rather self-conscious and pompous treatise on the qualities of the ideal governor, clearly intended for wider circulation, and not for Quintus' eyes alone. In the first letter he has mentioned in their turn all the members of Quintus' staff, pointing out that the governor is answerable for their honesty as well as his own. He now turns to the dangers of too easy friendships with residents of the province, first those of Roman (or Italian) extraction, then the natives themselves. On this subject much can be learnt from E. M. Forster's *A Passage to India*.

non quin possint: not that they cannot be; these *provinciales* are Romans who live in the province, most of whom are naturally there for business purposes.

qui potes?: how can you?

qui careant: the antecedent is *homines*, understood from *hominum*; they have left the delights of Rome willingly and permanently, in order to make money, not, like Quintus, unwillingly and out of a sense of duty; they are hardly likely therefore to be really in sympathy with him. To them he will be *alienus*, both in nature and because he is temporarily imposed on them from outside. This is perhaps the most perspicacious part of Marcus' homily.

praetores: governors, as usual, whatever their rank.

tui amantiorem: more fond of you, for your own sake, than for what they can get out of you.

adscribito: for this form of the imperative see note on p. 230, *dato*.

victuri: since they will not have to live with you in the future. *qui* is the old third declension ablative.

16. **Graecis**: the native inhabitants of the province; see note on p. 237, *Graecis*.

vetere Graecia: the usual Roman attitude is to praise the past glories of classical Greece and to lament the degeneracy of the present. Its clearest expression is in the *pro Flacco* (9–10), where Cicero complains that Greeks of his time combined to help each other out in the courts, and quotes, as a Greek saying, 'Da mihi mutuum testimonium.'

non nostris solum: they are envious not only of Romans but also of one another.

32. **publicani**: it is especially interesting to compare what Cicero says here with what he did in Cilicia nine years later.

His administration does not come badly out of the comparison.

coniunctum: in 60 Cicero still had hopes of his *concordia ordinum*, though already in December 61 he could write to Atticus of *illam a me conglutinatam concordiam* (*ad Att*. I. xvii. 19).

imperio tuo: Asia had no military problems, but was a happy hunting ground of the *publicani*.

abstinentem, continere: the nouns from these verbs frequently occur among the virtues expected of a governor.

facilem: approachable.

33. **ex civibus:** Romans; harbour dues had just been abolished in Italy.

male redemptis: especially as they have made a bad bargain in buying the taxes. This was the year of the famous complaint (*ad Att*. I. xvii. 9). The words *bene emptus* were used colloquially of a good bargain (bon marché), *male emptus* of a bad one.

ita fuerunt: the idea that taxes should be collected by private firms under contract was not a Roman one; the Roman practice was to take over existing systems as far as possible.

Sulla: this is the great war indemnity; the cities themselves had to employ contractors to collect it. Pompey, when in need of supplies for the second Mithridatic war, followed Sulla's *descriptio* in levying contributions *pro portione*; so did Flaccus in 62 (Cic. *Flacc*. 32). It has come to be believed that Sulla abolished the central auction for the taxes of Asia altogether. But it has to be remembered that at this time (85/4) he had no option; for one thing, *publicani* must have been high on the list of victims in the massacre of 88, and those who survived will have fled the country; for another, their head offices were in Rome, and since that was in the hands of Sulla's enemies, will not have dared to instruct them to collect money for him. The usual machinery was not available at this moment. When the civil war was over he could return to normal. Nor is the absence of censors in 80 and 75 decisive; we know that in these years the consuls let out public contracts (see note on p. 241, *consulibus*). When we next hear of the *censoria locatio* it is in 70, when there are censors again, but there is no hint in Cicero's language that this is a revival of something which has not happened for fifteen years (*II Verr.* III. 12. p. 127). There remains the notion that the man who transferred the juries to the senate must have had a hatred of the equestrian order — regardless of the fact that he put some three hundred equestrians into the senate (I have discussed this in *Greece and Rome* (1962); see also Brunt, *Latomus* (Jan.–Mar. 1956)). For the word *aequaliter*, obviously equivalent to Pompey's *pro portione*, see note on p. 244.

Rhodiis: the Rhodians had distinguished themselves by resisting the invasion of Mithridates in 88 (the failure of the siege and siege engine is described in *CAH* IX. p. 243). Sulla rewarded them at other peoples' expense, and this was not popular with their neighbours.

34. **illud Asia cogitet:** in spite of many individual injustices, this stands as a valid justification of the burdens imposed by Rome. Tacitus puts a similar claim into the mouth of Petilius Cerialis in Gaul in A.D. 70 (*H.* IV. 74: nam neque quies gentium sine armis, neque arma sine stipendiis, neque stipendia sine tributis haberi queunt).

35. **reliqua:** you can make them find taxpaying more tolerable if they appreciate that the collectors are reasonable men.

pactionibus: the amount to be collected was fixed in general terms by law, but there was ample scope for negotiating about means. These compacts between *civitates* and *publicani* were crucial, and it is clear that the *publicani* did not expect to get the worst of the bargain, especially if they lent the states the money with which to pay themselves. Marcus' advice on this point could lead to trouble, as he found later in Cilicia, where he had to adjudicate on some *pactiones* which had been illegally made (see Chap. IV). He was more prepared than most Romans to take thought for the provincials, but it is clear that, especially at this stage of his career, the friendship of the equestrian order ranks higher in his mind.

36. **societates:** these are the tax-collecting companies, whose head offices are in Rome.

voluntate: with good will; *diversa* is nom. pl.

desiderat: need.

The remainder of the letter is taken up by a warning that men

*are complaining of Quintus' bad temper, and that any failure
of his will be considered to implicate Marcus also.*

ii. 10. tempore ipso: it is just the right moment to be talking
about letters.

Flavius: as tribune in 60 he had tried to pass a *lex agraria*
to provide for Pompey's troops; although it failed to pass,
Pompey secured for him the praetorship for 58, after the necessary interval of a year. Flavius' behaviour shows us the immediate reaction of the Roman senator when his interests are
threatened — to appeal to someone who may have influence in
the right quarter. Marcus may have believed that Flavius had
grounds for his grievance, but he has not stopped to find out,
nor does he admit the possibility that Quintus may have been
right; clearly his only thought is that this is a friend of
Pompey, and must not be offended. Governors of provinces
were continually exposed to this sort of pressure.

procuratores: agents; Flavius must be a man of some wealth.

C. Fundanio: there was a Fundanius whom Cicero defended
in the courts, and on whose services, according to the author of
the *Petitio Consulatus*, he could count for his consular election
(*Com. Pet.* 19); it may be the same man.

Apollonidensis: the property was at Apollonis in Lydia, and
it is the local magistrates who will have to take action.

iudicare deberi: the fact that the money is owed should be
established in the courts, not by the governor himself. As far
as we can see, all that Quintus has certainly done is to freeze
Octavius' estate, so that outstanding debts can be paid before
it is handed on to the heirs; which seems quite right and
proper — provided that Naso has admitted the debt. If not,
then Fundanius should take the case to court, and Quintus is
anticipating the verdict. The vital fact is hidden from us.

Fundanio cupio: I wish him well.

nihil loci gratiae: as if the request which Marcus is now
making were not a glaring example of it.

aut quasi amicis: that you would be grateful to them if they
would obey, and make things difficult for them if they did not.

This is probably a normal enough formula for a governor's instructions.

11. **prorsus**: this collection of adverbs is as urgent as Cicero can make it.

remittas: to relent in your intention not to allow the money to be paid over.

et scilicet Pompei: now we come to the heart of the matter.

me dius fidius: I assure you; the origin of this strong assurance is 'may the god of faith destroy me if I lie'. It is sometimes written *medius fidius*.

ex tua iniuria: that you should think that I am being generous to Flavius by causing you to do injustice to Fundanius.

auctoritatem: to leave on record an authoritative decree or official letter.

ut opinor: these words do not, in Cicero, imply the existence of any doubt. They are used, as in English 'I believe', to introduce further information which is not common knowledge and not strictly essential.

commendarunt: doubtless in letters like *ad fam.* XII. xxi and XIII. ix. pp. 143, 144. Quintus had had quite a bombardment of letters about Flavius, and if Fundanius' claim was just (and Marcus' letter does not prove that it was not) he deserves credit for his courage.

Cicero, *II in Verrem*, IV. 32.

32. **Lilybitanum**: Cicero, having been quaestor in Lilybaeum, naturally had friends in the neighbourhood. He has obviously been back there to collect his evidence.

Boethi: according to Pliny (*N.H.* XXXIII. 55) he was a famous silversmith, and some of his works were to be seen in the temple of Minerva at Lindus on the island of Rhodes.

abstulisset: Verres, of course.

Venerius: one of Verres' *cohors*; see note on p. 270, *Venerios*.

sigillatos: adorned with figures in relief; they are silver cups.

binos: a pair; the plural *utrique* is also used of two when they make a pair (*e.g.* Tac. *A.* XV. 55, of a pair of conspirators).

promi: to be brought out (see note on p. 247, *prompsisset*).

Cibyratae: their names are given in the previous section,

Tlepolemus and Hiero; they were artists from Cibyra in Asia Minor. They had joined Verres when he was in Cilicia, and had come to Sicily with him; they specialised in detecting works of art for him to plunder.

HS mille: we do not know the size of the cups, but this is not likely to be their full value; according to Pliny (*N.H.* XXXIII. 53) up to five or even six thousand sesterces a pound was known to have been paid for antique silver — the latter price by Crassus, for two cups by Mentor, and considered fabulous (for comparison, at Christie's in June 1961 a George I circular dish by Mathew Walker of Dublin, weighing almost 14 oz., sold for £540: since 14 oz. troy is almost exactly the weight of the Roman pound, it seems that, in terms of antique silver, the sesterce at that time was the equivalent of about two shillings of our money).

luteum: worthless.

idem sibi videri: Verres agrees with his experts.

Cicero *II in Verrem*, II. 83–85, 88–101.

83. **adsidet:** the preposition has the notion of assisting; so *adesse*.

Thermitanus: Sthenius was a native of Thermae in northern Sicily (see map on p. 30). After the destruction of Himera by the Carthaginians, many of the inhabitants settled at Thermae, a few miles to the west, and the new city was considered to have taken the place of the old. Plutarch (*Pomp.* 10) calls Sthenius a man of Himera. Himera (that is to say Thermae) had sided with the Marians against Sulla, and Pompey was intending to punish the city when Sthenius persuaded him to spare the town. Sthenius — and Thermae — would become thereby a part of Pompey's *clientela*, and in harming them Verres made a powerful enemy. It may be true, as Badian suggests (*Foreign Clientelae 264–70*) that Pompey's prestige was endangered by this attack on his clients, and that he bestirred himself to ensure the condemnation of Verres. It is noticeable that the people of Messana, whom Pompey had insulted (see p. 174, note 9), were consistently friendly to Verres.

Deliacam: before 146 Delian bronze was the most famous in the world; Polyclitus used it, and the bronze Jupiter in the temple on the Capitol was made of it. But in the burning of Corinth a new alloy was accidentally found, and this bronze became more valuable than any other (interesting information about bronze and bronze statues can be found in Pliny *N.H.* XXXIV. 3 foll.). Sthenius was quite a collector.

nostrorum: Romans; Sthenius was not a typical helpless provincial, and Verres was unwise to try to rob him.

85. **Africani:** the Carthaginians had looted Himera; when the inhabitants settled down again at Thermae, and after the defeat of Carthage, Scipio returned to them as many of their treasures as he could.

88. **senatu:** the senate of Thermae.

adhuc: the only one up to that time.

alio loco: the title of Book IV is *de signis* (see especially IV, 32 above).

89. **hospitium:** this signifies a relationship in which you could naturally stay at your friend's house or he at yours.

atque adeo: 'or rather'. The point is that *emigrare* includes moving your belongings, and Verres had already taken away anything movable from Sthenius' house; all that was left was to walk out himself.

omnia: wife and all; hence Agathinus is an *adfinis*.

90. **ad se detulissent:** as soon as they should bring their case before him.

postulat ut: this *ut* is repeated at *ut de his omnibus*.

actio: there was at Thermae a procedure for trying such cases.

reddidisset: all the cities of Sicily had this right; Thermae is not in the list of *foederatae* or *liberae et immunes* in III. 13. p. 127; had it been so, Verres might have hesitated.

91. **cogniturum:** *cognitio* is the hearing of a case by a magistrate.

mulier: Callidama.

perspicuum: we do not know how much evidence Cicero had produced at the *actio prima*. A good many things in this story would need proof, including certainly the intention to inflict corporal punishment, and perhaps Sthenius' innocence.

de sententia: Heraclius' flight (II. 41. p. 115) is similarly described as *de amicorum et propinquorum sententia*; for the effect of this phrase see note on p. 228, *de amicorum sententia*.

92. **Venerios:** used of the temple slaves of Venus of Eryx, and then, insultingly, of Verres and his minions. We may compare these slaves with the notorious slaves of Venus of Corinth. A *denarius* of about this time has a vivid representation of the famous mountain temple at Eryx (Mattingly, *Roman Coins*, Plate XXI. 17).

horam tertiam: if the exact time of night is important, this is the usual way of stating it; *vigiliae* are used in military contexts. This being late autumn, Verres has stayed in court until eight o'clock in the evening, long after business should have stopped. At Rome, the courts had to adjourn by sunset.

93. **Sacerdote:** Verres' predecessor.

VIDERI: the praetor's formula for pronouncing the verdict in the extortion court is *fecisse videtur*.

HS D: probably five hundred thousand, *quingena milia sestertium* (see note on p. 225, *triciens*). Five hundred is too small a sum, and fifty million much too large.

vendere: one of the regular ways of enforcing payment of damages; but even if a man has been rightly convicted, he should be granted time for payment before this is done (see note on p. 231, *pignerator*).

tantulum: even the slightest.

94. **EIUS:** Sthenius: *nomen defero* of the accuser, *nomen recipio* of the magistrate.

rei capitalis adfinem: that he had anything to do with a capital case; this does not seem to be a deliberate echo of *adfinem* in the previous sentence.

egens: a word of reproach, frequently used of informers and suchlike persons (see, for instance, Cic. *Clu.* 66 and 70 of Staienus the bribery expert, and Tac. *A.* I. 74 of the typical *delator*).

absentis: at this stage the question is only how to get proceedings started; normally Pacilius should summon Sthenius to appear before the magistrate, and Sthenius must come; if he refuses, he can be dragged, either by Pacilius or by the magistrate's officials; when he appears, the charge is framed and the day appointed. At Rome, there was no other way of starting a case; here, it being impossible to bring Sthenius into court, Verres conducts these preliminaries without him, and though Cicero wants us to think that this was wrong, he does not actually say that it was illegal.

edicit: after this, Verres assumes that Sthenius, wherever he is, has had notice of the case, and if he does not appear he is deliberately defaulting — which is true enough.

95. **adverso tempore:** no one crossed the sea in winter if he could avoid it.

Cn. Lentulus: these are the consuls of 72.

placere: both this word and *si . . . videretur* are official language; *placet* is said by the Ayes, *non placet* by the Noes.

absentes homines: a special provision for capital cases. At Rome, if a man was being tried on a capital charge and absconded to avoid the consequences, the assembly, under the presidency usually of a tribune, pronounced that he had forfeited his citizen rights and his property; but that is not the same thing as sentencing a man who was never there in the first place. Verres is treating Sthenius as a man who has admitted his guilt by running away; that he could do so shows the extent of the governor's discretion.

NON PLACERE: a remarkable proposal to interfere with the governor's administration.

96. **consumerent:** a recognised form of senatorial obstruction; Cato later used it with effect against Caesar.

et terra et mari: to make sure that someone arrived in time, it being nearly midwinter.

fere xxx: the usual interval between the preliminary hearing and the trial itself.

97. **in integro:** no decision had been taken.

98. **ambitione:** the quest for useful friends.

99. **Vibone:** this is Vibo Valentia, sometimes called Hipponium, on the west coast of Bruttium; Velia is about 120 miles further north. Cicero describes how he hurried up the coast to reach Rome in time to prosecute Verres; he would not have run these dangers (as he calls them) if the presence of the prosecutor was unnecessary.

100. **Palicanum:** tribune of 71; he would have come into office on Dec. 10, 72, immediately after the condemnation of

Sthenius. A vigorous opponent of the oligarchy, he later aimed at the consulship, but he was of low birth, and in spite of his energy and eloquence the nobles succeeded in keeping him out.

me ipsum: the ex-quaestor of Sicily maintaining his interest in his old province.

eorum edicto: this is before the restoration of the full powers of the tribunes by Pompey in 70, but they still have the right to issue edicts.

101. **vertit stilum:** one end of the *stilus* is pointed, for writing on wax, the other is flat for rubbing out; hence the phrase *stilum vertere*.

facit: he entered it on the records that Sthenius had been present.

Livy, XLIII. 2.
The date is 171 B.C.

utriusque: the land frontiers of these provinces at this time are not easy to determine. Further Spain was the wealthier and more civilised, and Carthaginian occupation had started from the neighbourhood of Cadiz. It was in order to hold this that the nearer province also had to be held.

populorum: in the nearer province especially the unit of government at this time was the tribe.

quam hostes: slightly rhetorical, but others said the same; see Cic. *Imp. Pomp.* 13.

pecunias: the senate only agrees to investigate charges of extortion, not of other kinds of injustices or oppression. This narrow view was continued by the *quaestio perpetua*.

Canuleio: important legal organisation is usually a task for praetors, and the man who was going to Spain had a particular interest in these trials.

reciperatores: the usual procedure for actions between Romans and non-Romans (see Chap. III). Though this is a civil action, not a criminal trial, there is no question of mixed nationalities on the board; none but a senator is to sit in judgement on a senator. The Augustan *s.c. Calvisianum* (see p. 284) is a return to this procedure. The appointment of Roman *patroni* figures both in that and the *lex Acilia*.

quattuor: Cato had been governor of Hispania Citerior, and

the author of a law limiting what magistrates might demand
from provincials (see note on p. 211, *lege Porcia*). Members of
the Scipio family had distinguished themselves in the peninsula in the Hannibalic war. This Scipio was the son of the
Gnaeus Scipio who was killed in Spain in 211, and he had himself governed Hispania Ulterior as praetor in 194. (For the
perpetuation of such connections see p. 67.) Aemilius Paulus
was the victor of Pydna, the father of Scipio Aemilianus, and
had been praetor in Hispania Ulterior. Gallus was the only
one of the four who had not been consul and who, as far as we
know, had no connection with Spain; but he was a friend of
Aemilius Paulus, was a famous scholar and orator, and
obviously destined for high office (he was consul in 166). The
Spaniards have chosen four of the most distinguished men in
Rome to act for them. Their lack of success is the more
surprising.

A. Manlio: this is the year 178.

ampliatus: the case had to be reheard; if the judge's verdict
was *non liquet* the magistrate's order was *amplius cognoscen-
dum*; hence *ampliare* and *ampliatio*. The procedure is continued in the *quaestio perpetua*, and occurs in the *lex Acilia*.

praetor fuerat: the dates are 174 and 173. The magistrates
of this period are listed by Scullard in *Roman Politics 220–150*,
pp. 304–8. Nothing else is known of these peccant praetors.

de integro: at the second hearing the case has to be started
all over again.

solum vertisse: left the country; the phrase is especially
used of exile, which changes a man's status as well as his place
of residence. At this time they do not have to go very far.
exsulatum is a supine.

prohiberi: the subject of this verb is the Spaniards, who are
allowed to accuse undistinguished praetors, but are not allowed
to aim higher. Livy believes that greater men were being
shielded.

dilectum: this means that in sending him to Spain the senate
had authorised him to take legionary reinforcements from
Italy. This subject is discussed in Chap. II (Cicero was not
allowed to take them to Cilicia).

in futurum consultum: the decree deals with the kind of

complaints usually heard in the extortion court — purely financial injustice. Of these abuses, the first may be the *frumentum aestimatum* of Verres (p. 245); the second seems to be a practice whereby the governor buys up to a twentieth of the harvest at a low price (which he can then sell at a profit); the third reminds us of Scaptius (p. 38).

Extracts from the *Lex Acilia*

The beginning of this inscription is missing, and it contained the name of the proposer. It can however be taken as certain that this is C. Gracchus' law relating to the extortion court, and reasonably certain that it is the *lex Acilia*, that its proposer was M'. Acilius Glabrio, a tribune of 122, who was a son-in-law of the Mucius Scaevola who as consul in 133 had supported Tiberius Gracchus; this case is argued by Badian in *American Journal of Philology*, 1954. The law was recorded on a bronze tablet, fragments only of which have survived. On the back of the same tablet is the text of the *lex agraria* of 111, and since it would be impossible to see both sides of the tablet at the same time we are left wondering why the *lex Acilia* had its face turned to the wall twelve years later. Balsdon (*Papers of the British School at Rome*, 1938) has the suggestion that because this was a faulty copy — five lines of it are copied out twice — it was never exhibited, and in 111 someone had the idea of using the back of it to post up the *lex agraria*.

The lines of the text were long — about four hundred letters in each — and the edges of the tablet, with the beginning and end of the lines, were never found. The letters in italics are conjectural, but in the text of a law, with its set formulae and much repetition, they are less dubious than might appear. The Latin spelling is archaic, especially in the declension of the relative pronoun. These extracts are taken from Wordsworth, *Fragments and Specimens of Early Latin*, whose text is in two important places superior to that of Bruns, *Fontes Iuris Romani*.

1. **quoi**: dative, depending on *ablatum* in line 3; the sense is 'if from any Roman or provincial . . . by one who is dictator . . . money is taken . . . let there be a trial.'

ceivi Romano sociumve: *socium* is genitive plural; it is the usual word for a provincial. Bruns reads only *socium*, following Mommsen's dictum that there is no evidence that Roman citizens could prosecute under this law. If, however, it was under this law that senators could be called to account for taking bribes in other courts, it follows that Romans must have been able to initiate the prosecutions, and that Wordsworth's reading is correct. See Ursula Ewins in *JRS* (1960). To a study of provincial administration this does not make much difference, but it is important for the estimation of the scope and intention of Gracchus' law.

nominisve Latini: an intermediate status between *cives* and *peregrini*; it included the *ius conubii* (if a Roman married a 'Latin' the marriage was recognised and the children became Roman citizens), the *ius commercii* (contracts between Romans and 'Latins' would be upheld in Roman courts), and the *ius civitatis per honorem adipiscendae* (magistrates of a 'Latin' town became Roman citizens). It originated in Rome's alliance with the Latin League in 338, spread abroad in Italy by the creation of 'Latin colonies' (the settlers were mixed Romans and 'Latins', and their new status was that of the 'Latin name'), and when full citizenship was granted to all Italians south of the Po the Latin name was used, with no pretence of being confined to Latins, as a constitutional privilege, at first in Transpadane Gaul and, under the emperors, in the provinces also. It came to be used as a stepping-stone; the conception of gradual elevation to Roman citizenship owes much to Gracchus. The whole matter is discussed by Sherwin-White in *Roman Citizenship*, Chap. III, and, summarily, in *O.C.D. s.v. ius Latii*.

nationum: chiefly used of tribes less civilised than the Romans.

amicitiave: the Romans of the Republican period did not think that their empire stopped at the administrative boundaries; they would have considered, for instance, that it included the kingdoms of Deiotarus and Ariobarzanes. The clear frontiers drawn on most of our maps can be misleading.

2. **quei:** nominative singular.

dictator: this list of all the officers who can be prosecuted is

K

in descending order of power. The *magister equitum* has an *imperium*, but it is derived from that of the dictator, and ceases with it; he therefore comes after the praetors, whose *imperium* is their own. Censor after both of them, because he has no *imperium*, although in some ways the censorship was the senior of all the normal offices. The *tresviri capitales* were in charge of arrests and executions; the land board was appointed under the *lex agraria* of Tiberius Gracchus; the first four legions are the consular legions, numbered one to four, and their twenty-four military tribunes, being elected in the *comitia tributa*, have a kind of magisterial status; originally the consuls had been the commanders-in-chief, and two legions was the size of a consular army.

Elsewhere in this law it is laid down that none of these magistrates is to be prosecuted until he has ceased to hold his office.

aliqua: ablative, in apposition to legionibus; the first four legions, any one of them.

filius: a surprising extension of responsibility; perhaps there had been some scandals.

senator: we have seen (*ad fam.* XII. xxi. p. 143) that this rank, even without magisterial office, could be abused; it is probably under this heading that senators were accused for taking bribes in the courts.

amplius H.S.: unfortunately the figure is missing, and there is little basis for conjecture. The lowest known figure is that for the condemnation of C. Cato, whose restitution was assessed at 8,000 sesterces (presumably this was double the amount of his proved extortions, see 59 below; for Cato's case see note 26 on p. 195).

3. **pro imperio prove potestate:** by using his authority, military or civilian. This law is only aimed at abuses of power, not at acts done in a private capacity.

ipsei: this is the plaintiff; the dative repeats the original *quei ceivi*, and depends on *ablatum*.

potestate: authority over individuals (so *patria potestas*); **manus:** the particular authority of a man over his wife. **mancipium:** from *manu capio*, the formal ownership of goods or slaves.

suos: nominative singular; early spelling avoided *uu*, even when one of them was a consonant; so *servos*.

ablatum: varying degrees of force or fraud are covered by these words.

eius: the plaintiff; for this subjective genitive compare *quoius* in 9 below.

quaestio: the whole of the proceedings, divided into *iudicium*, the trial, *iudicatio*, the judgement, *litis aestimatio*, the assessment of the damages.

ex h. l.: *ex hac lege*; those who constitute this court shall hear this particular case.

9. **patroneis**: advocates; the provincial does not have to address the court himself. So in 171 the senate instructed the praetor to appoint advocates for the Spaniards (p. 160); see also the Cyrene edict (p. 170). This law also gives the plaintiff the right to reject an unsuitable *patronus*. It is noticeable that all its provisions are designed to help the plaintiff — the praetor is ordered, for instance, to assist him in the production of his witnesses. As Hardy points out (*Six Roman Laws*, p. 6), 'It seems to be assumed all through, and probably with justice, that the accused was well able to take care of himself'. The whole bias of the law, not only the change in the composition of the jury, shows Gracchus' verdict on the senate of his day.

eorum: the plaintiffs, although *qui petet* was singular.

ante k. Sept.: line 7 of the law contains the provision that if the accusation is made after the first of September the praetor shall appoint *recuperatores* instead of hearing the case himself in the *quaestio*. The proceeding before the *recuperatores* is more expeditious, and the intention is to make sure that the case is finished before the end of the year — when judge and jury would change and it would have to start all over again.

eis volet: *eis* is nominative.

dum nei quem: provided that none of them is a man to whom the defendant is related.

dolo malo: this is the legal term for malice aforethought; for the famous *exceptio doli* see note on p. 218, *exceptionem*.

quoiei: dative; the list of those debarred continues, and includes any family connection and men condemned of serious crime.

16. **CDLvireis**: a large number for the needs of a single court. The combined *decuriae* of Cicero's day were more numerous than this — though the number is not known for certain — but then there were seven courts to provide for. Liability to serve lasted for a year, but must have come round quite frequently.

rogatam: see note on p. 209, *rogaverunt*.

quisque eorum: each praetor peregrinus in the first ten days of his office. The fact that he is sometimes called *praetor* and sometimes *iudex* indicates that this *quaestio* is something between a civil and a criminal court.

HS cccc: it is most unfortunate that the text fails us at this very important point; there is also in the law a very similar formula for appointing the jurymen who are to serve for the rest of the year in which the law is passed, but here again the vital letters are missing. There is no doubt that later generations regarded the Gracchan jurymen as equestrians, and the conjecture adopted by Bruns makes them explicitly so: *quei hace in civitate equom publicum habebit habuerit:* those who are serving, or have served, in the cavalry. If Gracchus was looking for men who were not senators but were as like senators as possible, this might be his choice. But according to Pliny (*N.H.* XXXIII. 34), the middle class was at first called *iudices*, then *publicani*, and it was not until the time of Cicero that the name *equites* was used in this sense; which would be surprising if the *lex Acilia* already specified service in the cavalry. It is also possible that what Gracchus was looking for was experience in business administration, and knowledge of what was going on in the provinces; for this we should expect him to turn to the non-political rich; in that case, the lacuna would be likely to contain a property qualification — a type of qualification well known in Rome — and since 400,000 sesterces was later the minimum for an equestrian that is the figure which has been assumed for this passage; 'who has been assessed as worth four hundred thousand sesterces or more'. This is the view taken by Last in *CAH* IX. p. 892, and elsewhere in the book I have assumed that that is the correct reading.

tr. pl.: see the list in 2 above; here we start at the tribunes because the previous magistrates were excluded under the heading of senators; it is in fact usual for tribunes also to be senators, but that is not legally necessary, though, if not already members they have the right to attend its meetings. It is true that in line 1 also the other magistrates might be omitted for the same reason, but there the solemn declaration would lose its effectiveness.

a.d.a.: *agris dandis adsignandis.*

depugnavit: this compound is especially used of gladiators; that was considered to be a dishonourable trade, but it is interesting that it is considered possible that a gladiator might have qualified.

17. **quod circa**: because of which.

annis XXX: the age limits are what we should expect (the figure XXX survives in the identical formula in line 13). Thirty was the minimum age for the Roman senate, and therefore for local senates in some provinces (so at Halaesa, p. 97); there was no retiring age for senators, but under the empire at least they were not legally compelled to attend after the age of either sixty or sixty-five (the elder Seneca says that it was sixty-five, the younger Seneca that it was sixty; McAlindon in *C.R.* (1957) suggests that it was reduced by the emperor Claudius).

passus M.: the figure has to be supplied; the first milestone was considered to be the limit of the town; for instance it was the limit for the aediles in the *lex Julia municipalis*. A man did not escape service by living in the Campus Martius or on the Janiculan.

pater frater filiusve: making quite certain that the juryman had no ties with the defendant. With these regulations, both for *patronus* and *iudices*, compare the equivalent passages of the Cyrene edict, p. 172.

patrem tribum cognomenque: this is the Roman's full formal designation; the legal description of Domitius Ahenobarbus, for instance, was L. Domitius Cn. f. Fab. Ahenobarbus (Gnaei filius Fabia tribu).

K2

die: an ordinal numeral has to be supplied, but there is no evidence to judge by, and little point in speculating on the exact length of the interval.

18. **tributimque:** the names are to be arranged on the list in order of tribes.

suo magistratu: at his place of business.

de plano: from ground level, so that the ordinary man can see it.

describere: to make a copy.

facito recitentur: have them read out; a *contio* is an official meeting summoned by a magistrate.

49. **duae partes:** there had already been a vote by the jury on whether they are prepared to give a verdict; if more than a third of them have voted *non liquet*, the case must be heard again from the beginning. (The praetor's formula for this is *amplius*, and the procedure is known as *ampliatio*.) If those who vote *non liquet* are less than a third, then they take no further part, and the rest of the jury proceed to register their verdict. Since those who vote *non liquet* would be likely, if compelled to vote on the main issue, to vote for an acquittal, this procedure favours the prosecution; which was what Gracchus wanted. It had also the disadvantage that the jury were compelled to give their verdict immediately after hearing the witnesses, who might tell conflicting stories, no opportunity being given to the parties to sum up their cases. It was to meet this that the procedure of *comperendinatio* was introduced by the *lex Servilia* of Glaucia, which laid down an interval after which a second *actio* must take place. For the *non liquet* procedures see Greenidge, *Legal Procedure in Cicero's Time*, and, for *comperendinatio*, Balsdon, *PBSR*, 1938.

eis iudices: nominative.

50. **soueis:** *suis*.

sitellam: an urn; we have no means of knowing its diameter; *digitus* is an inch.

sorticolas: diminutive of *sors*, a lot. *A* is for *absolvo*, *C* for *condemno*.

51. **induci:** to be rubbed out; this word is used of smoothing letters on a wax tablet with the blunt end of the *stilus*.

52. **bracio aperto:** away from the folds of his toga. The juryman must show clearly that he is voting, but must conceal the vital letter. On one occasion Hortensius, when defending M. Terentius Varro in the extortion court, so coloured the wax on the tablets that he could tell which way the jurymen had voted, and whether they had earned their bribes; but that was after 80, when the senators were again supplying the jurymen.

When the votes have been counted, the praetor pronounces *fecisse videtur* or *non fecisse videtur*.

58. **ab eo:** the relation is *ab eo quei condemnatus erit . . .; aestimare quod quisque petet . . .; quisque quoius petitio erit. . . .*

iudices: the jurymen have pronounced the defendant guilty; they now have the more detailed task of stating which of the alleged offences they thought had been proved, and how much restitution should be made for each. No great speeches remain to be made, and the surviving literature does not tell us much about this stage.

ante h.l.: *ante hanc legem*; the Romans, too, thought that retrospective legislation was a bad thing; this simple restitution is the penalty which is already in force. It is probable that we have here the only penalty which was at this time inflicted for extortion; it is in essence a private suit; the praetor is *iudex*, the jury are his *consilium* (but under this law they give their votes formally by secret ballot, and he *must* give his verdict in accordance with their votes); the plaintiffs are *petitores*, the defendant is *is unde petitur*; the aim is pecuniary restitution, and apart from the fact that the restitution is now to be twofold there is no question of punishment — in the case of senators that can be left to the next censors. It is of course quite possible that in the course of his extortions the defendant will have done things which make him liable to prosecution in another court, and a conviction in this one would act as a *praeiudicium*, and make further prosecution more likely; so that he may prefer to go into exile. It is also possible that the amount to be restored may be so great that he would abscond with his movable property in order to save something from the wreck. This point is argued in full by Sherwin White in *JRS* (1952), in answer to M. I. Henderson (*JRS*, 1951).

59. **ad quaestorem:** the treasury is now involved; there follow regulations about the payment of the money. The praetor exacts it from the defendant and passes it on to the quaestor, and appoints a day for payment. If he does not succeed in exacting the full amount, a proportional distribution is made. The quaestor meanwhile keeps the money under seal, and if any plaintiff fails to collect his share, it eventually becomes the property of the treasury.

provincia: in its original sense of a sphere of duty; the use of the word in a geographical sense was derived from this, since the commonest sphere of duty was the administration of a given area.

The extant fragments of the law end with rewards to the successful prosecutor: if he is not a Roman citizen, he may, if he wishes, become one — the grant extending to his sons and grandsons — and be enrolled in the tribe of the condemned man; but this shall not make them liable to military service. If the successful prosecutor is 'of the Latin name' he may, if he prefers, take the right of *provocatio ad populum* in place of full citizenship. At the point where rewards for Roman citizens may have been enumerated the text fails us.

Extract from speech of Gaius Gracchus.

Gaius had been intimately concerned in the plans of his elder brother, and was already a marked man when he went as quaestor to Sardinia in 126. The nobility tried to keep him there, by not sending a successor, and he did stay two years. He then returned without leave, and an attempt was made to persuade the censors to degrade him. Part of his speech to them is preserved by Aulus Gellius (XV. 12), and this extract is taken from it. We conclude that he was successful, as he was elected tribune in the same year (124).

sumptum: Cicero was not the first to say this; nor was Gracchus. For Cato's attempts to control the abuse see Livy, XXXII. 27. p. 136, and the *lex Antonia*, p. 100; the expenses of governors and their staffs are discussed in Chap IV.

Chapter VI: AUGUSTAN EPILOGUE

Edicts of Augustus in Cyrene

I

αὐτοκράτωρ: **Emperor:** Augustus was the first man to use the military title *imperator* as a *praenomen*, in place of his original *praenomen* Gaius; it was not so used by his Julio-Claudian successors, but after the end of that dynasty it became the permanent *praenomen* of the emperor.

Σεβαστός: **Augustus:** Octavian understood the importance of words in forming thought, and took great trouble to choose a name to correspond with his position. It is said that he thought of Romulus, to be a second founder, but Romulus had been a king, and so that had to be avoided. The word Augustus was a little more than human, but less than divine, suited to a *divi filius* who was to redeem the world.

δημαρχικῆς: **tribunician:** the steps by which Augustus took this power are obscure, but from 23 B.C. onwards it became the most important title of the emperor; outside Rome he was a proconsul, in Rome he was a very special tribune. It had the advantages that it had nothing to do with the army, that it reduced the tribunes to the position of inferior colleagues, and that nobody really knew what its limits were. The tribunate was an annual office, and though Augustus held it for life the annual fiction was maintained, and from 23 the years of his reign are dated by this more often than by the names of the consuls.

αὐτοκράτωρ: **imperator:** the custom, going back at least to the second century, by which a successful general was saluted as *imperator* by his troops on the field of battle. Only the holder of an *imperium* could be so saluted, and under the empire all the salutations for successes by the armies in the emperor's provinces were taken by the emperor. They lost their spontaneous character, and became a way by which the emperor could give honour to the army, and at the same time emphasise that he was their real commander.

διναρίων: **denarii:** this sum is equivalent to ten thousand sesterces, and is evidently the qualification for the *album* *iudicum* in Cyrene; it is a small sum by the standards of the well-to-do at Rome; even Pompey's *tribuni aerarii* may have had to possess thirty times as much.

δοκοῦσί μοι: **I think that:** Augustus is giving instructions to the governor of a senatorial province, in which he is not the proconsul; he is therefore being extremely tactful. Since his proconsular *imperium* was in fact *maius* he had the right to give orders to any proconsul, and had there been any likelihood that this request would be disregarded he would doubtless have given it in the form of an order. His *auctoritas* was so great that he did not need to brandish his *imperium*.

Κρητικὴν: **Crete:** at its annexation in 67 the island was officially joined to the province of Cyrene.

πέντε καὶ εἴκοσι: **twenty-five:** at Rome such a minimum age would probably have been thirty, but there is a shortage of such men in the province.

σηκωθεισῶν: **made equal:** the word means to weigh in the balance; all the tablets must be of the same standard weight.

V

Γαίου Καλουισίου: **Gaius Calvisius:** these are the consuls of 4 B.C. The decree which follows is sometimes known as the *senatus consultum Calvisianum*.

ἐμοῦ πάροντος . . .: **in my presence . . .:** this corresponds to the Latin formula *scribendo adfuerunt*.

προγράμματι: **preamble:** evidently this will ensure that action is taken.

δῆλον ἔσται: **so that it may be clear:** for the propaganda of benevolence see p. 86.

ξυμβουλίου: **council:** so that he could guide senatorial business without having to appear to be personally dictating, and so that he could find out in advance what the feelings of the senate were — two very important things — Augustus had a committee appointed which he could consult. And since he did not want it to appear that he was only consulting his friends, the committee consisted of the two consuls, one of each of the other colleges of magistrates, and fifteen other senators chosen by lot, a new selection being made every six

months. Over the years a large number of senators will have
served on it, so that it helped to educate the senate in the
problems facing the emperor. The institution did not survive
Tiberius' retirement to Capri.

Χωρὶς τοῦ κεφαλῆς: the capital trial: the procedure now
being made available is similar to that in force before the
establishment of the *quaestio perpetua*, and which we found in
Livy, XLIII. 2 (p. 160); the intention is to make the procedure
quicker and less onerous. It is reasonable therefore that the
defendant shall not be on trial for his life; the penalty of this
court being simple restitution. If the provincials wanted
vengeance as well as recovery of what they had lost, a more
serious procedure was still available in the *quaestio*.

συνάγειν τὴν σύνκλητον: to summon the senate: this right
belongs to consuls, praetors and tribunes.

συνήγορον: advocate: compare the appointment of a *patronus*
in the *lex Acilia*, p. 161.

διακοσίων: two hundred: since at least 67 (the *lex Cornelia
de privilegiis*) this has been a recognised *quorum* for important
business. It is possible that this was the number sometimes
envisaged by the phrase *frequens senatus*.

γνώμην ἀποφάινεσθαι: the right to vote: the traditional formula for the consuls in summoning the senate was 'Senatores,
quibusque in senatu sententiam dicere licet'. When a man had
held an office which qualified for admission to the senate, he
was at once allowed to attend its meetings and vote, but until
the censors had entered him on the lists he was not really a
senator; some might be three years in this limbo, waiting for
the next census. When there was a division they could vote,
but were not called upon to speak. According to the learned
Varro, these were the same as the *pedarii*, because the final
division was done by moving to one side or the other, *pedibus
ire in sententiam*, and not until then could they indicate their
opinions. Since Sulla made entry into the senate independent
of the censors, it seems that this formula was a survival with
no present reference. By the time of Aulus Gellius (c. A.D. 150)
men are guessing at the meaning of *pedarius*, and he quotes two
other theories, neither very probable (III. xviii).

ἑβδομήκοντα: seventy: a higher age limit than the Gracchan

iudices; higher in fact than that for which attendance at the senate was compulsory (see note on p. 279, *annis XXX*).

ἐπ' ἀρχῆς ἢ ἐπ' ἐξουσίας: imperium or potestas: this includes all magistrates; a *iudex quaestionis* (usually an *aedilicius*) presided over a *quaestio perpetua* when there was no praetor available; the overseer of corn-measures was the *praefectus annonae*, not part of the organisation later created by Augustus, but an early Republican office about which, as is clear from Livy IV. 13, not much was by this time known. The formulae of the decree contain archaic survivals.

νόμωι 'Ιουλίωι: lex Julia: this is a law passed in Caesar's dictatorship, on the composition of juries in the *quaestiones perpetuae*; the law which ended the brief judicial career of the *tribuni aerarii*.

μεταπορευόμενοι: plaintiffs: here we have the Greek translation of *is qui petit* and *is unde petitur* (see the *lex Acilia*, p. 161).

τοσοῦτον: so much: this is the pre-Gracchan simple restitution (see note on p. 281, *ante h.l.*).

MAPS OF THE ROMAN EMPIRE

MAPS OF THE ROMAN EMPIRE

THE three maps which follow are intended to show the growth of the empire. The first two illustrate Ch. I, the third Ch. VI.

In order to show provinces on the map it has been necessary to draw lines marking the frontiers. In fact, the exact continental frontiers are in some cases not known today, and were not always known with certainty at the time. Of Illyricum it is even doubtful whether we ought to draw a line at all. In any case, the empire should not be considered as coming to a dead stop at the administrative boundary; the areas shaded with dots indicate the more settled and important of the client states, which can reasonably be considered part of the empire.

The third map is intended to show the frontier plan of Augustus, the *termini imperii*. The division into emperor's provinces (horizontal shading), senate's provinces, and client states represents the situation at his death. We do not know if he had any plans for Britain, in spite of the stories that he intended to invade.

Chronological list of the Republican provinces (some of the dates are not beyond dispute):

Sicilia	241	Cilicia (see Ch. II)	85
Sardinia	238	Gallia Cisalpina[2]	81
Hispaniae	197	Cyrene	74
Africa	146	Bithynia	74
Macedonia	146	Crete (joined to Cyrene)	67
Illyricum[1]	146?	Bithynia et Pontus	62
Asia	129	Syria	62
Gallia Transalpina	121	Gallia	51

---

[1] Sometimes joined to Macedonia, sometimes to Cisalpine Gaul; it is possible that it should not rank as a province until 33.

[2] Made part of Italy again by Caesar.

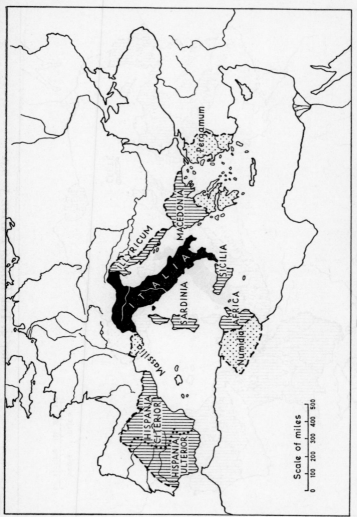

Map 3. The Roman Empire 133 B.C.

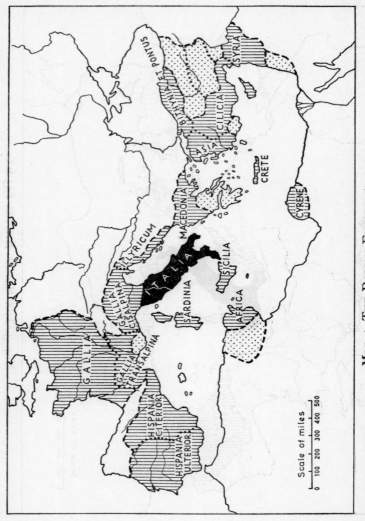

Scale of miles

0 100 200 300 400 500

Map 4. The Roman Empire 50 B.C.

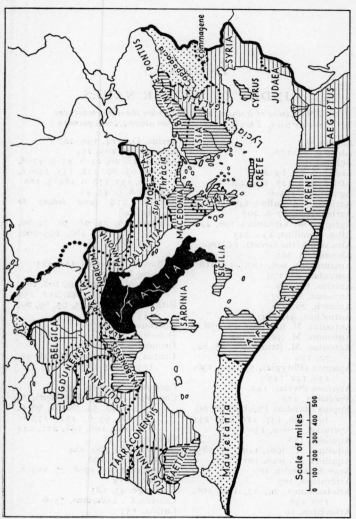

Map 5. The Roman Empire in the Augustan Plan

Scale of miles

0 100 200 300 400 500

INDEXES

INDEX OF PROPER NAMES

(The names of Romans are listed under the name most commonly used. This is usually, but not always, the cognomen.)

INDEX OF ROMAN LAWS

GENERAL INDEX